Principles of Web Design, Second Edition

by Joel Sklar

THOMSON

COURSE TECHNOLOGY

Australia • Canada • Mexico • Singapore • Spain • United Kingdom • United States

THOMSON

COURSE TECHNOLOGY

Principles of Web Design, Second Edition

by Joel Sklar

Product Manager: Tricia Boyle	**Associate Product Manager:** Janet Aras	**Cover Designer:** Joseph Lee, Black Fish Design
Managing Editor: Jennifer Locke	**Editorial Assistant:** Christy Urban	**Compositor:** GEX Publishing Services
Acquisitions Editor: Bill Larkin	**Associate Marketing Manager:** Angela Laughlin	**Manufacturing Coordinator:** Denise Powers
Development Editor: Lisa Ruffolo	**Production Editor:** Danielle Power	

BRIEF
Contents

PREFACE   xiii

CHAPTER ONE
Variables in the Web Design Environment   1

CHAPTER TWO
Web Site Design Principles   27

CHAPTER THREE
Planning the Site   63

CHAPTER FOUR
Planning Site Navigation   87

CHAPTER FIVE
Creating Page Templates   119

CHAPTER SIX
Web Typography   165

CHAPTER SEVEN
Graphics and Color   201

CHAPTER EIGHT
HTML Frames   239

CHAPTER NINE
Working with Forms   273

CHAPTER TEN
Publishing and Maintaining Your Web Site   303

APPENDIX A
HTML Reference   317

APPENDIX B
CSS Reference   333

GLOSSARY   349

INDEX   353

TABLE OF
Contents

PREFACE   xiii

CHAPTER ONE
Variables in the Web Design Environment   1
The Current State of HTML   2
    HTML: Then and Now   2
    HTML and the World Wide Web Consortium   2
    The Limitations of HTML   3
    The Need for Style Sheets   3
    Organizing Information with Hypertext   5
XML: An Open Standard for Structuring Data   5
    XML Describes Data   6
    XML Syntax Rules   7
XHTML: The Future of HTML   8
    Benefits of Moving to XHTML   8
    Style Sheets Are Required   9
    Stricter Syntax Rules   10
How Web Browsers Affect Your Work   11
    Browser Compatibility Issues   11
    Creating Cross-Browser Compatible Pages   12
    Solving the Browser Dilemma   14
Coding for Multiple Screen Resolutions   14
    Fixed Resolution Design   15
    Flexible Resolution Design   17
Bandwidth Concerns   19
    Working with the Cache   20
    Should You Use an HTML Editor?   21
Chapter Summary   22
Review Questions   22
Hands-on Projects   23
Case Project   24

CHAPTER TWO
Web Site Design Principles   27
Design for the Computer Medium   28
    Craft the Look and Feel   28
    Make Your Design Portable   28
    Design for Low Bandwidth   30
    Plan for Clear Presentation and Easy Access to Your Information   30

Design the Whole Site   31
    Create Smooth Transitions   33
    Use a Grid to Provide Visual Structure   34
    Use Active White Space   35
Design for the User   40
    Design for Interaction   42
    Design for Location   44
    Guide the User's Eye   45
    Keep a Flat Hierarchy   48
    Use the Power of Hypertext Linking   50
    How Much Content Is Enough?   53
    Design for Accessibility   55
Design for the Screen   56
    Reformat Content for Online Presentation   57
Chapter Summary   59
Review Questions   59
Hands-on Projects   60
Case Project   61

CHAPTER THREE
Planning the Site   63

Create a Site Specification   64
Identify the Content Goal   64
Analyze Your Audience   66
    Identify Technology Issues and Constraints   68
    Identify Software Tools   69
Build a Web Site Development Team   69
Create Conventions for Filenames and URLs   70
    File Naming   71
    URL Usage   72
Set a Directory Structure   73
    Relative versus Absolute Paths   75
    Building a Relative File Structure   75
Diagram the Site   77
    Create the Information Structure   78
Chapter Summary   83
Review Questions   84
Hands-on Projects   85
Case Projects   86

CHAPTER FOUR
Planning Site Navigation   87

Creating Usable Navigation   88
    Locating the User   89
    Limiting Information Overload   90
Building Text-Based Navigation   91
Linking with a Text Navigation Bar   92
    Linking to Individual Files   94
    Adding Internal Linking   96
    Adding an Internal Navigation Bar   97
    Linking to External Document Fragments   100
    Adding Page Turners   103
Adding Contextual Linking   105

Using Graphics for Navigation and Linking 107
Using Text Images for Navigation 107
Using Icons for Navigation 108
Using the alt Attribute 111
Chapter Summary 114
Review Questions 115
Hands-on Projects 116
Case Projects 117

CHAPTER FIVE
Creating Page Templates 119
Understanding Table Basics 120
Using Table Elements 120
Defining Table Attributes 122
Spanning Columns 124
Spanning Rows 125
Formatting Tables 126
Choosing Relative or Fixed Table Widths 126
Determining the Correct Fixed Width for a Table 129
Adding White Space in a Table 130
Removing Default Table Spacing 131
Table Pointers for Well-Designed Tables 132
Writing Easy-to-Read Table Code 132
Removing Extra Spaces 133
Centering Tables 134
Stacking Tables 134
Nesting Tables 135
Creating a Page Template 137
Building the Basic Table Structure 138
Setting a Fixed Width 139
Creating the Page Banner Cell 140
Creating the Feature Article Cell 142
Creating the Link Column Cells 143
Setting the Column Widths 145
Completing and Testing the Template 147
Evaluating Examples of Page Templates 154
Two-Column Template 154
Two-Column with Banner Template 155
Three-Column Template 156
Three-Column with Banner Template 157
Three-Column Sectioned Template 158
Three-Column Main Sectioned Template 159
Chapter Summary 160
Review Questions 161
Hands-on Projects 162
Case Project 163

CHAPTER SIX
Web Typography   **165**
   Type Design Principles   166
      Choose Fewer Fonts and Sizes   166
      Use Available Fonts   167
      Design for Legibility   168
      Avoid Using Text as Graphics   169
   Controlling Typography with the <font> Element   170
      Setting Font Size   170
      Specifying Font Alternates   170
      Setting Font Color   171
      Using the <font> Element   171
   Controlling Typography with Cascading Style Sheets   172
      CSS Basics   173
      CSS Selection Techniques   175
      CSS Font Properties   177
      Specifying Block-Level Space Values   185
   Building a Style Sheet   188
      Setting Up Document Divisions   189
      Styling the Standard Paragraph   190
      Styling the Chapter Number   191
      Styling the Chapter Title   193
      Styling the Credit and Book Title   195
   Chapter Summary   198
   Review Questions   199
   Hands-on Projects   199
   Case Project   200

CHAPTER SEVEN
Graphics and Color   **201**
   Understanding Graphics File Formats   202
      GIF   202
      JPG   204
      PNG   205
      SVG   205
      Using Interlacing and Progressive Display   206
      Where You Can Find Images   207
      Choosing the Right Format   208
   Computer Color Basics   208
      Color Depth   209
      Dithering   209
      Using Non-Dithering Colors   209
   Choosing a Graphics Tool   210
      Using the <img> Element   211
      Replacing img Attributes with Style Sheet Properties   212
      Specifying alt and title Attribute Text   213
      Specifying Image Width and Height   214
      Sizing Graphics for the Page   218
      Removing the Hypertext Border from an Image   218
      Aligning Text and Images   219
      Adding White Space Around Images   221
      Using Single-Pixel Rules   222
      Using Background Images   224

Working with Hexadecimal Colors   227
   Universal Color Names   228
   Setting Background Page Color   228
   Using Background Color in Tables   229
   Changing Link Colors   231
Working with Images and Color   231
Chapter Summary   236
Review Questions   236
Hands-on Projects   237
Case Project   238

CHAPTER EIGHT
HTML Frames   **239**
Understanding Frames   240
   Frame Benefits   240
   Frame Drawbacks   241
Frame Syntax   242
   The <frameset> Element   242
   The <frame> Element   243
   The <noframes> Tag   245
   Nesting Frames   246
   Restricting Resizing   247
   Controlling Scroll Bars   248
   Controlling Frame Borders   249
   Controlling Frame Margins   251
Targeting in Framesets   252
   Naming Frames   252
   Targeting Named Frames   253
   Using Special Target Names   255
Planning Frame Content   259
   Frames and Screen Resolution   259
   Designing Effective Frames   260
   Mixing Fixed and Variable Frames   260
Working with Framesets   265
Chapter Summary   269
Review Questions   270
Hands-on Projects   271
Case Project   272

CHAPTER NINE
Working with Forms   **273**
Understanding How Forms Work   274
Understanding Form Syntax   275
   Using the Forms Element   275
   Creating Input Objects   276
   Using the Select Element   284
   Using the textarea Element   286
   Creating Input Groupings   287
Building Forms within Tables   288
Building and Testing a Sample Form   290
   Adding a List Box List and Radio Buttons   292
   Adding a File Element and Submit Button 294

Chapter Summary   296
Review Questions   297
Hands-on Projects   297
Case Project   301

CHAPTER TEN
Publishing and Maintaining Your Web Site   **303**
Publishing Your Web Site   304
   Choosing a Web Hosting Service Provider 304
   Registering a Domain Name   306
   ISP Comparison Checklist   306
   Using the File Transfer Protocol to Upload Files   307
Testing Your Web Site   308
   Testing Considerations   309
   User Testing   309
Refining and Updating Your Content   311
Attracting Notice to Your Web Site   311
   Working with Search Engines   311
   Use Meaningful Titles   312
   Using <meta> Elements   312
   Be Careful with Frames   313
   Use alt Text with Images   314
   Submit URLs to Search Engines   314
Chapter Summary   314
Review Questions   315
Hands-on Projects   315
Case Project   316

APPENDIX A
HTML Reference   **317**
Core Attributes   318
Alphabetical HTML Reference   318
Categorical HTML Reference   323
   Global Structure Elements   323
   Text Elements   324
   List Elements   325
   Table Elements   325
   Link Elements   326
   Inclusion Element   327
   Style Sheet Element   327
   Formatting Elements   327
   Frame Elements   328
Numeric and Character Entities   328

APPENDIX B
CSS Reference   **333**
CSS Notation Reference   334
Alphabetical CSS Property Reference   334

CSS Properties by Category 339
    Font and Text Properties 339
    Box Properties 340
    Background Properties 342
    Visual Properties 342
    Classification Properties 343
CSS Measurement Units 344
ISO 369 2-Letter Language Codes 344

GLOSSARY **349**

INDEX **353**

Preface

Principles of Web Design, Second Edition will help you plan and develop well-designed Web sites that combine effective navigation with the judicious use of graphics, text, and color. You will learn how to create Web sites that let users easily and quickly access your information, regardless of browser type, connection speed, or computing platform. Whether you are building a site from scratch or redesigning an existing site, the principles presented in this text will help you deliver your Web content in a more interesting, accessible, and visually exciting way.

THE INTENDED AUDIENCE

Principles of Web Design, Second Edition is intended for the individual that has a knowledge of HTML and wants to apply those skills to the task of designing attractive, informative Web pages. To work effectively with the content of this book you need to understand the basics of HTML at the code level. You may have taken an introductory class in HTML, or taught yourself HTML with the help of a book or the Web. You should be able to build a simple Web page that includes text, hyperlinks, and graphics. Additionally, you should be comfortable working with computers and know your way around your operating system, whether Windows, Macintosh, or UNIX.

THE APPROACH

As you progress through the book, you will practice the design techniques by studying the supplied coding samples, looking at the example pages and Web sites, and applying the principles to your own work. Each chapter will conclude with a summary, project ideas, and review section that highlights and reinforces the major concepts of each chapter. To complete the case project you should complete each chapter in sequence.

OVERVIEW OF THIS BOOK

The examples and exercises in this book will help you achieve the following objectives:

- Apply your HTML skills to building designed Web pages
- Effectively use graphics, typography, color, and navigation in your work
- Understand the affects of browser and computing platform on your design choices
- Learn to build portable, accessible Web sites that clearly present information
- Gain a critical eye for evaluating Web site design

In **Chapter 1** you will explore the variables in Web design and learn how Web browser, connection speed, and other factors affect your work. You will also explore the current state of HTML and preview the new markup languages that will change the future of the Web. **Chapter 2** covers the basic design principles that you will apply as you work through the book. You will look at a variety of Web sites and learn to focus on both the user's needs and information requirements of your site. In **Chapter 3** you will learn about the process of planning your Web site before you start coding. You will also learn about important file naming and directory conventions, as well as create a flowchart that depicts the information structure of your site. **Chapter 4** discusses basic navigation principles and how to build navigation schemes that meet your user's needs with the creative use of hypertext linking. **Chapter 5** explains how you can use the HTML table elements to create page templates and take a page concept from design to HTML code. **Chapter 6** demonstrates the principles of using creative typographic design in the Web environment, and focuses on using Cascading Style Sheets to manipulate a wide variety of type properties. **Chapter 7** explains the effective use of images and color on your Web site, including image file formats, correct use of the <img> element, and computer color basics. **Chapter 8** discusses the benefits and drawbacks of HTML frames, and explains how frames can be the solution for solving specific information design problems. In **Chapter 9**, you will learn how to work with HTML form elements to build interactive Web pages that collect information from a user and process it on the Web server. Finally, in **Chapter 10** you will learn how to publish your site to the Web and plan for ongoing site maintenance and updates.

FEATURES

Principles of Web Design, Second Edition contains many teaching aids to assist the student's learning.

- **Chapter Objectives**: Each chapter in this book begins with a list of the important concepts to be mastered within the chapter. This list provides you with a quick reference to the contents of the chapter as well as a useful study aid.
- **Illustrations and Tables**: Illustrations help you visualize common components and relationships. Tables list conceptual items and examples in a visual and readable format.

- **Tips**: Chapters contain Tips designed to provide you with practical advice and proven strategies related to the concept being discussed.

- **Chapter Summaries**: Each chapter's text is followed by a summary of chapter concepts. These summaries provide a helpful way to recap and revisit the ideas covered in each chapter.

- **Review Questions**: End-of-chapter assessment begins with a set of approximately 15 to 20 review questions that reinforce the main ideas introduced in each chapter. These questions ensure that you have mastered the concepts and have understood the information you have learned.

Hands-on Projects: Although it is important to understand the concepts behind Web design topics, no amount of theory can improve on real-world experience. To this end, along with conceptual explanations, each chapter provides Hands-on Projects related to each major topic aimed at providing you with practical experience. Some of these include researching information from people, printed resources, and the Internet, as well as installing and using some of the technologies discussed. Because the Hands-on Projects ask you to go beyond the boundaries of the text itself, they provide you with practice implementing Web design skills in real-world situations.

Case Projects: The case projects at the end of each chapter are designed to help you apply what you have learned to business situations much like those you can expect to encounter as a Web designer. They give you the opportunity to independently synthesize and evaluate information, examine potential solutions, and make recommendations, much as you would in an actual design situation.

TEACHING TOOLS

The following supplemental materials are available when this book is used in a classroom setting. All of the teaching tools available with this book are provided to the instructor on a single CD-ROM.

Electronic Instructor's Manual. The Instructor's Manual that accompanies this textbook includes:

- Additional instructional material to assist in class preparation, including suggestions for lecture topics. It is critical for the instructor to be able to help the students understand how to use the help resources and how to identify problems. The Instructor's Manual will help you identify areas that are more difficult to teach, and provide you with ideas of how to present the material in an easier fashion.

- Solutions to all end-of-chapter materials, including the Review Questions, and when applicable, Hands-on Projects, and Case Projects.

ExamView®. This textbook is accompanied by ExamView, a powerful testing software package that allows instructors to create and administer printed, computer (LAN-based), and Internet exams. ExamView includes hundreds of questions that correspond to the topics covered in this text, enabling students to generate detailed study guides that include page references for further review. The computer-based and Internet testing components allow students to take exams at their computers, and also save the instructor time by grading each exam automatically.

PowerPoint Presentations. This book comes with Microsoft PowerPoint slides for each chapter. These are included as a teaching aid for classroom presentation, to make available to students on the network for chapter review, or to be printed for classroom distribution. Instructors can add their own slides for additional topics they introduce to the class.

Data Files. Files that contain all of the data necessary for the Hands-on Projects and Case Projects are provided through the Course Technology Web site at *www.course.com*, and are also available on the Teaching Tools CD-ROM.

Solution Files. Solutions to end-of-chapter Review Questions, Hands-on Projects, and Case Projects are provided on the Teaching Tools CD-ROM and may also be found on the Course Technology Web site at *www.course.com*. The solutions are password protected.

Distance Learning. Course Technology is proud to present online test banks in WebCT and Blackboard, as well as MyCourse 2.0, Course Technology's own course enhancement tool, to provide the most complete and dynamic learning experience possible. Instructors are encouraged to make the most of your course, both online and offline. For more information on how to access your online test bank, contact your local Course Technology sales representative.

Read This Before You Begin

The following information will help you as you prepare to use this textbook.

To the User of the Data Files

To complete the steps and projects in this book, you will need data files that have been created specifically for this book. Your instructor will provide the data files to you. You also can obtain the files electronically from the Course Technology Web site by connecting to *www.course.com* and then searching for this book title. Note that you can use a computer in your school lab or your own computer to complete the steps and Hands-on Projects in this book.

Using Your Own Computer

You can use a computer in your school lab or your own computer to complete the chapters, Hands-on Projects, and Case Projects in this book. To use your own computer, you will need the following:

- **A Web browser**, such as Microsoft Internet Explorer 5.0 or later, Netscape Navigator version 6.0 or later, or Opera version 5.0 or later.
- **A code-based HTML editor**, such as Macromedia Homesite, or a text editor such as Notepad on the PC or SimpleText on the Macintosh.

TO THE INSTRUCTOR

To complete all the exercises and chapters in this book, your users must work with a set of user files, called a Data Disk, and download software from Web sites. The data files are included in the Instructor's Resource Kit. They may also be obtained electronically through the Course Technology Web site at *www.course.com*. Follow the instructions in the Help file to copy the user files to your server or standalone computer. You can view the Help file using a text editor, such as WordPad or Notepad.

After the files are copied, you can make Data Disks for the users yourself, or tell them where to find the files so they can make their own Data Disks. Make sure the files are set up correctly by having students follow the instructions in the "To the User of the Data Files" section.

Course Technology Data Files

You are granted a license to copy the data files to any computer or computer network used by individuals who have purchased this book.

Visit Our World Wide Web Site

Additional materials designed especially for this book might be available for your course. Periodically search *www.course.com* for more information and materials to accompany this text.

ACKNOWLEDGMENTS

Thanks to the team at Course Technology for their support and encouragement during the writing of this book. A special thanks to Lisa Ruffolo, a superb editor who made working on this project a pleasure.

Thanks to the reviewers who provided plenty of comments and positive direction during the development of this book:

Dan Dao, Richland College

Connie Farthing, St. Gregory's University

Dorothy Harman, Tarrant County College

Kathy Harris, Northwestern Oklahoma State University

Doug Hulsey, Virtual Professor Corporation/Limestone College

Ella McManus, Central Piedmont Community College

Thanks to the students in my HTML Authoring and Design class at Northeastern University, who never cease to amaze me with their creativity and enthusiasm for this new medium.

Thanks to Debra Cote for use of examples from her student project Web site. Thanks to the F.A. Cleveland Elementary School for use of examples from their Web site.

This book is dedicated to my wife Diana and to my daughter Samantha, who put up with too many days of Dad at the computer, and too few days at the beach. Thanks for your encouragement, support, patience, and love.

1

VARIABLES IN THE WEB DESIGN ENVIRONMENT

When you complete this chapter, you will be able to:

- ◆ Describe the current state of HTML
- ◆ Understand XML, an open standard for structuring data
- ◆ Understand XHTML, the future of HTML
- ◆ Describe how Web browsers display your work
- ◆ Code for multiple screen resolutions
- ◆ Understand bandwidth concerns

In this chapter you will explore the variable factors that affect Web design. You will learn how the **Hypertext Markup Language (HTML)**, the language used to create documents on the World Wide Web, is constantly evolving, and preview the new markup languages that will change how you design for the Web. You will see how Web browsers affect the way users view your content, and how variations in the user's browser choice, screen resolution, and connection speed pose specific challenges to creating Web pages that display properly in different computing platforms. Finally, you will consider what type of software tool you should use to create your HTML code.

THE CURRENT STATE OF HTML

In this section you will explore the evolution of HTML and its future as a markup language for creating Web documents. You will analyze current design limitations of HTML, the need for style sheets that allow separation of style from structure, and the usage of hypertext as a means for organizing information.

HTML: Then and Now

When Tim Berners-Lee first proposed HTML at the European Laboratory for Particle Physics (CERN) in 1989, he was looking for a way to manage and share large amounts of information among colleagues. He proposed a web of documents (at first, he called it a mesh) connected by hypertext links and hosted by computers called hypertext servers. As the idea developed, Berners-Lee named the mesh the World Wide Web. He created an application of the **Standard Generalized Markup Language (SGML)**, a standard system for specifying document structure, and called it the Hypertext Markup Language. HTML greatly reduces the complexity of using SGML to facilitate transmission of documents over the Internet.

When Berners-Lee created HTML, he adopted only the elements of SGML necessary for representing basic office documents such as memos and reports. The first working draft of HTML included elements such as titles, headings, paragraphs, and lists. HTML was intended for simple document structure, not for handling today's variety of information needs. As the Web has developed and expanded, the demands to transport data for transactions such as shopping and banking online has far outgrown the capabilities of HTML. The need for new markup languages and standards to address these demands is handled by the **World Wide Web Consortium (W3C)**.

HTML and the World Wide Web Consortium

HTML has progressed significantly since it was first formalized in 1992. After the initial surge of interest in HTML and the Web, a need arose for a standards organization to set recommended practices that would guarantee the open nature of the Web. The W3C was founded in 1994 at the Massachusetts Institute of Technology to meet this need. The W3C, led by Tim Berners-Lee, sets standards for HTML and provides an open, nonproprietary forum for industry and academic representatives to add to the evolution of this new medium. The unenviable goal of the W3C is to stay ahead of the development curve in a fast-moving industry. The various committees that comprise the W3C look to expand and set standards for the many new Web technologies that have emerged. These include XHTML, XML, and other markup and style languages. You will learn more about these new companion technologies to HTML later in this chapter.

Visit the W3C site at *www.w3.org* to find out more about HTML, XML, CSS, and the history and future of the Web. You can look up individual element definitions, test your code for validity, or keep up-to-date on the latest Web developments.

The Limitations of HTML

HTML is a **markup language**, a structured language that lets you identify common sections of a document such as headings, paragraphs, and lists. An HTML file includes text and HTML markup elements that identify these sections. The HTML markup elements indicate how the document sections appear in a browser. For example, the <h1> element tags in the following code indicate that the text is a first-level heading:

```
<h1>Welcome to My Web Page</h1>
```

The browser interprets the HTML markup elements and displays the results, hiding the actual markup tags from the user. In the previous code, the user sees only the text "Welcome to My Web Page" formatted as a level-one heading.

HTML adopts many features of SGML, including the cross-platform compatibility that allows different computers to download and read the same file from the Web. Because HTML is cross-platform compatible, it does not matter whether you are working on a Windows PC, Macintosh, or UNIX computer. You can create HTML files and view them on any computer platform.

HTML is not a What You See Is What You Get (WYSIWYG) layout tool. It was intended only to express logical document structure, not formatting characteristics. Although many current HTML editors let you work with a graphical interface, the underlying code they create is basic HTML. However, because HTML was not designed as a lay-out language, many editing programs create less-than-standard code to accomplish a certain effect. You cannot rely on the HTML editor's WYSIWYG view to test your Web pages. Because users can view the same HTML file with different browsers and on different machines, the only way to be sure of what your audience sees is to preview your HTML files in the browsers you anticipate your audience will use.

Despite its limitations, HTML is ideal for the Web because it is an open, non-proprietary, cross-platform compatible language. All of the markup tags are included with every document and usually can be viewed through your browser. Once you are familiar with the HTML syntax, you will find that one of the best ways to learn new coding techniques is to find a Web page you like and view the source code.

The Need for Style Sheets

Style elements such as <font> were introduced by browser developers to help HTML authors bypass the design limitations of HTML. Designers and writers who are accustomed to working with today's full-featured word processing programs want the same ability to manipulate and position objects precisely on a Web page as they can on the printed page. Again, this is not what HTML was designed to do; like SGML, it was intended to represent document structure, not style.

Mixing style information within the structure, as is the case in most of the Web today, limits the cross-platform compatibility of the content. The display information that is embedded in Web pages is tailored towards one type of display medium, the computer screen. With style sheets, the display properties are separate from the content. This accommodates the diverse variety of devices that are becoming available to browse the Web. Whether you come to the Web with a Personal Digital Assistant (PDA), a Personal Communication Services (PCS) telephone, or Windows CE device, the Web server can determine the type of requesting device and supply a style sheet that matches the device. Figure 1-1 illustrates this concept.

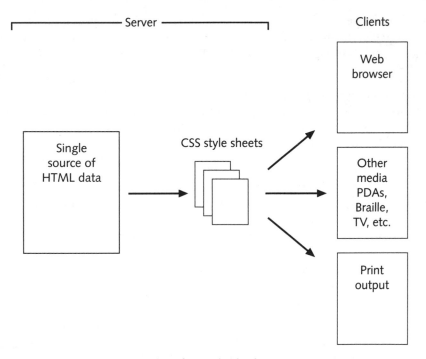

Figure 1-1   Formatting data for multiple destinations

This separation of style and structure was accomplished in 1996 by the W3C's specification for a Web style language. The style language, named **Cascading Style Sheets (CSS)**, allows authors to create style rules for elements and express them externally in a document known as a **style sheet**. CSS rules are easy to create and very powerful. For example, assume that you want all of your <h1> headings to appear green and centered everywhere on your Web site. For every instance of an <h1> element, you would have to include the following code in a standard HTML document:

```
<font color="green"><h1 align="center">Some Heading
Text</h1></font>
```

Using a CSS rule, you can express the same style as follows:

```
h1 {color: green; text-align: center;}
```

You can place this rule in an external style sheet and then link every page on your site to that style sheet; with much less code you can achieve the same result. Later, if you want to change the <h1> color to red, you simply revise the style sheet rule to change every page on your site.

Until recently, the adoption of CSS as a standard for style has been limited because of poor and uneven support by the major browsers. The newer browsers, such as Internet Explorer 6.0, Netscape Navigator 6.2, and Opera 6.0, offer more complete and consistent support for CSS. The current trend is to rely more heavily on style sheets to control the visual display of your content. You will learn more about CSS in the "Web Typography" chapter.

Organizing Information with Hypertext

The most engaging aspect of browsing the World Wide Web is the linking of information on related topics using **hypertext**, a non-linear way of organizing information. When using a hypertext system, you can jump from one related topic to another, quickly find the information that interests you, and return to your starting point or move onto another related topic of interest. As a hypertext author, you determine which terms to create as hypertext links and where users will end up when they click a link.

On the Web, clickable hyperlinks, which can be text or images, can connect you to another Web page or allow you to open or download a file, such as a sound, image, movie, or executable file. Although the basic one-way nature of a hypertext link has not changed since the Web was developed, the nature of the destination content has changed greatly. The different types of linked content and media have continually evolved as the Web grows into a richer, more interactive environment. Taking advantage of these new technologies in any Web site often requires users to have better connection speeds than they normally have with a modem. You will read more about connection speed as a design variable later in this chapter.

XML: AN OPEN STANDARD FOR STRUCTURING DATA

The first and only version of the **Extensible Markup Language (XML)** was released by the W3C in 1997. Like HTML, XML is also a subset of SGML, but has no predefined elements like <h1> or <p>. XML is a **meta-language**. The PC Webopaedia defines the meta prefix as meaning "about," so a meta-language is a language about a language. XML is thus a language that lets you describe a markup language, allowing you to create your own elements to meet your information needs. This flexibility significantly distinguishes XML from HTML and its predefined elements. XML provides a format for describing structured data that can be shared by different applications across multiple platforms. The ability to handle data efficiently over the Internet became important as the Web evolved to allow data-intensive tasks such as online shopping, banking, and stock trading.

XML Describes Data

The power of data representation in XML comes from separating display and style from the structure of data. XML elements describe only data, not presentation. Whereas HTML contains elements that describe a word as a paragraph or heading, XML declares an element to be a book title, item price, or phone number, for example. Once the data is structured in XML, it can be displayed across a variety of media, such as a computer display, television screen, or handheld device, using an associated style sheet that contains the appropriate display information.

XML is also valuable because it allows access to more meaningful searches for information, development of flexible applications, and multiple views of data. XML also is based on a non-proprietary standard that supports the open nature of the Web. Consider the following example.

Suppose you want to sell audio CDs on the Web. Currently, the markup code for a page from your online catalog looks like the following:

```
<body>
    <h1>Songs of the World</h1>
    <h2>Artist: World Singers</h2>
    <p>Format: CD</p>
    <p>Price: $12.95</p>
    <p>Track List</p>
    <ul>
    <li>A Song</li>
    <li>Another Song</li>
    </ul>
</body>
```

Using XML, you could code your catalog this way:

```
<recording>
    <title>Songs of the World</title>
    <artist>Artist: World Singers</artist>
    <format>CD</format>
    <price>12.95</price>
    <tracklist>
    <track number="1">A Song</track>
    <track number="2">Another Song</track>
    </tracklist>
</recording>
```

Notice how the data is structured by the elements in the two preceding examples. The HTML elements have no inherent meaning or connection to the data. They simply describe text types and display information. If a customer wants to search for a particular recording, the search program must read each line of code to find the title or artist based on the content. In contrast, the XML code has meaningful element names that could match the field names in a database. The search program could look quickly for a particular element that matches the user's request. An invoicing program could extract the price easily and list it on the customer's invoice. The possibilities are endless because the element names match and describe the data they contain.

Both people and machines can read XML code. Some years from now, someone could open your XML file and understand what you meant by using <headline> and <paragraph> as markup elements. The cross-platform, independent nature of XML supports a variety of data applications currently migrating to the Web. XML lets you display data on many devices without changing the essential data descriptions.

XML Syntax Rules

XML contains a number of syntax rules that are different from those in HTML. As you will see later in this chapter, XHTML conforms to XML syntax rules, so you only have to learn the syntax rules once for both languages.

Documents Must Be Well-Formed

Well-formed means that a document adheres to the syntax rules described in this section. Any document that does not meet the syntax rules will not be accepted as an XML document.

Elements Must Nest Correctly

You can nest XML tags, but they must not overlap. Each set of opening and closing tags must completely contain any elements that are nested within. For example, the following is incorrect XML syntax:

```
<paragraph><bold>some text… </paragraph></bold>
```

The closing tag for the bold attribute must come before the closing tag for the paragraph element. The correct nesting syntax follows:

```
<paragraph><bold> some text… </bold></paragraph>
```

XML Is Case-Sensitive

XML, unlike HTML, is case-sensitive. An XML browser will interpret <PARAGRAPH> and <paragraph> as two different elements. For this reason, use all lowercase characters for element and attribute names.

End Tags Are Required

In HTML, certain elements such as the <p> element had optional closing tags. This is not allowed in XML, where non-empty elements need a closing tag. For example, the following two <p> elements do not have closing tags:

```
<p>This is the first paragraph. <p>This is the second
paragraph.
```

In XML (and XHTML) the following example is correct:

```
<p>This is the first paragraph.</p> <p>This is the second
paragraph.</p>
```

Empty Elements Are Signified by a Closing Slash

Empty elements must either have a closing tag or be marked empty by a slash (/) in the single tag. For example, the <br> element, when rendered in XHTML, becomes <br/>.

Attribute Values Must Be Contained in Quotes

All attribute values in XML must be contained within quotes, unlike those in HTML. The following is incorrect XML syntax:

```
<h1 align=center>Heading</h1>
```

The correct syntax follows:

```
<h1 align="center">Heading</h1>
```

As you can see, these syntax rules are simple and fairly easy to implement. They ensure clean, more compatible code, allowing the use of XML data across a variety of destination devices and media. Your HTML code can benefit from following these syntax rules as well, which is another of the reasons for XHTML, as you will read in the next section.

XHTML: The Future of HTML

HTML has progressed through a number of versions since its inception. The latest standard is version 4.0, which was released by the W3C in late 1997. This is the last release of HTML in its current state. The next generation of HTML is called the **Extensible Hypertext Markup Language (XHTML)**. The W3C released the version 1.0 of XHTML in January 2000.

Benefits of Moving to XHTML

The W3C released the XHTML 1.0 standard in August of 1999. XHTML is a reformulation of the HTML 4.0 specification in XML. One of the significant advantages of making HTML part of XML is the stricter syntax, as described previously in this chapter's XML section. As more sites start to adopt XHTML, they will have to clean up any

1

code that does not match the standard. With more Web sites using cleaner code, browsers have to do less work judging between what is correct code and what is not. Additionally, XHTML is designed to appear properly in browsers that support HTML 4.0.

HTML was originally designed for limited document expression and has not adapted well to the exploding interest in the Web. Because XHTML is based on XML, it will be extensible, allowing developers to address future markup needs easily. XHTML is also designed to support the variety of new devices that will be accessing the Internet as new technologies emerge. Any XHTML-compliant software will be able to access and display XHTML regardless of the computer or display type.

Because XML allows better data handling, the new version of XHTML will work better with database and workflow applications. The next generation of HTML will include advanced support for form elements, defining them more for data handling than presentation, and allowing data to pass between applications and devices with greater ease. Tables will emphasize a data model that allows their content to be rendered based on the presentation device. For example, tabular data for stock pricing information could be sent to multiple destinations and displayed to best fit the user's individual display type. This arrangement gives the same data greater value; though it only needs to be generated once, it can be displayed in many ways.

Style Sheets Are Required

Because XHTML is an application of XML, you must use style sheets to render style in XHTML. Separating data from style means that the same information can be directed to various display devices simply by changing the style sheet. When different style sheets are used, the contents of the same Web page can be displayed on a computer monitor, TV screen, handheld device, or cellular phone screen. This data-once, destination-many format liberates the data and structure of XHTML documents to be used in a variety of applications. A script or applet would redesign the data presentation as it is requested from the server and apply the proper style sheet based on the user's choice of device.

There are two style-sheet languages currently available for use with XML or XHTML. These are:

- **Cascading Style Sheets (CSS)**—CSS has recently gained a lot of popularity based on increasing browser support. CSS is an easy-to-use style language that controls only how documents are displayed.

- **Extensible Style Language (XSL)**—As an application of XML, XSL both describes page formatting and allows XML documents to be transformed from one type to another. XSL supports the use of CSS style rules within an XSL style sheet, so the two style languages complement each other.

Stricter Syntax Rules

XHTML follows the syntax rules of XML described previously in this chapter. To review, here are the syntax rules that you must follow in XHTML:

- Documents must be well-formed

- Elements must nest symmetrically

- Element names are case-sensitive

- End tags are required

- Empty elements are signified by a closing slash

- Attribute values must be contained in quotes

If you anticipate working with XHTML in the future, you should consider following these syntax rules in your HTML code now. This will ensure that the HTML you are creating today will work with XHTML in the future. If you have legacy HTML code, consider revising it to meet XHTML syntax standards. The following code shows an example of HTML code that is common on the Web today. Although not syntactically correct, this code would be displayed properly in the browser:

```
<H1>Some plain HTML code</h1>
<P ALIGN=CENTER>This is a paragraph of text.
<IMG SRC="xml.gif">
<H3>A bulleted list</H3>
<UL>
<LI>Item one
<LI>Item two
<LI>Item three
```

Converting this code to syntactically correct XHTML means applying the stricter syntax rules listed earlier, resulting in the following code:

```
<h1>Some plain HTML code</h1>
<p align="center">This is a paragraph of text.</p>
<img src="xml.gif"/>
<h3>A bulleted list</h3>
<ul>
<li>Item one</li>
<li>Item two</li>
<li>Item three</li>
</ul>
```

 Many shareware and commercial software programs will assist you in bringing your code up to XHTML standards. These include HTML Tidy at *http://www.w3.org/People/Raggett/tidy/* and Tidy GUI at *http://perso.wanadoo.fr/ablavier/TidyGUI/*.

HOW WEB BROWSERS AFFECT YOUR WORK

One of the greatest challenges facing HTML authors is designing pages that multiple browsers display properly. Every browser contains a program called a **parser** that interprets the markup tags in an HTML file and displays the results in the **canvas area** of the browser interface, as illustrated in Figure 1-2. The logic for interpreting the HTML tags varies from browser to browser, resulting in many possibly conflicting interpretations of the way the HTML file is displayed. As a Web page designer, you must test your work in as many different browsers as possible to ensure that the work you create appears as you designed it. Although you may consider your work cross-browser compatible, you may be surprised to see that the results of your HTML code look very different when viewed with different browsers.

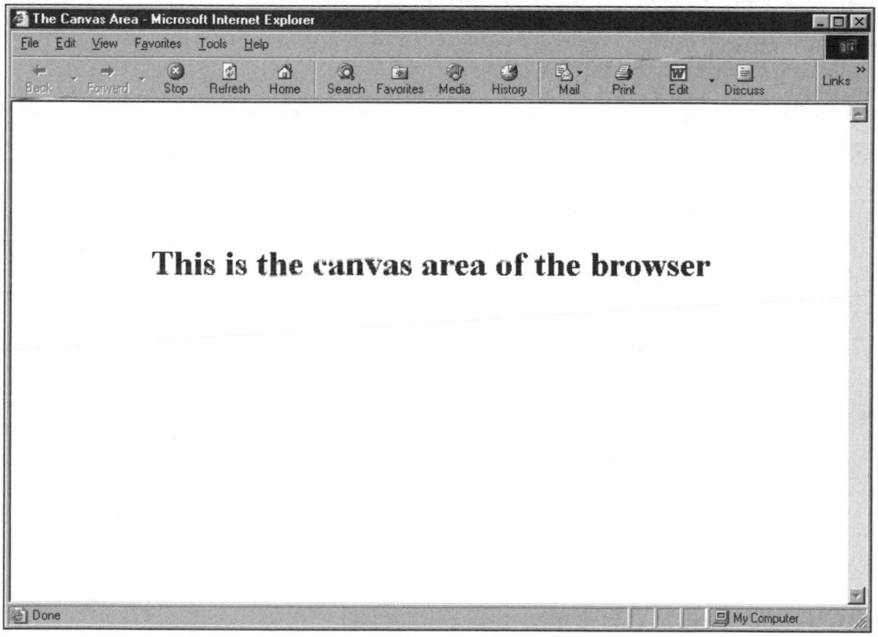

Figure 1-2   The canvas area of the browser

Browser Compatibility Issues

As different browsers competed for market share, a set of proprietary HTML elements evolved for the use of each particular browser. Some examples of these elements are <font> and <center>, which were developed specifically for the Netscape browser. <font> eventually became part of the HTML 3.2 specification, but it has been designated a deprecated element in HTML 4.0. **Deprecated elements** are those that the W3C has identified as obsolete and will not be included in future releases of HTML. However, it is likely that such elements will be supported by browsers for some time. The browser developers would be doing users a disservice (and possibly losing market share) if they removed support for these elements.

Confusing the compatibility issue further are the elements that are strictly proprietary, such as <marquee> (Internet Explorer only), which creates scrolling text, and <blink> (Netscape Navigator only), which makes text blink on and off. These elements work only within the browser for which they were designed and are ignored by other browsers. Because proprietary elements like these go against the open, portable nature of the Web, they are not included in the standard maintained by the W3C. Avoid using proprietary elements unless you are sure that your audience is using only the browser for which they were designed.

The newer browsers such as Internet Explorer 6.0, Netscape 6.0, and Opera 6.0 offer much better support for the standards released by the W3C. The browser software companies have found that the Web development community benefits from the increased support of the standards. More consistent browsers allow better visual design and increased interactivity for all users.

Most HTML authors do not have the luxury of knowing the age, type, or operating system of the browser that will be used to view their Web pages. Browser and version choices can vary widely based on a number of variables. Many individuals and organizations are reluctant to upgrade software simply because a new version has been released. Other users may have older computers that do not have the processing speed or disk space to handle a newer browser. Although it is a good idea to test with the latest browsers, it also is prudent to test your work in older browsers to maximize the number of people who see your Web pages as you intend.

As discussed earlier, not only are new browsers released frequently, but older browsers still are used by many Web users. The newer browsers support desirable features, such as Cascading Style Sheets, that are not supported by older browsers. Including newly supported features in your page design may significantly affect the way your page is viewed if the browser cannot interpret the latest enhancements. Browsers exhibit subtle differences across computing platforms as well.

Creating Cross-Browser Compatible Pages

How can you handle the demands of different browsers while designing attractive Web pages? Some HTML authors suggest that you use an older version of HTML to ensure portability. Others say that you should push the medium forward by coding to the latest standard and using the most recent enhancements. Some Web sites recommend that you use a particular brand and version of browser to access the site. Let us examine each of these methods to determine the best way to design your site.

 If you would like to download a particular browser, or find out which browser is currently the most popular, visit one of these Web sites:
BrowserWatch at *browser.evolt.org/*
CNET Browser Info at *www.browsers.com*

1

Lowest Common Denominator Coding

Although it can be difficult to create pages that are always displayed properly, it is not impossible. One way to create portable pages is to use a lowest-common-denominator approach. This approach provides the greatest acceptance across browsers, because the authors choose to code their HTML using the next-to-last release of HTML. For example, when the browsers supporting HTML 4.0 were released, many continued coding to the HTML 3.2 standard, knowing that their HTML would render more consistently because the browsers understood all of the 3.2 specifications. This safer method of coding is widely supported among sites that are interested in the greatest accessibility. Maintaining coding specifications of a previous release of HTML does not mean that your site has to be visually uninteresting, although you may have to sacrifice the latest enhancements. Reliable visual and information design techniques, discussed in Chapter 2, can let you overcome many functional limitations.

Cutting-Edge Coding

Another strategy to adopt when designing your Web site is to stay at the cutting edge. By requiring the latest software, some designers insist that their users keep up with them. This design strategy can result in visually exciting and interactive sites that keep pace with the latest technology. Often the user must have not only the latest browser version but also plug in enhancements that render certain media types such as Macromedia Flash animations. **Plug-ins** are helper applications that assist a browser in rendering a special effect. Without the plug-in, your user will not see the results of your work. Often when a new browser is released, these plug-ins are included for the most widely adopted enhancements. The risk of the cutting-edge approach is that many users may not be able to see the content as it was designed. Sites that use the latest enhancements also may require significant download times for the special effects to load on the user's computer. If sites that adopt the latest technologies do not make sure that their users keep up with the latest browser versions and plug-ins, their information may go unread.

Browser-Specific Coding

Some Web sites are coded for one particular browser or brand of browsers only. The author may have wanted to use a unique enhancement for the site, or may have found that the site did not render properly in other browsers. Although this may seem the most expedient coding method, consider the consequences. A site coded for only one browser may alienate a significant number of readers who immediately leave because they do not have the correct browser. On the Web, you never can be sure of the type of browser your user has. However, this method of browser-specific coding may be viable on a company **intranet**, where you know or you can specify that all users have the same brand and version of browser. For the general Web it is the least desirable choice, because you are limiting the availability of your site.

Solving the Browser Dilemma

You must test your work in as many browsers as possible during the entire development process to make sure that your pages will render properly. Knowing your audience is a major step towards correctly implementing your site. For example, you may be building a site that discusses the latest in technology trends. This site will attract computer-savvy users, so you can code for the latest browsers. On the other hand, if you are creating a site that will attract the general public, you should code for the lowest common denominator and make sure your pages appear as designed in every browser. Many general Web users access the Web via America Online, Inc. (AOL), so test your work using their browser as well. In an academic environment you may encounter readers that use Lynx, a text-only browser. For this type of audience, avoid using too many graphics, and make sure that all of the graphics you include have alt attributes, which provide alternate text information about images. (You'll learn more about alt attributes in the "Graphics and Color" chapter.) If you want to include animations or effects that require a plug-in, use a development tool that already is supported by the major browsers. Make sure that the most important content on your site is rendered in a way that does not rely on the new technology so that users with older browsers still get your message. Finally, if you are designing for an intranet and can mandate the type of software your viewers use, you can work with only one browser in mind.

CODING FOR MULTIPLE SCREEN RESOLUTIONS

No matter how carefully you design pages, you can never know how users view your work because you do not know their monitors' screen resolution. A computer monitor's **screen resolution** is the width and height of the computer screen in pixels. Most monitors can be set to at least two resolutions, whereas larger monitors have a broader range from which to choose. User screen resolution is a factor over which you have no control.

Screen resolution is a function of the monitor's capabilities and the computer's video card. The three most common screen resolutions (traditionally expressed as width $\times$ height in pixels) are 640 $\times$ 480, 800 $\times$ 600, and 1024 $\times$ 768. Some users choose the highest resolution of 1024 $\times$ 768, allowing them to display more on the screen. They may have multiple application windows open at the same time. Users at 800 $\times$ 600 usually maximize their browser to full screen, whereas those working at 640 $\times$ 480 may see additional scroll bars if content does not fit on their screen.

Be careful when making the decision to code at higher resolutions. Any content outside the user's window will require the use of horizontal scroll bars. Although vertical scroll bars are the norm, users consider horizontal scroll bars annoying. Figure 1-3 shows a Web page coded at 800 $\times$ 600 and viewed at 640 $\times$ 480 with horizontal scroll bars. The user must repeatedly scroll from left to right when reading. Users do not like to scroll horizontally to read text, so be sure to minimize the need for horizontal scrolling as much as possible.

Fixed Resolution Design

Figures 1-3 through 1-5 show the same Web page viewed at different screen resolutions.

Figure 1-3   Fixed design at 640 X 480

Figure 1-4   Fixed design at 800 X 600

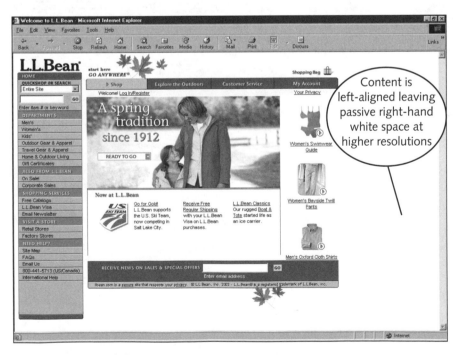

Figure 1-5   Fixed design at 1024 X 768

Notice that the page is designed to display its content within an 800 × 600 screen resolution without making the user scroll, indicating that 800 × 600 is the base screen resolution of this Web site. Users viewing the page at 640 × 480 do not see all of the content and must scroll both horizontally and vertically. Users viewing the page at 1024 × 768 see the content aligned to the left side of the page, and the passive white space on the right side of the page fills in the remainder of the screen. You will read more about the use of active and passive white space in the "Web Site Design Principles" chapter.

Flexible Resolution Design

In contrast, Figures 1-6 through 1-8 show a Web page that has been designed to adapt to different screen resolutions.

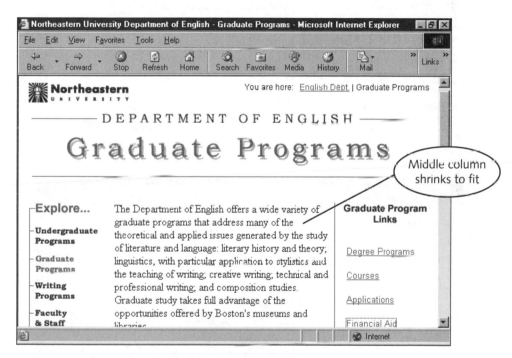

Figure 1-6   Flexible design at 640 X 480

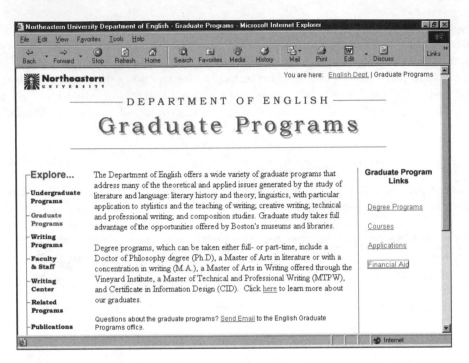

Figure 1-7   Flexible design at 800 X 600

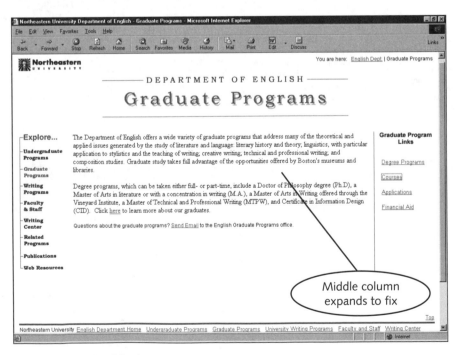

Figure 1-8   Flexible design at 1024 X 768

The Web page shown in Figures 1-6 to 1-8 was designed for an 800 × 600 resolution but is adaptable to other resolutions as well. As the screen resolution changes, the middle column expands or contracts to accommodate the varying screen width, while the outside columns remain fixed. Notice that the design fits without horizontal scrolling on even the lowest screen resolution. The designers accomplished this adaptability through variable rather than absolute table widths. You will learn about this technique in the "Creating Page Templates" chapter.

As a Web designer, you decide how to code your Web site to handle different screen resolutions. Most Web sites were once coded to the lowest possible screen resolution, which is 640 × 480. Now that monitors are getting bigger and less expensive, the majority of Web users probably have their screen resolution set to 800 × 600, which is the current standard resolution for most Web sites. If you know your audience is consistently using a higher resolution, you can code to it. Otherwise, code to the lowest resolution to make sure that your content fits most screens. Remember to test at different resolutions to ensure that your user can view your pages properly.

BANDWIDTH CONCERNS

Although many cable and media providers would have you believe otherwise, it will still be a while before most computer users gain high-speed access to the Web. According to Cable Datacom News (*http://www.cabledatacomnews.com/*), "At the end of 2001 U.S. broadband penetration reached 10 percent." Access via cable modem is currently the most reliable high-speed connection to the Web for home users. Corporations rely primarily on T1 or Integrated Services Digital Network (ISDN) connections. Digital Subscriber Line (DSL), a new technology that allows voice and high-speed Internet access on the same line, is available to only 5 to 10 percent of all the households in the U.S. Table 1-1 describes the more common types of connection technologies.

Connection speed is another factor that should influence your Web page design. Most users simply will not wait longer than 10-20 seconds for a page to load. If your pages download slowly, your users probably will click to go to another site before they see even a portion of your content. Many designers make the mistake of not testing their pages at different connection speeds. If you do not test, you cannot appreciate what it is like for users to connect at different speeds to your site, and you may lose valuable visitors.

Because the single biggest factor influencing the speed at which your pages render is the size and number of graphics on your Web pages, you should keep your page designs simple with few graphics. As a rule of thumb, no single image on your Web site should exceed 10 to 15K. If you know your users all have faster access, you can design your pages to match. For the general public you can consider 56 Kbps as a base connection speed because many users still use modems. You will learn more about how to prepare your images to download quickly in the "Graphics and Color" chapter.

Table 1-1   Common Types of Connection Technologies

Technology	Speed	Notes
Regular telephone line	Up to 56 Kbps	This is still the most common method of connecting to the Internet. However, you're lucky if you can consistently maintain a connection speed over 44 Kbps.
ISDN basic	64 Kbps to 128 Kbps	ISDN offers good speed and allows a constant connection to the Internet, but is fairly expensive. ISDN is more common in urban areas and is primarily used by business.
Digital Subscriber Line	512 Kbps to 8 Mbps	For DSL to work well, you must be located within 18,000 feet of your local telephone office. DSL uses a single existing phone line to carry both voice and data, and allows a constant connection to the Internet.
Cable modem	512 Kbps to 52 Mbps	Cable modems are fast and allow a constant connection to the Internet. You don't have to dial up to connect. Many cable systems are rushing to install Internet access, but most households will wait at least 2–5 years.

Working with the Cache

All Web pages are stored on computers called Web servers. When you type a Uniform Resource Locator (URL) address in your browser, it connects to the appropriate Web server and requests the file you specified. The server serves up the file so your browser can download it. The first time you visit a site, the entire contents of the HTML file (which is plain text) and every image referenced in the HTML code is downloaded to your hard drive. The next time you visit this site, your browser downloads and parses the HTML file. The browser checks to see if it has any of the specified images stored locally on the computer's hard drive in the **cache**. The cache is the browser's temporary storage area for Web pages and images. The browser always tries to load images from the cache rather than downloading them again from the Web.

You can make use of the browser's caching capabilities by reusing graphics as much as possible throughout your site. Once an image is downloaded, it remains in your user's cache for the number of days specified in the user's preference settings. Most users do not change the settings, so there is a good chance your graphics will remain on the user's hard drive a while. Every time the user revisits your site, the cached graphics load locally rather than from the Web server. The browser's caching capability is a great argument for standardizing the look of your site by using the same navigation, branding, and background graphics throughout. Not only will the consistency reassure users, but also your pages will load faster.

Should You Use an HTML Editor?

You can create or generate HTML code to build Web pages in many ways. Until recently, the tool most widely accepted was Notepad, the simple text editor that comes with Windows versions from 95 to XP. On the Macintosh, the equivalent tool is TeachText or SimpleText. Many sites on the Web are coded using these text editing tools, which are easy to use and still relied upon by top-notch HTML authors. They also are the best way to learn HTML because you have to enter every tag by hand. However, fewer designers use simple text editors now that increasingly robust HTML authoring packages have appeared.

There are a variety of HTML editing programs, such as Adobe PageMill, Microsoft FrontPage, and Macromedia Dreamweaver, to name a few. Some code-based HTML editors, such as Macromedia HomeSite, forgo a WYSIWYG approach. They have become popular because they include many powerful enhancements that Notepad lacks, such as multiple search-and-replace features and syntax checking, while still allowing you to manipulate code at the tag level.

Many of the latest office applications now convert documents to HTML. For example, you can create a flyer in your word processor and export it to create an HTML page. You can even create slides in Microsoft PowerPoint or Lotus Freelance Graphics and export them to HTML. This hands-off approach leaves much to be desired for an HTML author because you give up control over the finished product. Additionally, the practice of converting content from a program such as Microsoft Word to HTML is notorious for creating less-than-standard HTML code. You are better off moving away from one of the office applications to a dedicated HTML authoring package if you are serious about creating attractive, portable Web sites.

As with the browsers, authoring packages interpret tags based on their own built-in logic. Therefore, a page that you create in an editing package may look quite different in the editing interface than it does in a browser. Furthermore, many editing packages create complex, less-than-standard code to achieve an effect specified by the user. The more complex code can cause compatibility problems across different browsers. Remember that HTML is a relatively simple language that is not meant to express complex layouts. Many Web page designers, spoiled by the ease of use of today's powerful word processors, build complex pages with complicated text effects and spacing. When the editing program has to translate this for display with simple HTML, it must resort to a variety of methods that may result in code that is difficult to update or debug. HTML authors who are used to coding by hand (in Notepad or another text editor) often are surprised to see the code an HTML editing package has generated. To code effectively with HTML, you must be comfortable working directly at the code level. Though you may choose to use one of the many editing packages to generate the basic layout or structure for your page or to build a complex table, be prepared to edit the code at the tag level to fix any discrepancies. You probably will end up working with a combination of tools to create your finished pages.

CHAPTER SUMMARY

Many variables affect the way users view your Web pages. As an HTML author, your goal should be to code pages that are accessible to the largest audience possible. As you plan your Web site, make the following decisions before implementing your site.

▫ Decide whether to use Cascading Style Sheets. The style enhancements and control offered by this style language are formidable, but are not evenly supported by older browsers. Implement CSS gradually, testing for browser compatibility as you go.

▫ Choose the suite of browsers you will use to test your site. Although you will include the latest versions of Netscape and Internet Explorer, consider testing in older versions of each browser as well. Test with Opera if your site has a large international audience. If you have a large academic audience, test in Lynx.

▫ Decide how browser-specific your site will be. Your goal is to create a site that is widely accessible to multiple browsers. If you have a narrow audience or specific requirements, you may want to specify one browser as the primary method for viewing your site.

▫ Choose the type of editing tool you will use to create your HTML code. You may want to use a WYSIWYG editor to create the general page layout and then rely on Notepad to make corrections to your code. Alternately, a code-based editor such as Macromedia HomeSite lets you work directly with code while enjoying enhancements that Notepad doesn't support.

▫ Resolve to test your work continually as you build your site. Test with multiple browsers at different screen resolutions and at different connection speeds. If you can, view your site on multiple platforms such as PC, Macintosh, and UNIX as well.

REVIEW QUESTIONS

1. HTML is a subset of which markup language?

2. List three characteristics of HTML that make it ideal for the World Wide Web.

3. What are the benefits of viewing source code on the Web?

4. What work does the World Wide Web Consortium perform?

5. What is a deprecated element?

6. What is a proprietary element?

7. What style language allows the separation of style from structure in HTML?

8. What are the advantages of using an external style sheet?

9. What feature distinguishes XML from HTML?

10. What are the two types of style languages designed for use with XML?

11. Explain how XML lends itself to customized data applications.

12. What improvements does XHTML promise over existing HTML?

13. Explain how different browsers affect the display of a Web page.

14. Describe the characteristics of lowest-common-denominator coding.

15. Describe how coding using the latest technology can prevent users from accessing your site.

16. List the three most common screen resolutions.

17. Explain how screen resolution affects the display of a Web page.

18. List four common types of Internet connection technologies.

19. Explain how the browser's caching capability improves download time.

HANDS-ON PROJECTS

1. Visit the World Wide Web Consortium Web site (*www.w3.org*). Find and describe the three types of XHTML 1.0—Transitional, Strict, and Frames—and explain why you might use each.

2. View and copy the source code of a Web site into your text editor. Critique the code for syntax errors and non-standard usage of HTML. Try to determine the version of HTML to which the page is coded.

3. Visit the World Wide Web Consortium Web site (*www.w3.org*). Find the Cascading Style Sheets specification. List and describe ten style properties that you can affect with a style rule.

4. Visit the World Wide Web Consortium Web site (*www.w3.org*) and examine the Web Accessibility Initiative (WAI). Describe how you would design a page that meets the WAI guidelines.

5. Describe three common mistakes that Web designers make when building a Web site.

6. Test the HTML conversion capabilities of a standard office application.

   a. Use your favorite word processing, spreadsheet, or presentation graphics program that supports conversion to HTML.

   b. Create a document and export it to HTML.

   c. Examine and evaluate the HTML code. Look for non-standard coding techniques or tricks that the program uses to render content into HTML. Write a detailed description of your findings.

7. Test cross-browser compatibility.

   a. Make sure you have recent versions of both Netscape Navigator and Internet Explorer installed on your computer.

   b. Browse a variety of Web sites. Make sure to view various pages of the sites in both browsers.

   c. Write a detailed description of how successfully the various sites appear in both browsers. Look for text, layout, and graphic inconsistencies.

8. View source code in a browser.

In the following steps you view the source code from a live Web page in your browser. Choose the instructions for the Internet Explorer 6.0, Netscape 6.2, or Opera 6.0.

To view source code in Internet Explorer 6.0 or Opera 6.0:

❑ Click View on the menu bar, and then click Source. Your system's text editor, either Notepad, SimpleText, ort WordPad opens and displays the page's source code. You then can save the file to your own hard drive and manipulate the code.

To view source code in Netscape Navigator 6.2:

❑ Click View on the menu bar, then click Page Source. The page's source code opens in another window of Netscape. You can copy and paste text from this window into your own text or HTML editor, then manipulate and test the code. You cannot edit directly in the Page Source window.

Whenever you copy code from a Web site, remember to respect the author's copyrights on any original material. Although page layouts cannot be copyrighted, any original text or graphics are the property of the author and should be properly cited.

CASE PROJECT

To complete the ongoing case study for this book, you must create a complete stand-alone Web site. The site must contain between six and ten pages, displaying at least three levels of information. You can choose your own content. For example, you can do a work-related topic, a personal interest site, or a site for your favorite non-profit organization. The site will be evaluated for cohesiveness, accessibility, and design. At the end of each chapter you will complete a different section of the project. For Chapter 1, get started by creating a project proposal, as in the following outline. As you progress through the chapters of the book, you will complete different facets of the Web site construction, resulting in a complete Web site.

Project Proposal

Create a one- or two-page HTML document stating the basic elements you will include in your Web site. Create this document using your favorite HTML editor or Notepad. At this stage your proposal is primarily a draft. At the end of the next chapter you will have a chance to modify the proposal and supplement the design details.

Include the following items, if applicable:

- **Site title**—Specify the working title for the site.
- **Developer**—Identify yourself and anyone else who will work on the site.
- **Rationale or focus**—Explain the content and goals of the site, such as billboard, customer support, catalog/e-commerce, informational, or resource. Refer to Chapter 3 for help on content types.
- **Main elements outline**—The main features of the site.
- **Content**—Estimate the number of individual Web pages.
- **Target audience**—Describe the typical audience for the site.
- **Design considerations**—The design goals for the site.
- **Limiting factors**—The technical or audience factors that could limit the design goals of the site.

2

WEB SITE DESIGN PRINCIPLES

When you complete this chapter, you will be able to:

♦ Design for the computer medium
♦ Design the whole site
♦ Design for the user
♦ Design for the screen

This chapter covers the basic design principles that you will apply to your Web page designs as you work through this book. By examining a variety of Web sites, you will learn to focus on both the user's needs and the information requirements of the content you want to deliver, while planning a site that is easy to navigate and quick to download.

The sample Web pages in this chapter come from a wide range of sites. The Web is so far-reaching in content and design that no collection of pages represents what is typical. Most of the samples illustrate good design principles, although some contain design defects as well. In truth, almost every site has one flaw or another, whether it is confusing accessibility, over-ambitious design, or poor download time. Judge the samples with a critical eye. Look for elements of design that you can transfer to your own work. As you progress through the book, you will practice and apply these principles to your own Web design efforts.

DESIGN FOR THE COMPUTER MEDIUM

When designing a Web site, remember the destination is a computer monitor, not the printed page. As a Web page designer, you must create Web pages specifically for the computer screen. You must consider how the layout, fonts, and colors will appear onscreen. As an HTML author, you must consider the nonlinear nature of hypertext, weaving the appropriate links and associations into the information. Give users the options to follow the information path they desire by providing appropriate links to related topics. Make them feel comfortable at your site by letting them know where they are and where they can go.

Craft the Look and Feel

The interface that the user must navigate often is called the look and feel of a Web site. Users look and feel when they explore the information design of your site. They read text, make associations with links, view graphics, and, depending on the freedom of your design, create their own path through your information. The look and feel is both the way your Web site works and the personality it conveys to the user. Not only should you plan for a deliberate look and feel, but you must test your design against the variable nature of the Web. You want to ensure that the greatest number of users can navigate your site reliably.

Make Your Design Portable

To be successful, your Web site design must be portable and accessible by users who have different browsers, operating systems, and computer platforms. Many designers make the mistake of testing in only one environment, assuming that their pages look the same to all of their users. No matter how much Web design experience you gain, always remember to test in different environments even when you feel confident of your results. For example, Figures 2-1 and 2-2 show the same page displayed in Netscape Navigator 6.0 and Netscape Navigator 4.75. The page is coded with Cascading Style Sheets (CSS) code that the older version of Netscape cannot interpret. Notice that the page contains a link informing users that they must use an updated browser to view the site. As you can see by comparing the two figures, Netscape 4.75 has significant problems with CSS that render the page unreadable.

You can avoid problems like these by testing for compatibility. Viewing your pages in the browsers your users are likely to have, testing on the popular operating systems, and checking the site on more than one computer platform ensure that your site is accessible to the greatest number of users. Consider analyzing your audience and building a profile of your average user. Perhaps many of them have moved up to a newer browser, allowing you to build pages that can take advantage of newer technologies such as the CSS example shown here. You will read more about analyzing your audience in the "Planning the Site" chapter.

2

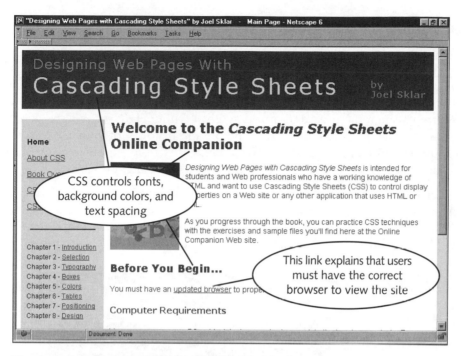

Figure 2-1 Netscape 6.0 correctly displays the CSS styles

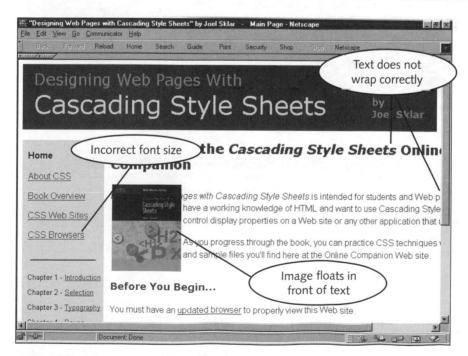

Figure 2-2 Netscape 4.75 has problems with CSS

Design for Low Bandwidth

Plan your pages so that they are accessible at a variety of connection speeds. If your pages download slowly because they contain large, detailed graphics or complicated animations, your users will leave before they ever see your content. According to Keynote Systems (*www.keynote.com*), which measures Web performance, the average user clicks away from a site if the page does not download within eight seconds. As you learned in Chapter 1, it will be a few more years before the majority of your users have a consistent, high-speed connection to the Web. Until that time, consider users with a lower bandwidth when you design the look and feel of your site.

The Petco Web site (*www.petco.com*) main page, illustrated in Figure 2-3, contains 71 separate images totaling 84 Kb in file size. Although most of these images average only 1 Kb or 2 Kb each, the sheer number of images that must be sent to the user's computer means a lengthy download time, especially for first-time visitors.

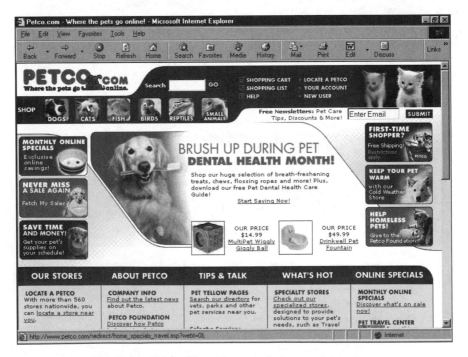

Figure 2-3　The Petco Web site main page is image-intensive

Plan for Clear Presentation and Easy Access to Your Information

Your information design—the presentation and organization of your information—is the single most important factor in determining the success of your site. Your graphics and navigation options—the look and feel of your site—must present a variety of options to the user without detracting from their quest for information. A visitor to your site may choose to browse randomly or look for specific information. Often users arrive at a page looking for data low in the hierarchy of information. Sometimes users arrive at your site seeking a specific piece of information, such as a telephone number or order form. Anticipate and plan for the actions and paths that users are likely to choose when they traverse your site. Provide direct links to the areas of your site that you feel are most in demand.

The screen's low resolution makes the computer monitor a poor reading medium. The light source coming from behind the text tires the user's eye. Environmental factors such as glare or physical distance from the screen affect the user as well. To counter this, design your information so it is easy to read. Many Web sites fail this criterion by using too many fonts, colors, and lengthy passages of text. Break text into reasonable segments that make for easier on-screen reading. Think about providing contrasting colors that are easy to read and easy on the eye, such as dark colors against a light or white background.

Keep in mind that readers have different habits when reading online. Compared to how they read printed text, they scan more and read less online, skimming long pages quickly as they scroll through the text. Include plenty of headings so users can find content quickly. Control the horizontal length of your text to provide complete, easy-to-read columns. Keep the "seven plus or minus two" rule of information design in mind; that is, users cannot comprehend more than seven plus or minus two steps or segments of information at one time. For example, a well-written procedure would contain no more than nine steps. Rather than presenting long scrolling pages, break information into smaller chunks and link them with hypertext.

DESIGN THE WHOLE SITE

When designing your site, plan the unifying themes and structure that will hold the pages together. Your choices of colors, fonts, graphics, and page layout should communicate a visual theme to users that orients them to your site's content. The theme should reflect the impression that you or your organization wants to convey. For example, Figure 2-4 shows the White House Web site main page. This mainly text-filled page has a restrained, newspaper-like feel. The content is primarily news and information links.

The use of subdued colors, familiar, business-oriented fonts, and structured, linear columns underscores the content and emphasizes the news and informational theme. The White House also maintains a Web site for children (*www.whitehousekids.gov*), as illustrated in Figure 2-5.

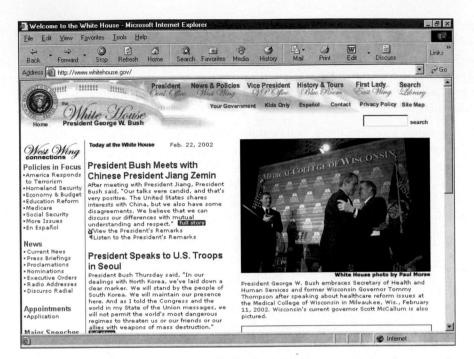

Figure 2-4   The White House Web site main page

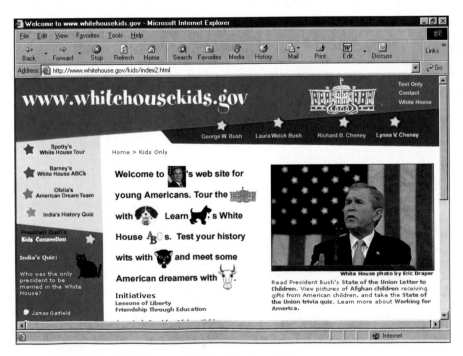

Figure 2-5   The White House Web site for children

While the site for adults communicates a serious impression, the site for children combines bright colors, an open, friendly font, a dynamic structure, and simple, appealing graphics to present a livelier, more playful theme.

When you design the whole site, you must consider more than each individual page. For a well-integrated site, create smooth transitions, use a grid to provide visual structure, and use active white space. Each technique is explained in the following sections.

Create Smooth Transitions

Plan to create a unified look among the sections and pages of your site. Reinforce the identifying elements of the site and create smooth transitions from one page to another by repeating colors and fonts and by using a page layout that allows different hierarchical levels. Avoid random, jarring changes in your format, unless this is the effect you want to achieve. Consistency creates smooth transitions from one page to the next, reassures viewers that they are traveling within the boundaries of your site, and helps them find information.

Think of users turning the pages of a periodical when they browse from Web page to Web page. Although each page should be a complete entity, it also is a part of the whole site. The overall design of a page at any information level should reflect the identity of the site. For example, Figures 2-6 and 2-7 show the main page and a secondary-level page from the National Public Radio Web site (*www.npr.org*).

Figure 2-6   The National Public Radio Web site main page

Because these pages share the same color scheme, navigation icons, and identifying graphics, the Web site offers a smooth transition from the main page to the secondary page and a unified look and feel.

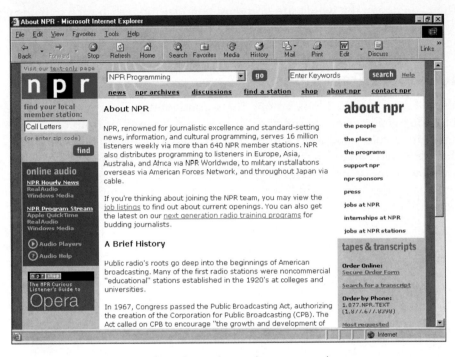

Figure 2-7   The National Public Radio Web site secondary page

Use a Grid to Provide Visual Structure

The structure of a Web page is imposed by the grid or page template you choose for your page design. The **grid** is a conceptual layout device that organizes the page into columns and rows. You can impose a grid to provide visual consistency throughout your site. You can use the grid to enforce structure, but you also can break out of the grid to provide variety and highlight important information.

HTML authors use the HTML table elements to build the grid for their pages. Although originally designed for tabular data, the table elements were used by designers as a tool for building the type of columnar grid structure they were accustomed to using in traditional print media. Most current Web sites use tables in one form or another to give their pages structure and consistency. With table borders turned off, the user cannot tell the layout is held together by a table; they see a coherent, well-structured page. The reliance on tables as a design tool will eventually wane as more users adopt newer browsers that support CSS, which allows columnar positioning without tables.

Use Active White Space

White spaces are the blank areas of a page, regardless of the color you choose to give them. Use white space deliberately in your design, rather than as an afterthought. Good use of white space guides the reader and defines the areas of your page. White space that is used deliberately is called **active white space** and is an integral part of your design that structures and separates content. Sometimes the strongest part of a design is the active white space. Passive white spaces are blank areas that border the screen or are the result of mismatched shapes. Figure 2-8 illustrates active versus passive white space.

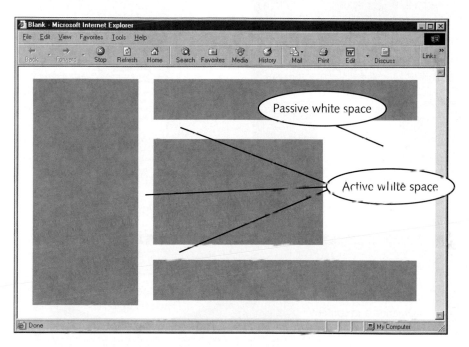

Figure 2-8   Areas of active and passive white space

Content presentation can become confused when designers do not use enough active white space to separate and define content. The Scientific American Web site (*www.sciam.com*) illustrated in Figure 2-9 would be easier to scan if it used more active white space between the content areas.

A lack of active white space creates the impression that a page contains too much information and that it will be difficult to find the piece of information you want. In contrast, the Christian Science Monitor Web site page (*www.csmonitor.com*) in Figure 2-10 shows good use of active white space, making it much easier to read. Plenty of active white space reduces clutter and clarifies the organization of your ideas.

Figure 2-9 More white space would diminish the clutter

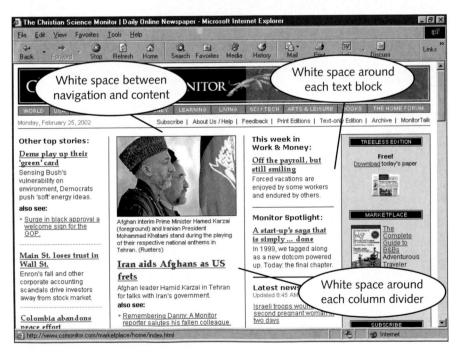

Figure 2-10 Active white space enhances legibility

Provide grounding for the user by placing navigation elements in the same position on each page. Users orient themselves quickly to your navigation structure. Use the same navigation graphics throughout the site to provide consistency and avoid the need to download a wide variety of graphics.

Apply some of these principles to two mainstream Web sites. Figures 2-11 and 2-12, from the National Gallery of Art Web site *(www.nga.gov)*, demonstrate a smooth transition between pages.

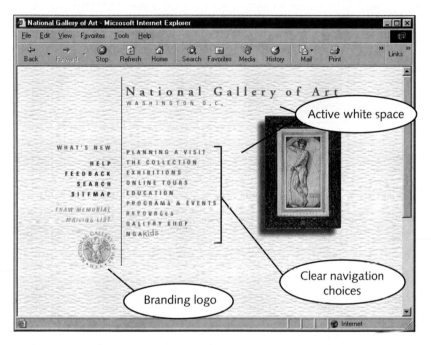

Figure 2-11   National Gallery of Art Web site main page

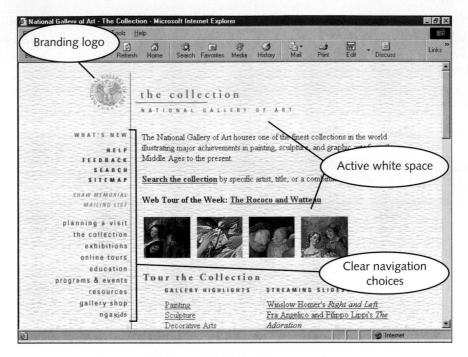

Figure 2-12   National Gallery of Art Web site secondary page

The main page and secondary page share a number of characteristics:

- Consistent background texture
- Consistent placement of navigation information
- Two-column layout
- Vertical rule that provides structure
- Consistent font usage
- Logo that brands the site
- Generous areas of active white space

The continuity between these pages reinforces that they are part of a larger piece of work. The understated fonts and colors and the quiet background graphics provide an appropriate museum-like impression. One design rule to note—the logo should remain in the same place on all pages for consistency. Users may otherwise look for reasons the logo has moved, which distracts them from your message.

The NASA Human Spaceflight Web site (*www.spaceflight.nasa.gov/*), illustrated in Figures 2-13 and 2-14, has a much different look but still applies the same principles as the National Gallery of Art Web site. In these two pages from the NASA site, the top banner and navigation graphic provide continuity. The unifying colors and typefaces tie the pages together. The consistent page width and the white space on the left and right sides of the page enforce the same visual structure for both pages, even though the content column widths are different. Notice that the main page is designed for scanning the various links and options the site offers, while the secondary page is designed for reading about the selected subject.

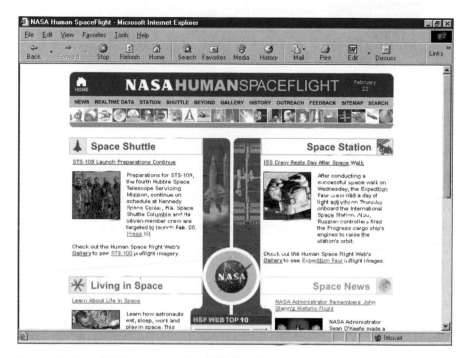

Figure 2-13   NASA Human Spaceflight Web site main page

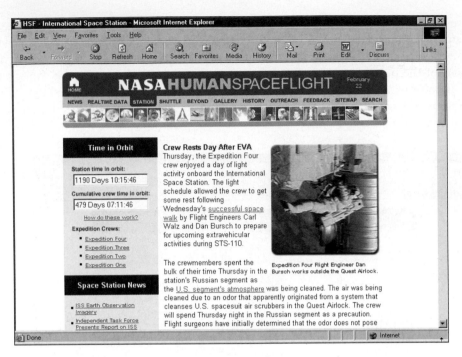

Figure 2-14   NASA Human Spaceflight Web site secondary page

DESIGN FOR THE USER

Keep your design efforts centered solely on your user. Knowing your audience answers almost all design questions—if it serves the audience, keep it; if it is potentially distracting or annoying, eliminate it. Find out what users expect from your site. If you can, survey them with an online form. Create a profile of your average user by compiling responses to basic questions. What do users want when they get to your site? Are they trying to find customer support and troubleshooting help, or do they want to buy something? Do they want to read articles or search for information? Once you know what your users want from your site, you can evaluate how the design reflects the audience profile.

Compare the main pages from the following sites and consider their target audiences. The E! online Web site (*www.eonline.com*), shown in Figure 2-15, is an entertainment news site. The four-column main page contains competing content that draws the user's eye, such as animations, a Java text scroll, bright colors, and familiar shapes. The overall effect is decidedly similar to television—familiar territory for E! online's audience.

Linguafranca's Web site (*www.linguafranca.com*) in Figure 2-16 projects a strong journal-like layout. The main page components are textual. The journal's logo is a black-and-white line drawing rather than a photograph. Strong contrasting colors highlight the links. The layout evokes a paper-based journal, which is exactly what the literary-minded user might enjoy in an online journal.

2

Figure 2-15   A hectic design for E! online's audience

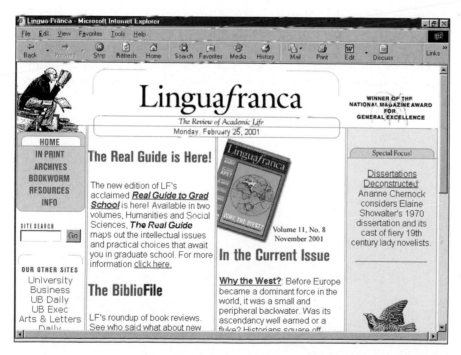

Figure 2-16   A paper-based design for Linguafranca's audience

These two examples demonstrate how the design suits the audience's visual expectations—the look of the site. However, you also should consider the ways users interact with the content—the feel of the site.

Design for Interaction

Think about how the user wants to interact with the information on your Web page. Design for your content type, and decide whether the user is likely to read or scan your pages.

For example, suppose your page is a collection of links, such as a main page or section page. Users want to interact with these types of pages by scanning the content, scrolling if necessary, pointing to graphics to see if they are hyperlinked, and clicking linked text. Design for this type of user interaction by using meaningful column headings, linked text, and short descriptions. Organize links into related topic groups and separate groupings with white space, graphics, or background color.

Suppose the page is an article that contains large blocks of text. Your user is accustomed to interacting with pages of text by scrolling and possibly clicking hyperlinked words of interest. The links may be in the body of the article or contained in a sidebar. Design your pages for this type of content by keeping paragraphs short for online consumption. Make reading easier by using a text column that is narrower than the width of the screen. Keep your text legible by providing enough contrast between foreground and background colors. Provide links that allow the user to jump quickly to related content.

Two screens from the Northeastern University English Department Web site (*www.casdn.neu.edu/~english/*) illustrate the difference between designing for reading and for scanning. Figure 2-17 shows a page designed for scanning. Users look through a variety of links to find a topic of interest. Once they choose a link, they jump to a page designed for reading, as illustrated in Figure 2-18. Note in both pages the user location identifier. This simple path statement lets users quickly see their place in the hierarchy of information and jump to any page in the path.

2

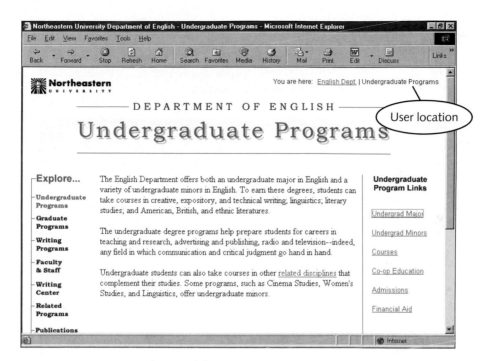

Figure 2-17   Page is designed for scanning

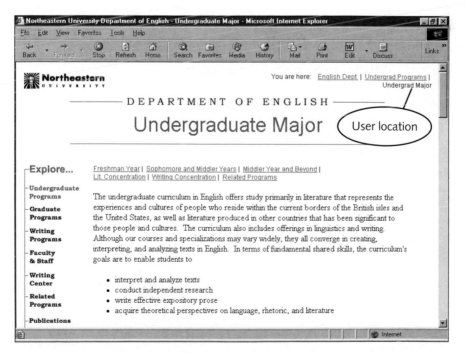

Figure 2-18   Page is designed for reading

Design for Location

It is difficult to predict the user's exact viewing path. There is, however, general agreement on the relative areas of screen importance. Figure 2-19 depicts the sections of screen "real estate" ranked in order of importance.

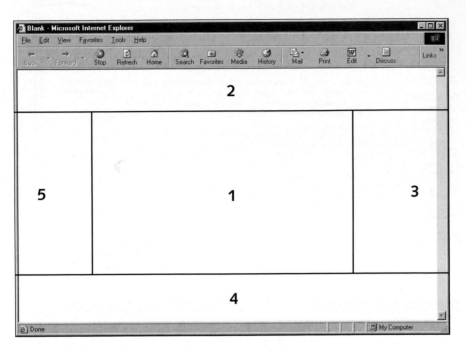

Figure 2-19   Relative areas of screen importance

During page design, rank the information you want to display, and then position the most important in the middle of the window, the next most important across the top, and so on, with the least important or static information in the left margin. For example, Figure 2-20 shows the Cabela's Outdoor Gear (*www.cabelas.com*) main page with the areas of importance overlaying the content.

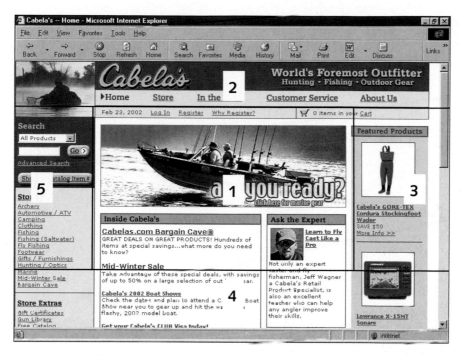

Figure 2-20   Areas of screen importance applied to the Cabela's Web site

Note that the newest content and feature information are displayed in area 1. The company logo and main navigation banner are displayed in area 2. Featured products that change often are placed in area 3. Reading content is in area 4. Area 5 is used for links that appear consistently but are of secondary importance. When planning your page layout, think location. The positioning of your content defines its importance to the user.

Guide the User's Eye

The user can traverse a page in a variety of ways. Human engineering studies show a wide range of results when tracking a user's eye movements. As you plan your design to guide the user's eye, consider the following two examples of online reading habits.

As a function of normal reading habits, the user's eye may move from left to right and back again, as in Figure 2-21.

Figure 2-22 shows this viewing pattern applied to the Linguafranca Web site. This page's columnar design encourages a paper-based reading pattern, enforcing the appropriate literary journal feel for the content.

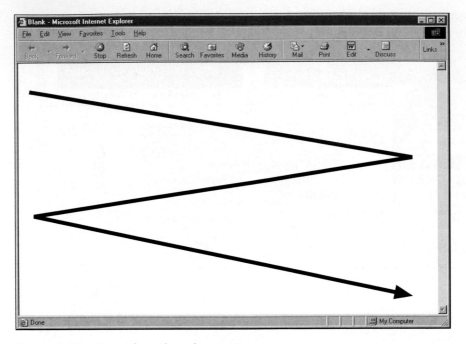

Figure 2-21   Paper-based reading pattern

Figure 2-22   Using the reading-based viewing pattern to view a site

In contrast, when viewing landscape-based displays, such as televisions, the user may scan information following a clockwise pattern, as shown in Figure 2-23.

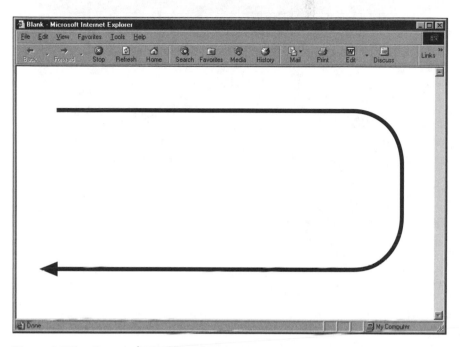

Figure 2-23 Screen-based viewing pattern

Figure 2-24 shows this viewing style overlaying the Library of Congress Web site (*www.loc.gov*). As the user's eyes sweep over the page, they can take in most of the main content areas. This page encourages a screen-based reading pattern.

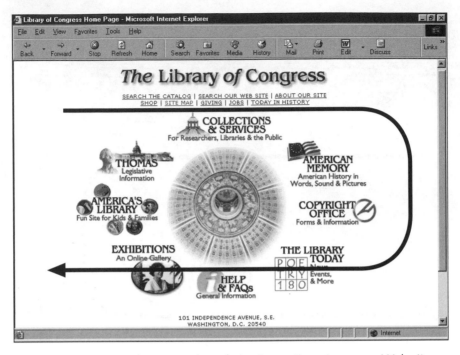

Figure 2-24   Using the screen-based viewing pattern to scan a Web site

Knowing these common user habits can help you decide where to focus the user's attention by object placement, text weight, and color use. Think about your grid structure and how you want to break out of it to attract attention. Use text weight and size to communicate relative importance of information. Break sections up with rules or active white space. Use shapes and color to reinforce location or topic. Get to know your users, and consider the two sample viewing methods described earlier as you experiment with content placement based on the way these users view the page.

Keep a Flat Hierarchy

Do not make users navigate through too many layers of your Web site to find the information they want. Structuring your Web site to include section- or topic-level navigation pages allows users to find their path quickly. Provide prominent navigation cues that quickly take your users to the content they desire. For example, a standard navigation bar consistently placed on every page reassures users that they will not get lost, and lets them move through the site with flexibility.

Consider providing a site map that graphically displays the organization of your Web site. Figure 2-25 shows a site map from the Yale Journal of Health Policy, Law, and Ethics Web site (*www.yale.edu/yjhple/*).

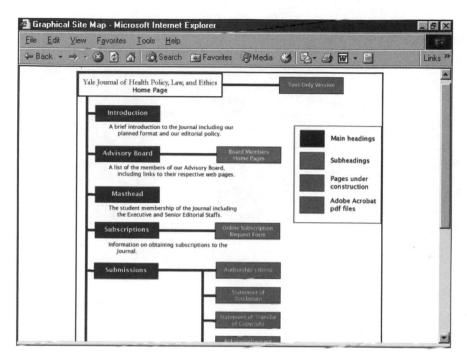

Figure 2-25   A graphical site map

This graphical view of the Web site shows all the individual pages and the section in which they reside. Users can click to go directly to a page or orient themselves to the site's content. The color-coded design indicates the different content types.

Figure 2-26 shows a text-based site map from the Environmental Protection Agency Web site (*www.epa.gov/*). Text-based site maps are more popular than graphics-based maps because they are accessible whether graphics display properly or not.

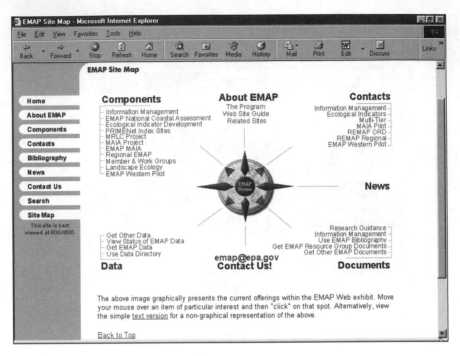

Figure 2-26   A text-based site map

Use the Power of Hypertext Linking

Unlike paper-based authors, as a hypertext author you have the luxury of adding clickable text and images where necessary to guide users through your information. This powerful ability comes with a measure of responsibility. You make the decisions that determine how users move through your site and process information. Readers browsing through magazines can flip to any page in any order they desire. You can replicate this nonlinear reading method on your Web site with links that let users move from page to page or section to section. With thoughtful hypertext writing, you can engage readers in a whole new way.

Many sites have separate columns of links and topics, but not enough provide links within the text. This is a powerful hypertext feature that is not used often enough. Weave your links into your prose to offer a variety of paths. Avoid using the meaningless phrase "Click Here" as the hypertext link. Instead provide a helpful textual clue to the destination of the link.

Figure 2-27 shows a page from *Arctic Dawn, The Journeys of Samuel Hearne* (*http://web.idirect.com/~hland/sh/title2.html*). This is an online hypertext version of an explorer's journal from the 1700s. Note how the hypertext links are worked directly into the text. When users click a link, they move to another page of information; from that page they can either go back or move to another page of information, and so on. The abundant hypertext links allow users to create a view of the site's information that is uniquely their own.

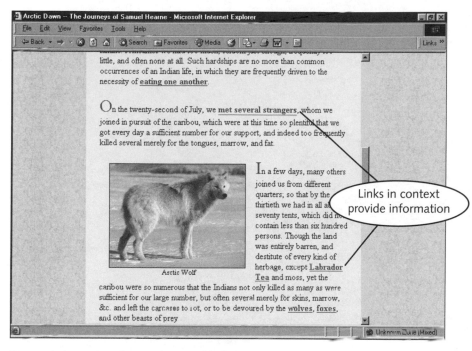

Figure 2-27   Good use of textual links

Provide plenty of links to let the user get around quickly. Use links to let the user return to the navigation section of your page, to a site map, or to the main page. Do not make the user scroll through lengthy columns. Provide links that let users jump down the page, jump back to the top of the page, or that show a clear way back to higher levels of your content.

Provide a hypertext table of contents, as in Figure 2-28, that lets the users pick the exact topic they want to view.

The benefit of a hypertext table of contents is the color-coding that shows the users which pages they have visited. By default, links are blue when new; they change to purple after they have been visited. A hypertext table of contents instantly shows the users where they have been and where they have yet to go.

Glossaries and other densely packed documents become much easier to navigate with the addition of hypertext. Figure 2-29 shows a hypertext glossary that provides plenty of navigation choices for the user.

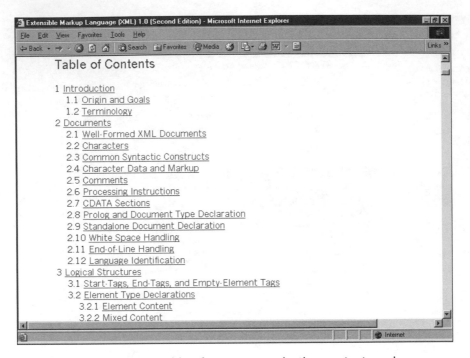

Figure 2-28   Hypertext table of contents tracks the user's viewed pages

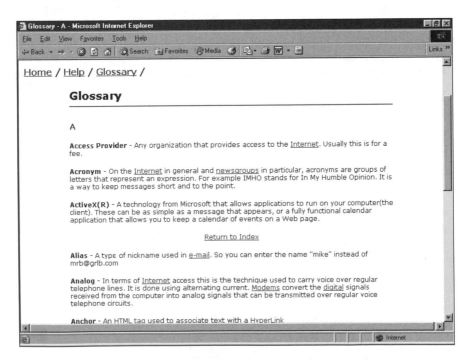

Figure 2-29   Hypertext glossary with plenty of navigation choices

Provide alternate methods of linking to accommodate a variety of users. It is generally a sound idea to duplicate image links with text links in case users have turned off images in their browsers, use a text-based browser, or if images fail to download. Providing meaningful alt attribute values in the <img> tag also can provide the necessary navigation information if images do not display. (See Chapter 4 for more information about including alt attribute values in the <img> tag.) Figure 2-30 shows a Web page that has meaningful alt values for every image. If the images do not appear, the user still can navigate the site.

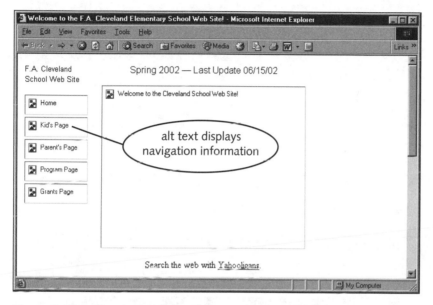

Figure 2-30   Good use of alt attribute values

How Much Content Is Enough?

You can crowd only so much information onto any one Web page. Be conscious of the cognitive load of the user, who often thinks that Web pages hold too much information. Yahoo's Web site (*www.yahoo.com*) in Figure 2-31 offers a dizzying array of Web resources.

The page is designed for scanning, so the user may spend a few seconds looking for a particular topic before moving on by selecting a link. Similarly, the About.com Web site (Figure 2-32) squeezes a large amount of varied information into a small space.

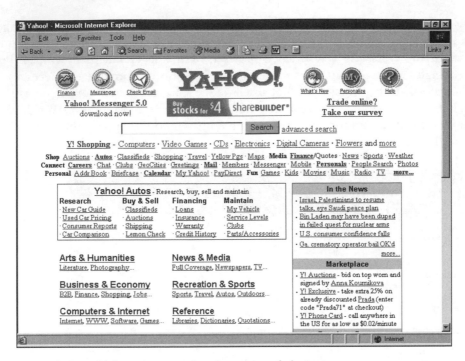

Figure 2-31   Yahoo.com—a dizzying array of choices

Figure 2-32   So much content, so little time...

Resist the temptation to overload users with too much information. Provide enough clues to let them find the content they want, and use links to divide content between pages.

Design for Accessibility

Any large audience for a Web site includes users who want to access your content despite certain physical challenges. Designing for accessibility means developing Web pages that remain accessible despite any physical, sensory, and cognitive disabilities, work constraints, or technological barriers on the part of the user. Most mainstream Web sites are so heavily image- and media-intensive that they are not suitable for adaptive devices such as screen readers, voice browsers, and Braille translators. Many of the guidelines necessary for developing accessible content naturally lend themselves to creating good design.

 The W3C supports a comprehensive accessibility initiative, available at *www.w3.org/WAI/*. Here you find a large variety of guidelines and standards to build more accessible Web content. You can learn more about the adaptive devices for accessible browsing at *www.w3.org/WAI/References/Browsing*.

Building more accessible content does not mean that you have to forgo more challenging Web designs. Often the best way to provide a more accessible site is by building alternatives to the traditional navigation choices, or by offering a text-based version of your content. When designing for accessibility, consider these tips from the W3C (also found at *www.w3.org/WAI/References/QuickTips/*).

- **Images and animations**—Use the alt attribute to describe the function of each visual.

- **Multimedia**—Provide captioning and transcripts of audio, and descriptions of video.

- **Hypertext links**—Use text that makes sense when read out of context. For example, avoid "Click Here."

- **Page organization**—Use headings, lists, and consistent structure. Use CSS for layout and style where possible.

- **Scripts, applets, and plug-ins**—Provide alternative content in case active features are inaccessible or unsupported.

- **Frames**—Use the noframes element and meaningful titles.

- **Tables**—Make line-by-line reading sensible. Summarize.

- **Validity**—Check your work and validate your code using validators from the W3C.

You can verify that physically challenged people can access your Web pages easily by using Bobby, a Web-based tool developed by the Center for Applied Special Technology (CAST) (available at *www.cast.org/bobby*). Bobby checks your pages by applying the W3C's Web contents accessibility guidelines to your code and recording the number and type of incompatibility problems it finds. Bobby looks for elements such as consistent use of ALT attributes, appropriate color usage, compatibility with screen readers, and ease of navigation. You can use Bobby online if your pages are live, or you can download Bobby to test your work on your own machine. Unfortunately, many mainstream Web sites fail Bobby's requirements for accessibility because they use tables as a page layout device and lack support for Cascading Style Sheets.

DESIGN FOR THE SCREEN

The computer monitor, the destination for your Web pages, is very different from print-based media. You must take the following differences into account when planning your Web site:

- The shape of a computer screen. Although most paper-based media are portrait-oriented, the computer screen is landscape-oriented—that is, wider than it is tall. Your page design must reflect the space where it is displayed and read.

- While a piece of paper reflects light, a computer screen has light passing through it from behind. This affects your choices of colors and contrasts. Design pages that provide enough contrast for the user to read, but not so much that the colors distract from the content. Avoid light text on a light background and dark text on dark backgrounds. For example, the bobdylan.com Web site, illustrated in Figure 2–33, uses red links on a black background, making the links illegible.

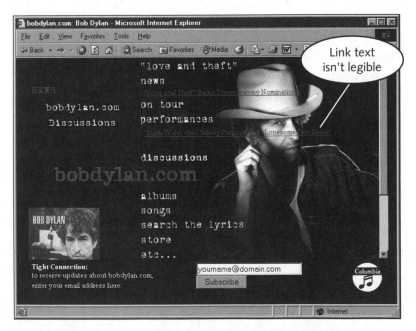

Figure 2-33   Hard-to-read links on a dark background

■ Computer screens use a much lower resolution than the printed page. Graphics and text that look fine on a laser printer at 600 dpi are coarse and grainy at 72 dpi, the typical resolution for a computer monitor. Because of the screen graininess, italic text is especially hard to read in paragraph format, as illustrated in Figure 2-34.

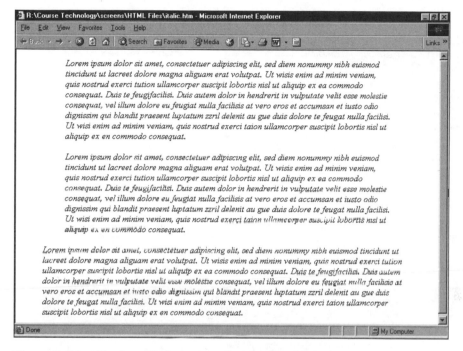

Figure 2-34   Blocks of italic text are hard to read

Reformat Content for Online Presentation

Although tempting, it often is a poor choice to take documents that are formatted for print and post them online without considering the destination medium. In most cases, a document that is perfectly legible on paper is hard to negotiate online. The text length, font, and content length do not transfer successfully to the computer screen. Figures 2-35 and 2-36 show the same section of text from Lewis Carroll's *Alice in Wonderland*. Figure 2-35 is formatted as if it were a page from a book.

Note that the text in Figure 2-35 is dense and fills the screen in large gray blocks. In contrast, Figure 2-36 shows text that has been designed for online display.

The text width is short and easy to read without horizontal scrolling. The white space creates a text column that enforces the vertical flow of the page. The illustrations break up the text and relieve the user's eye. The differences between these two pages show that text must be prepared thoughtfully for online display.

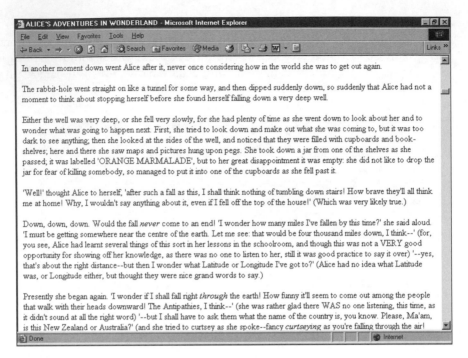

Figure 2-35 Text formatted for paper

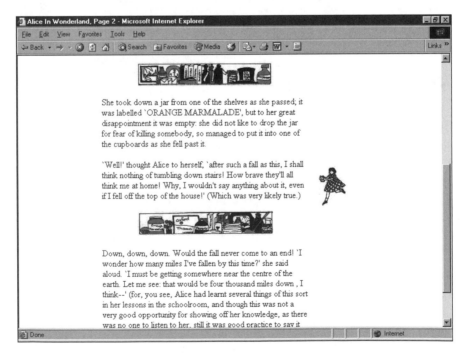

Figure 2-36 Text formatted for the Web

CHAPTER SUMMARY

Web sites have a wide variety of looks. It is easy to see why so many Web designers get caught up in the medium and forget their message. The lure of technology makes it easy to forget that you still are trying to communicate with words and pictures, just as humans have for centuries. Adapting those elements to online display for effective communication is the challenge.

Plan a site that stands out and delivers its message. If you stick with the principles you learned in this chapter, you can present information that is both accessible and engaging.

❑ Design specifically for the computer medium, considering how the page layout, fonts, and colors you use appear on the screen.

❑ Craft an appropriate look and feel and stick with it throughout your site. Test and revise your interface by paying close attention to the demands of online display.

❑ Make your design portable by testing in a variety of browsers, operating systems, and computing platforms, and use as low a bandwidth as possible.

❑ Plan for easy access to your information. Provide logical navigation tools, and do not make users click through more than two or three pages before they get what they want.

❑ Design a unified look for your site. Strive for smooth transitions from one page to the next. Create templates for your grid structure and apply them consistently.

❑ Use active white space as an integral part of your design. Use text, color, and object placement to guide the user's eye.

❑ Know your audience and design pages that suit their needs, interests, and viewing preferences.

❑ Leverage the power of hypertext linking. Provide enough links for the users to create their own path through your information.

❑ Design your text for online display, considering the differences between the screen and the page.

REVIEW QUESTIONS

1. What is another name for the interface the user must navigate in a Web site?
2. What is a common mistake Web designers make when testing their site?
3. What is a prime reason users may leave a Web site?
4. What is the single most important factor in determining the success of a Web site?
5. What important factor degrades the legibility of your information?
6. Name three ways to create a unified look for your site.

7. How does a grid layout enhance Web design?

8. Which HTML elements can you use to create a visual grid?

9. Explain active vs. passive white space.

10. List three ways to create a smooth transition between pages of a Web site.

11. List two benefits of consistently placing navigation tools.

12. Describe the difference between reading and scanning a page.

13. Name three ways to focus a user's attention.

14. Describe why using "Click Here" as link text is ineffective.

15. Describe the benefits of textual linking.

16. Describe the benefits of a hypertext table of contents.

17. Why is the alt attribute so important to navigation?

18. Name three differences between paper-based and screen-based design.

19. Describe a good strategy to format text for online display.

HANDS-ON PROJECTS

1. Browse the Web for examples of good Web design.

    a. Using a screen capture program, capture Web pages that show two levels of information from the Web site. For example, capture the main page of a Web site and a secondary page.

    b. Indicate with screen callouts the unifying characteristics of the pages, such as shared colors, fonts, graphics, and page layout.

    c. Indicate the areas of active white space and passive white space.

    d. Describe whether the design of the site is appropriate for the content.

2. Browse the Web for examples of poor Web design.

    a. Using a screen capture program, capture Web pages that show two levels of information from the Web site. For example, capture the main page of a Web site and a secondary page.

    b. Indicate with screen callouts the jarring or distracting inconsistencies of the site, such as abrupt changes in any design element including theme and layout. (A callout is an arrow or line that connects to explanatory text. Many figures in this book have callouts, including Figure 2-1.)

    c. List detailed recommendations for improving the site design.

3. Write a short essay critiquing a Web site's design. Describe the structural layout of the site and determine whether information is presented clearly and is easily accessible.

4. Browse the Web for sites that use unique navigation methods. Write a short essay describing why the method is or is not successful.

5. Find a Web site that you think needs improvements in its design.

   a. Print two pages from the site.

   b. Make copies of the originals, and set the originals aside.

   c. Using scissors, cut out the main elements of each page. Rearrange the elements and paste them in a design you feel improves the site.

   d. Compare and contrast the original with your improved design.

CASE PROJECT

Visualize the page design for your site by sketching a number of page layouts for different information levels of the site. For example, sketch the main page, a secondary page, and a content page. You do not have to be concerned with the exact look of the elements, but be prepared to indicate the main components of the pages, such as headings, navigation cues, link sets, text areas, and so on.

Start to organize your site. Create a visual diagram that indicates the main page, section pages, content pages, etc. Indicate the links between the pages. Indicate whether you will provide alternate navigation choices such as a table of contents and site map.

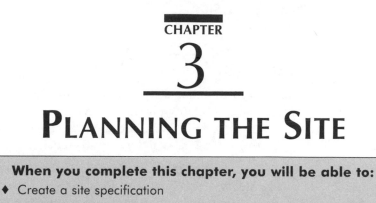

PLANNING THE SITE

When you complete this chapter, you will be able to:

♦ Create a site specification

♦ Identify the content goal

♦ Analyze your audience

♦ Build a Web site development team

♦ Create conventions for filenames and URLs

♦ Set a directory structure

♦ Diagram the site

A good Web site design requires a detailed initial planning phase. Before starting to code your site, pick up a pencil and paper and sketch out your site design. Creating the stylistic conventions and conceptual structure of your site beforehand saves time during development. This chapter walks you through planning and building a framework for your site, resulting in less recoding when you actually sit down at the computer.

CREATE A SITE SPECIFICATION

What are your objectives for building a Web site? You may want to increase communication among employees, gain visibility, provide a service, attract new customers, or simply show the world you can code HTML. Because properly maintained Web sites take a lot of work, make sure you have valid and achievable goals for your site.

Start your planning by creating a **site specification**, which is the design document for your site. If you completed the Hands-on Projects and Case Study at the end of Chapter 1, you created a basic draft of a project proposal. You can use some of that information in your site specification. After you read this chapter, you will be able to answer a number of additional questions about your site. You can return to the site specification as you build your site to help maintain your focus. Answer the following questions in your site specification:

- Why are you building the Web site? Write a two- or three-paragraph mission statement that briefly states the site's goals. What do you or your company or organization hope to gain from creating and maintaining a Web site?

- How will you judge the success of the site? What are the measuring factors you can use to assess the effectiveness of the site?

- Who is the target audience? What characteristics do they share? How will you find out more about them?

- What are the limiting technical factors affecting your site?

IDENTIFY THE CONTENT GOAL

Consider carefully what type of site you are building. What you want the Web site to accomplish and what your users want from your site may differ. For example, site designers are often concerned with the visual aspects of a Web site, such as the quality of the graphics and the use of animation. Your users probably care more about how quickly they can find information. Adopt your user's perspective. Think about the type of content you are presenting and look to the Web for examples of how best to present it. The following types of Web sites demonstrate ways to focus your content.

- *Billboard*—These sites establish a Web presence for a business or commercial venture. In many cases they are informational and offer no true Web-based content, acting as an online brochure rather than offering Web-based interaction. Many businesses build this type of site first and then slowly add functions such as online ordering and product demonstrations as they become more comfortable with the medium.

- *Publishing*—Most major newspapers and periodicals now publish both to print media and to the Web. These Web sites are some of the most ambitious in breadth and depth of content, often containing multiple levels of information with many page templates. Many publishing sites use special software to create Web pages using content from the same databases that produced the paper-based versions. This allows their authors to write the article once, but have it published to multiple destinations, such as the daily newspaper and the Web site.

- *Portal*—Portals act as a gateway to the Web and offer an array of services including searching, e-mail, shopping, news, and organized links to Web resources. Many of the major search engines have been converted into portals to attract more users. These sites are often heavy with advertising content, which is their main source of revenue.

- *Special interest, public interest, and nonprofit organization*—These sites include news and current information for volunteers, devotees, novices, a specific audience, or the general public. No matter what your special interest, you can find a Web site devoted to it. Public-service Web sites contain links, information, downloadable files, addresses, and telephone numbers that can help you solve a problem or find more resources. Nonprofit organizations can state their manifesto, seek volunteers, and foster a grass-roots virtual community

- *Virtual gallery*—The Web is a great place to show off samples of all types of art and design. Photographers and artists can display samples of their work; musicians can post audio files of their songs; writers can offer sections of text or complete manuscripts. However, keep in mind that any copyrighted material you display on a Web site can be downloaded to a user's machine without your permission. Software companies such as Digimarc (*www.digimarc.com*) offer digital watermarking technology that lets artists embed digital copyright information in their electronic files as a deterrent to piracy of proprietary content. This information cannot be seen or altered by the user.

- *E-commerce, catalog, and online shopping*—The Web has become a viable shopping medium that will continue to expand as more users improve their Internet access and learn to trust the security of online commerce. Web commerce already has begun to compete successfully with traditional retailing, offering many advantages over mail-order shopping, such as letting the customer know immediately whether an item is in stock. Other types of commerce on the Web include stock trading, airline ticketing, and auctions. Many software vendors offer turnkey systems that can be integrated with existing databases to speed the development of a commerce site. A good e-commerce site provides users with quick access to the item they want, detailed product descriptions, and easy, secure ordering.

- *Product support*—The Web is a boon to consumers who need help with a product. Manufacturers can disseminate information, upgrades, troubleshooting advice, documentation, and online tutorials through their Web site. Companies that provide product support information on the Web often find that the volume of telephone-based customer support calls decreases.

Software companies especially benefit from the Web; users can download patches and upgrades and use trial versions of software before they buy.

- *Intranet and extranet*—An intranet is a smaller, limited version of the Internet on a company's private local area network (LAN) accessible only to those who have access to their network. Many companies have telecommuting employees who need access to company policies, documentation, parts lists, pricing information, and other materials. These employees can be reached via an **extranet**, which is a part of the private intranet extended outside the organization via the Internet. Many organizations mandate a particular browser for employee use, making the Web designer's job a little easier, because they only have to code and test for one browser.

ANALYZE YOUR AUDIENCE

If possible, analyze your audience and produce an **audience definition**, a profile of your average user. If you are building a new site, work from your market research and try to characterize your average user. If you have an existing user base, contact your typical users and try to answer the following questions:

- What do users want when they come to your site?

- How can you initially attract them and entice them to return?

- What type of computer and connection speed does your typical visitor have?

Obtaining answers to these questions is especially difficult when your medium is the Web. Though your users may fit no common profile, there are a fews ways you can gather information about them. One way is to include an online feedback form in your site. Figures 3-1 and 3-2 show a portion of an online survey from the IBM Life Sciences Web site (*www-3.ibm.com/solutions/lifesciences/feedback.html*).

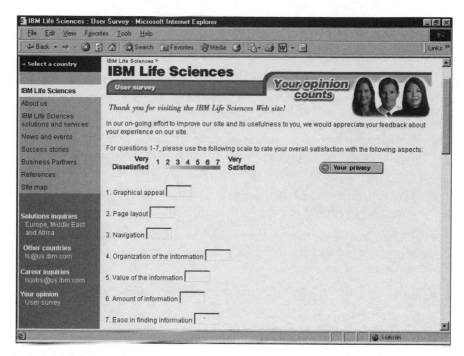

Figure 3-1   User feedback form part 1

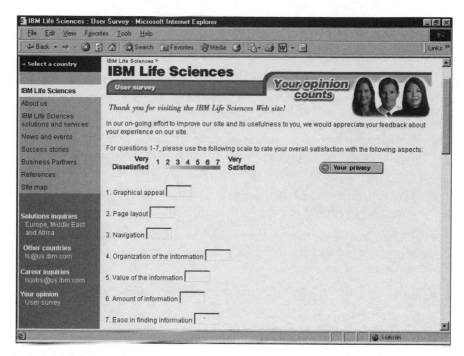

Figure 3-2   User feedback form part 2

The survey asks users about their experiences visiting the Web site. It uses both scaled and open-ended questions to elicit a variety of responses from the user concerning the visual and information design of the site.

If you cannot survey your users, or if you feel you are not getting good survey results, try to adopt a typical user's perspective as you define your audience. Here are some questions to consider:

- Who are the typical members of your audience? Are they male or female? Do they have accessibility issues? What is their level of education? What is their reading and vocabulary level? What is their level of technical aptitude?

- Why do people come to your site? Do they want information? Do they want to download files? Are they looking for links to other Web sites?

- Do you have a captive audience, such as a base of loyal customers that want up-to-date information? Are you designing for an intranet, where users are employees of an organization?

- If users are unfamiliar with the site will they know what you offer?

- How often will users return to your site? Why would they come back?

- What computing platform do your users use? What is their typical connection speed? What type of browser do they use? If you are on an intranet, is there a standard for browsers, connection, and screen resolution?

- Whose skills do you need to build the site? Who will create the graphics, code the pages, and write the text? Do you have the talent and economic resources that you need? Will the results meet the expectations of your users?

Refine your content and presentation even after your site is built and running. Continue soliciting user feedback to keep your site focused and the content fresh.

Identify Technology Issues and Constraints

Make your best effort to identify any technological factors—limitations or advantages—that members of your audience share. As you read in Chapter 1, you have to make assumptions about the user's browser, connection speed, operating system, and screen resolution. If you think your user is the average person browsing the Web, you may have to adopt lowest-common-denominator settings to satisfy the widest audience. If you feel that you have a primarily high-tech or computer-savvy audience, higher resolution or connection speed may apply. If you are designing an intranet site, you may have the luxury of knowing your users' exact operating systems and browser versions. Whatever the particulars, make sure to design at an appropriate level, or you risk losing visitors.

Identify Software Tools

Determining the software requirements for your Web site is important during the planning process. Try to choose software that matches the complexity and needs of your site so that you do not end up with a tool that is either under-equipped or over-specialized. Simple Web sites, including many student sites, can be built with text editors like Notepad or SimpleText. As your site and skills grow, you can move up to more robust tools such as Macromedia Homesite (*www.macromedia.com*) or SoftQuad HotMetal Pro (*www.softquad.com*). Finally, tools like Macromedia Dreamweaver, Microsoft FrontPage, and Adobe GoLive (*www.adobe.com*) offer complete coding, design, and site management capabilities. You may also need graphics tools (discussed in the "Graphics and Color" chapter), database software, and online credit/shopping programs, based on the needs of the different members of your Web site team, as described in the next section.

One popular type of software is **shareware**, programs that you can download and use for a trial period. Users can then register the software for a relatively small fee compared to commercially produced software. Because shareware is usually developed by individuals or small software companies, registering it is important to support future development efforts. Some of the most popular and commonly used programs are shareware, such as WinZip, from Nico Mak Computing, Inc., at *www.winzip.com*. WinZip lets you work with .ZIP archive files, the PC standard for file compression and archiving. If you are sending or receiving files via e-mail, you need WinZip to compress and uncompress them. If you have a Macintosh, you can use Stuffit to compress your files. Stuffit Deluxe and Stuffit Lite, created by Aladdin Systems, Inc., are available in shareware versions at *www.aladdinsys.com*. If you are a PC user and someone sends you a Stuffit file, you can expand it with Aladdin's Expander program, which also is available free of charge at the Aladdin site. Shareware programs are also available to help you with Web site development. Two great shareware sites that have WinZip as well as hundreds of other programs are Shareware.com (*www.shareware.com*) and Tucows.com (*www.tucows.com*).

BUILD A WEB SITE DEVELOPMENT TEAM

Although one person can maintain small Web sites, larger sites require groups of people filling a variety of roles. Of course, the line between these roles can be blurred, and many aspects of site design require collaboration to solve a problem. The following are examples of the types of talent necessary to build a larger, well-conceived site.

- *Server administrators*—Get to know and appreciate the technical people that run your Web server. They take care of the sticky technical issues such as firewalls, modem ports, internal security, file administration, and back-up procedures. Consult with them to determine your Web site's default filename and directory structure. They also can generate reports of how many visitors your site is attracting, where the visitors are coming from, and what pages they like best.

- *HTML coders*—These are the people responsible for creating the HTML code, troubleshooting the site, and testing the site across different operating systems and Web browsers. Most HTML coders are now using HTML editing programs to create code, but any self-respecting HTML author knows how to open the HTML file in a text editor and code by hand. Knowing how to work directly with the code frees you from dependency on one particular authoring tool and makes you more desirable to companies hiring HTML authors.

- *Designers*—Designers are the graphic artists responsible for the look of the site. They use graphic design software, such as Adobe PhotoShop or Macromedia Fireworks. Designers are responsible for the page template design, navigation icons, color scheme, and logos. If your site uses photographic content, the designers are called upon to prepare the photos for online display. They might also create animations and interactive content using Macromedia Flash.

- *Writers and information designers*—Writers prepare content for online display, including hypertext information and navigation paths. Additionally, many writers are responsible for creating a site style guide and defining typographic conventions, as well as consistency, grammar, spelling, and tone. They also work closely with the designers to develop page templates and interactive content.

- *Software programmers*—Programmers write the programs you need to build interaction into your site. They may write a variety of applications, including Common Gateway Interface (CGI) scripts, Java scripts, and back-end applications that interact with a database. Commerce sites especially need the talents of a programming staff.

- *Database administrators*—The people who are responsible for maintaining the databases play an important role in commercial Web sites. They make sure that your data is accessible and safe.

- *Marketing*—The marketing department can generate content and attract visitors to the site.

CREATE CONVENTIONS FOR FILENAMES AND URLS

Before you sit down at the keyboard, plan the file-naming conventions for your site. Find out from your system administrator what type of operating system your Web server uses. Typically you develop your Web site locally on a PC or Macintosh and upload the files to the Web server as the last step in the publishing process. If the Web server runs a different operating system from your local development system, any filename or directory structure inconsistencies encountered in transferring your files to the server may break local URL links.

File Naming

A filename's maximum length, valid characters, punctuation, and sensitivity to uppercase and lowercase letters vary among operating systems, as described in Table 3-1.

Table 3-1 File Naming Conventions

Operating System	Filename Conventions
ISO 9660 Standard	The filename consists of a maximum of eight letters followed by a period and a three-letter extension. Allowed characters are letters, numbers, and the underscore "_"
DOS and Windows 3.x (FAT file system)	The same as ISO 9660 but with the following additional characters allowed: $ % ' ` - @ ^ ! & [ ] ( ) #
Microsoft Windows/NT, NTFS, and Windows 95 VFAT, Windows 98 FAT32, Windows 2000 NTFS, Windows XP NTFS	Maximum 255 letters, all characters allowed except \ / * " < >	
Macintosh	Maximum 31 letters, all characters allowed except the colon (:)
UNIX	Maximum 255 letters, all characters allowed except the forward slash (/) and spaces

Case Sensitivity

If you have an image file named Picture.gif, for example, and you reference that file as <img src="picture.gif">, the image will be displayed properly on a Macintosh or Windows machine. On a UNIX server, however, the image will not load properly because UNIX is case-sensitive; Picture.gif and picture.gif are recognized as two different files. It is best to use lowercase letters for all filenames, including filenames in your HTML code.

Character Exceptions

Like case sensitivity, character use also is incompatible between operating systems. For example, the filename *my stuff.htm* is valid on a Windows PC or Macintosh, but not on a UNIX machine because of the space in the filename. If you transfer a Web site containing *my stuff.htm* to a UNIX server, the links to the file will not work. As another example, the filename *<section2>.htm* is valid on a Macintosh or UNIX machine, but the file would not be recognizable to a Windows NT server because the <> characters are not allowed. It is best when naming your files to leave out special characters such as <, >, /, \, &, *, and blank spaces.

File Extensions

You must use the correct file extensions to identify your file to the browser. HTML text files must end in .htm or .html; whichever you choose, set it as a standard convention for your site. Be careful to add this extension when you are working in Notepad, which defaults to saving as .txt. You also must correctly identify image file formats in the file extensions. Joint Photographic Experts Group (JPEG) files must end in .jpg or .jpeg; Graphics Interchange Format (GIF) files must end in .gif; and Portable Network Graphic (PNG) files must end in .png.

Solving the Filename Dilemma

The best way to overcome the restrictions of case sensitivity, character exceptions, and file extensions is to use the convention specified by the International Standards Organization (ISO) for all your files. This convention (often called 8.3, pronounced "eight-dot-three") specifies a maximum of eight characters followed by a period and a three-character extension. Allowed characters are letters, numbers, and the underscore character. Here are some examples of 8.3 filenames:

- mypage.htm
- chap_1.htm
- picture1.jpg
- logo.gif

If you use the 8.3 file-naming convention on your development system, you will have fewer filename problems when you transfer your files to the Web server, regardless of the server's operating system. By sticking with this filename format, you ensure that your files can be transferred across the greatest number of operating systems. Do not forget to use lowercase characters and omit special characters from your filenames to maximize compatibility.

The Default Main Page Name

Every Web site has a default main page that appears when the browser requests the directory of the site rather than a specific file. The URL for such a page always includes a trailing (forward) slash, as in *www.mysite.com/*. In this instance the Web server provides the index file, which usually is named index.htm. Windows NT, however, defaults to an index filename of default.htm, and other servers may be set to other names such as main.htm or home.htm. Before you start coding, check with your system administrator to verify the correct main page filename.

URL Usage

Although you may know that URLs are the addresses you type into your browser to access a site, you may not realize that there are two types of URLs: complete and partial.

Complete URLs

A **Uniform Resource Locator (URL)** is the unique address of a file's location on the World Wide Web. A **complete URL** includes the protocol the browser uses, the server or domain name, the path, and the filename. Figure 3-3 shows an example of a complete URL.

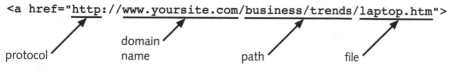

<a href="http://www.yoursite.com/business/trends/laptop.htm">

protocol   domain
name   path   file

Figure 3-3   Parts of a complete URL

In this example, *http* is the protocol, and *www.yoursite.com* is the domain name. The path shows that the destination file, *laptop.htm*, resides in the *business/trends* folder. Use complete URLs in your HTML code when linking to another server.

> When you are browsing the Web, you do not need to enter the protocol because the browser defaults to http://. However, when creating links in your code, you must always include the protocol with a complete URL; otherwise the browser does not know how to connect to the location you specify.

Partial URLs

Use a partial URL when you are linking to a file that resides on your own computer or server. **Partial URLs** omit the protocol and domain or server name, and specifies the path to the file on the same server. Files that reside in the same directory need no path information other than the filename. The following code shows an example of a partial URL.

```
<a href="laptop.htm">link text</a>
```

SET A DIRECTORY STRUCTURE

When you complete your site, you publish your files on the Web by transferring them to a Web server. A typical Web server has a user area that contains folders for each user; your files are stored in your user area, and files from other Web sites are stored in their user areas. The directory structure of the Web server affects the format of your site's URL.

Figure 3-4 shows a typical Web server directory structure. If you do not register a domain name for your site, you will have a URL that reflects your path in the public area of the Web server. A user enters the following address in the browser to access User2's Web site: *www.webserver.com/user2/*.

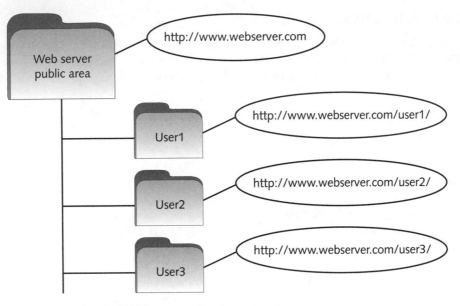

Figure 3-4   Typical Web server directory structure

A domain name is an alias that points to your actual location on the Web server, as shown in Figure 3-5. User2 has purchased the domain name www.mysite.com. The actual path to User2's content has not changed, but the visitor to the site sees only the domain name. Now User2 can advertise the Web site with an easy-to-remember URL.

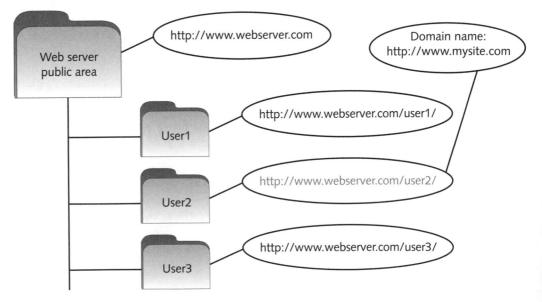

Figure 3-5   Domain name hides the actual path

Relative Versus Absolute Paths

You will probably build your Web site on a computer that is different from the computer that hosts your site. Keep this in mind when you are designing the directory and file structure. Because your files will be transferred to another computer, any URLs you specify to link to other pages in your site must include paths that are transferable. This is why you should never specify an absolute path in your partial URLs. An absolute path points to the computer's root directory, indicated by a leading (forward) slash in the file path:

```
/graphics/logo.gif
```

If you include the root directory in your partial URLs, you are basing your file structure on your development machine. If the files are moved to another machine, the path to your files will not apply, and your site will include links that do not work because the browser cannot find the files.

Relative paths tell the browser where a file is located relative to the document the browser currently is viewing. Because the paths are not based on the root directory, they are transferable to other computers.

Building a Relative File Structure

The easiest way to ensure that all your path names are correct is to keep all of your HTML and image files in the same directory. Because all files are kept together, the only information you need to put in the src or href attribute is the filename itself. In Figure 3-6, User2 has simplified the directory structure. To reference the file logo.gif, User2 adds the following code in one of the HTML files:

```
<img src="logo.gif">
```

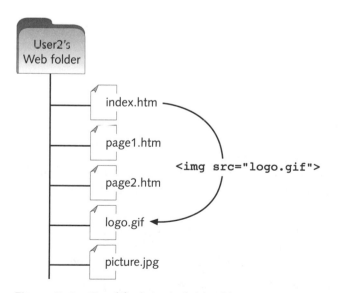

Figure 3-6 Simplified single folder file structure

The simple directory structure shown in the preceding example is fine for a small Web site, but as your site grows you may want to segregate different types of content into separate folders for ease of maintenance. Take a look at the relative file structure for User2's Web site as depicted in Figure 3-7. Notice that User2's Web folder contains three HTML files and one subfolder named images, which contains the graphics and pictures for the Web site.

To include the image file logo.gif in index.htm, User2 adds the following code to index.htm:

```
<img src="images/logo.gif">
```

The path in the SRC value tells the browser to look down one level in the directory structure for the graphics folder and find the file logo.gif. The path to the file is relative to the file the browser is viewing. This type of relative file structure can be moved to different machines; the relationship between the files will not change, because everything is relative within the Web folder.

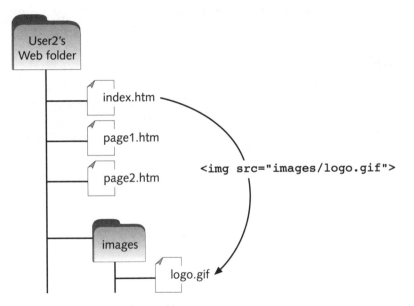

Figure 3-7   Basic relative file structure

User2's Web site may need a more segregated directory structure, as shown in Figure 3-8. In this example, common files such as the index and site map reside in the top-level folder. Multiple subfolders contain chapter and image content. Two linking examples are illustrated in this figure:

- *Example 1*—To build a link from page1.htm (in the chapter1 folder) to index.htm, use ../ in the path statement to indicate that the file resides one level higher in the directory structure, as shown in the following code:

```
<a href="../index.htm">Home</a>
```

- *Example 2*—To include the image file logo.gif in page1.htm, use ../ to indicate that the file resides in the images folder, which is one level higher in the directory structure, as shown in the following code:

```
<img src="../images/logo.gif">
```

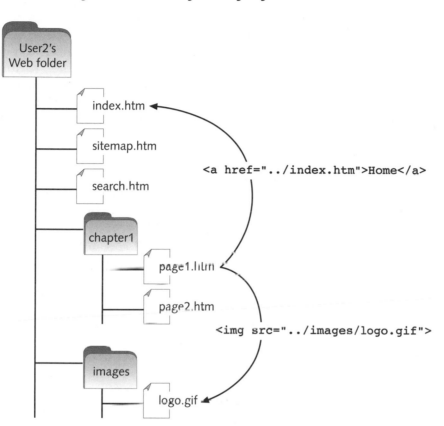

Figure 3-8   More segregated relative file structure

Diagram the Site

Plan your site by creating a flowchart that shows the structure and logic behind the content presentation and navigation choices you offer. You can sketch your site with paper and pencil or create it using flowcharting software. Sometimes it is helpful to use sticky notes or cards to plan the structure visually. This method lets you easily move pages from one section or level to another. Whichever method you choose, this preliminary planning step is one of the most important in planning your site. You can move pages and whole sections of content freely, plan navigation paths, and visualize the entire site. This is the stage at which to experiment. Once you have started coding the site, it is much more difficult and time-consuming to go back and make major changes. Remember to adhere to the file naming conventions for each of your pages.

Create the Information Structure

Think about your users' information needs and how they can best access the content of your site. How should your information design map look? Review the sample structures provided in this section and judge how well they fit your information. Your design may incorporate several different structures, or you may have to adapt the structures to your content. Each sample structure is a template; you may have more or fewer pages, sections, topics, or links. You may choose to use bidirectional links where only single-direction links are indicated. Use these examples as starting points and design from there.

Linear Structure

The linear information structure, illustrated in Figure 3-9, guides the user along a straightforward path. This structure lends itself to book-type presentations; once into the content, users can navigate backward or forward. Each page can contain a link back to the main page if desired. Pages may also contain links to a related subtopic. If the users jump to the subtopic page, they only can return to the page that contains the subtopic link. This structured navigation returns them to the same point in the content path.

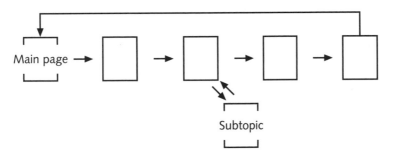

Figure 3-9 Linear information structure

Tutorial Structure

The tutorial structure illustrated in Figure 3-10 is perfect for computer-based training content such as lessons, tutorials, or task-oriented procedures. The tutorial structure builds on the simple linear structure in Figure 3-9. The user navigates through the concept, lesson, and review pages in order. Because the lessons use hypertext, users can leave the lesson structure and return at any time. They also can choose the order of lessons and start anywhere they wish. Notice that the table of contents, index, and site map pages are linked to—and from—all pages in the course. Within each lesson users can navigate as necessary to familiarize themselves with the content before they review. This structure can be adapted to fit content needs; for example, the group of pages in the illustration could be one section of a larger training course.

Web Structure

Many smaller Web sites follow the Web-type content structure illustrated in Figure 3-11, which is nonlinear, allowing the user to jump freely to any page from any other page. If you choose to use this type of content structure, make sure that each page includes clear location information and a standardized navigation bar that not only tells users where they are, but where they can go.

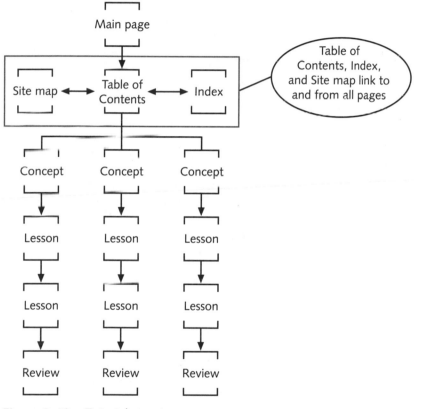

Figure 3-10   Tutorial structure

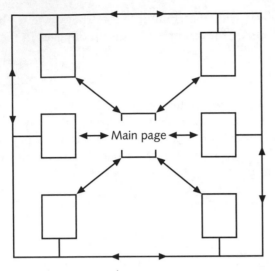

Figure 3-11   Web structure

Hierarchical Structure

The hierarchical structure illustrated in Figure 3–12 is probably the most commonly used information design. It lends itself to larger content collections because the section pages break up and organize the content at different levels throughout the site. Navigation is primarily linear within the content sections. Users can scan the content on the section page and then choose the content page of their choice. When they finish reading the content, they can return to the section page. The site map allows users to navigate freely throughout the site. A navigation bar on each page lets the user jump to any section page, the main page, and the site map.

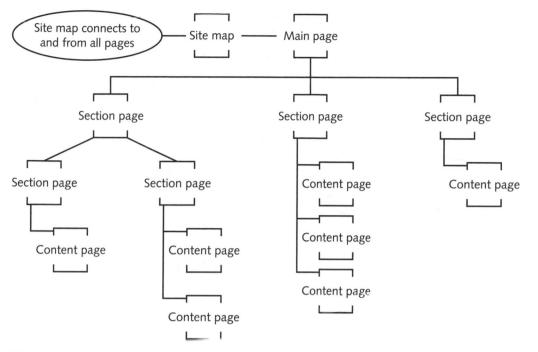

Figure 3-12 Hierarchical structure

Cluster Structure

The cluster structure illustrated in Figure 3-13 is similar to the hierarchical structure, except that every topic area is an island of information, with all pages in each cluster linked to each other. This structure encourages exploration within a topic area, allowing the user to navigate freely through the content. All pages contain a navigation bar with links to the section pages, main page, and site map.

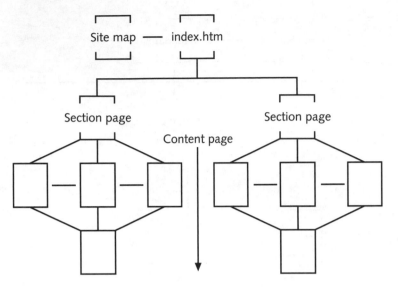

Site map — index.htm

Section page

Content page

Section page

Figure 3-13   Cluster structure

Catalog Structure

The catalog structure illustrated in Figure 3-14 is ideally suited to electronic shopping. The user can browse or search for items and view specific information about each product on the item pages. Users can add items to their shopping cart as they shop. When they are finished, they can review the items in their shopping cart and then proceed to checkout, where they can enter credit card information and finalize the order.

This type of Web site requires back-end data transaction processing to handle the shopping cart tally, process credit card information, and generate an order for the warehouse. Businesses that want to set up an electronic commerce site can purchase ready-made commerce software packages or develop their own from scratch.

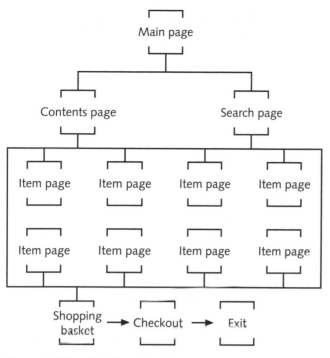

Figure 3-14   Catalog structure

CHAPTER SUMMARY

A successful Web site is the result of careful planning. The steps you take before you actually start coding the site save you time, energy, and expenses in the long run. Remember these guidelines for successful planning:

☐ Start with pencil and paper; your ideas are less restricted and you easily can revise and recast without recoding.

☐ Write a site specification document. You will find it invaluable as a reference while building your site.

☐ Identify the content goal by adopting your users' perspective and learning what they expect from your site.

☐ Analyze your audience and create an audience profile. Focus your site on the user's needs and continue to meet those needs by adapting the site based on user feedback.

☐ An effective site is most commonly the result of a team effort. Leverage different skill sets and experience to build a Web site development team.

◻ Plan for successful implementation of your site by creating portable file-naming conventions. Build a relative file structure that can be transferred to your Web server without a hitch.

◻ Select a basic information structure for your site and then manually diagram it, customizing it to the needs of your site.

REVIEW QUESTIONS

1. List three technology constraints that can affect the way a user views your Web site's content.

2. Consult your Web server administrator when you need to determine the _____ and _____ for your site.

3. Name two inconsistencies that can cause broken links when you upload your files to a Web server.

4. List three characteristics of filenames that vary by operating system.

5. The international standard for filenames often is called _____.

6. Which computer operating system is case-sensitive?

7. Rename the following files so that they are compatible across all operating systems:

   My file.htm   _____

   case:1.htm   _____

   #3rdpage.htm   _____

8. What is the default home page filename for a Web site?

9. What are the two types of URLs?

10. What are the four parts of a complete URL?

11. What type of URL links to another server?

12. What type of URL links within a server?

13. What affects the format of the URL for your Web site?

14. What is the benefit of purchasing a domain name?

15. What symbol indicates an absolute path?

16. Why should you never specify an absolute path in partial URLs?

17. What is the benefit of building a site with relative paths?

18. Files that reside in the same directory need only the _____ to refer to each other.

19. List two benefits of diagramming your site before you start coding.

HANDS-ON PROJECTS

1. Browse the Web and find a site you like. Write a brief statement of the Web site's goals.

2. Browse the Web and find Web sites that fit the following content types:

   a. Billboard

   b. Publishing

   c. Special interest

   d. Product support

   Write a short summary of how the content is presented at each Web site and describe how each site focuses on its users' needs.

3. Browse the Web and find a site that does not contain a user survey form. Write a 10- to 15-question user survey that you would use on the site. Tailor the questions to the site's content and goals.

4. Find a billboard-type Web site. Write an analysis of the site that includes functions and features you would add to extend the site's effectiveness for its users.

5. Visit *www.winzip.com* and download the latest version of WinZip. If you have a Mac, visit *www.aladdinsys.com* and download the shareware version of Stuffit.

   a. Read the product documentation and install the program on your computer.

   b. Find a document that you have created with your word processing software. Note the file size.

   c. Compress the file. Note the new file size.

6. Browse the Web to find examples of the following site structures and describe how the content fits the structure. Think about how the chosen structure adds to or detracts from the effectiveness and ease of navigation of the site. Determine whether the site provides sufficient navigation information. Print examples from the site and indicate where the site structure and navigation information are available to the user.

   a. Linear

   b. Hierarchical

7. Browse the Web to find a site that uses more than one structure type and describe why you think the site's content benefits from multiple structures. Consider the same questions as in Project 3-6.

8. Are there other structure types that are not described in this chapter? Find a site that illustrates a different structure content. Create a flowchart for the site and determine how it benefits from the different structure type.

CASE PROJECTS

Write a site specification for the site you defined in Chapters 1 and 2. Include as much information as possible from the project proposal you completed at the end of Chapter 1. Make sure to include a mission statement. Determine how you will measure the site's success in meeting its goals. Include a description of the intended audience. Describe how you will assess user satisfaction with the site. Include technological issues that may influence the site's development or function.

Prepare a detailed flowchart for your site using the preliminary flowchart you created at the end of Chapter 2. Create a filename for each page that matches the ISO 9660 standard. Indicate all links between pages. Write a short summary that describes the flowchart. Describe why you chose the particular structure, how it suits your content, and how it benefits the user.

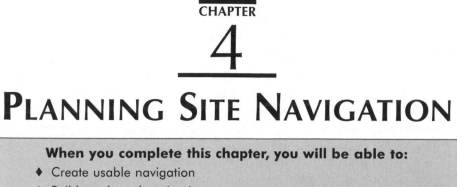

CHAPTER

4

PLANNING SITE NAVIGATION

When you complete this chapter, you will be able to:

♦ Create usable navigation

♦ Build text-based navigation

♦ Link with a text navigation bar

♦ Add contextual linking

♦ Use graphics for navigation and linking

The free-flowing nature of information in a nonlinear hypertext environment can be confusing to navigate. Help your users find content easily rather than making them hunt through a maze of choices. Let your users know where they are at all times and where they can go within your Web site. In this chapter you will learn to build user-focused navigation within the hypertext environment to accomplish these goals. Then you will get a chance to apply these skills in a Hands-on Project.

CREATING USABLE NAVIGATION

The PC Webopaedia defines hypertext as a system "in which objects (text, pictures, music, programs, and so on) can be creatively linked to each other…You can move from one object to another even though they might have very different forms." Hypertext was envisioned in the 1960s by Ted Nelson, who described it as non-sequential writing in his book *Literary Machines*. Nelson's basic idea of connecting content through hypertext linking influenced the creators of the Web. With hypertext-linked content, users can traverse information in any order or method they choose, creating their own unique view.

Hypertext is a distinctly different environment in which to write and structure information. In traditional paper-based media, users navigate by turning pages or referring to a table of contents or index separate from the information they are reading. In a hypertext document, users can connect instantly to related information. The hypertext forms of traditional navigation devices, such as tables of contents and cross-references, can be displayed constantly alongside related content. The user can explore at will, jumping from one point of interest to another. Of course, the ease of navigation depends on the number of links and the context in which they were added by the hypertext author.

In HTML, hyperlinks are easy to create and add no additional download time when they are text-based. When you are planning your site navigation, do not skimp on navigation cues, options, and contextual links. You can add graphics easily to create attractive navigation elements, as most Web designers do. Remember that every graphic you add to your Web site increases the download time for the user; keep your navigation graphics simple, and reuse the same graphics throughout your Web site. Once the navigation graphics are loaded in the user's cache, the server does not have to download them again. Use an alternate set of text links in the event that the user cannot or will not view your graphics. You will learn more about this later in this chapter.

Effective navigation includes providing not only links to other pages in the Web site, but also cues to the user's location. Users should be able to answer the following navigation questions:

- Where am I?
- Where can I go?
- How do I get there?
- How do I get back to where I started?

To allow users to answer these questions, provide the following information:

- The current page and what type of content they are viewing.
- Where they are in relation to the rest of the Web site.
- Consistent, easy-to-understand links.
- Alternatives to the browser's Back button that let users return to their starting point.

Locating the User

Figure 4-1 shows a page from the WebMonkey Web site (*www.webmonkey.com*) that displays a number of user-orienting features.

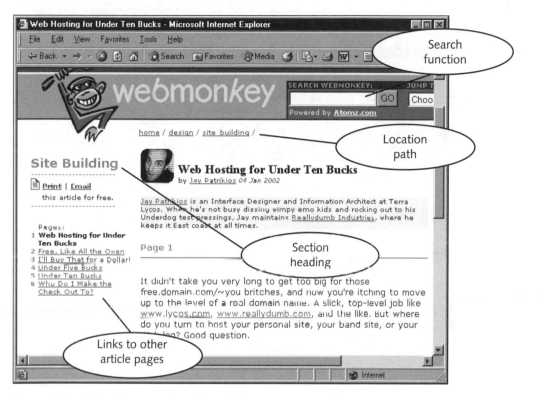

Figure 4-1 Providing user location cues

The navigation cues on this page offer many options without disorienting the user. A search option lets the user search the entire WebMonkey site. A linked path at the top of the page shows the user's location within the site hierarchy. Users can see they are in the Site Building section, which is contained in the Design section. Users can click any of the links in the path to move through the content structure. This location device is especially effective in guiding users who may have arrived at this page from somewhere outside this Web site. The section heading in the left column identifies the current section, and the links beneath this heading let the user jump to the section's other pages. Using these navigation devices, users can choose to jump directly to a page, search for information, or move back up through the information hierarchy.

Figure 4-2 shows a section page from the Frontend.com Web site (*www.frontend.com/ usability_infocentre/index.html*), which also offers the same types of helpful navigation devices as the page from the WebMonkey Web site.

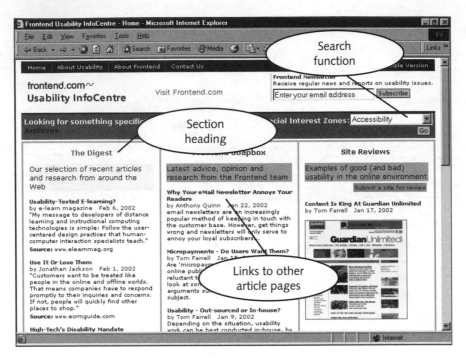

Figure 4-2   Variety of navigation cues

Limiting Information Overload

Many Web sites tend to present too much information at one time. Lengthy files that require scrolling or arrays of links and buttons can frustrate and overwhelm the user. You can limit information overload in the following ways:

- **Create manageable information segments**. Break your content into smaller files, and then link them together. Provide logical groupings of choices. Notice that the Web site in Figure 4-2 breaks up content with logical headings.

- **Control page length**. Do not make users scroll through never-ending pages. Long files also can mean long downloads. Provide plenty of internal links to help users get around, and keep the pages short. You can judge your page length by pressing the Page Down key; if you have to press it more than two or three times to move from the top to the bottom of your page, break up the file.

- **Use hypertext to connect facts, relationships, and concepts**. Provide contextual linking to related concepts, facts, or definitions, letting the users make the choices they want. Know your material, and try to anticipate the user's information needs.

BUILDING TEXT-BASED NAVIGATION

Text-based linking often is the most effective way to provide navigation on your site. It can work in both text-only and graphical browsers, and does not depend on whether your images display properly or not. Although you may want to use linked graphics for navigation, always include a text-based set of links as an alternate means of navigation.

In the following set of steps you will link a series of sample Web pages using text-based navigation techniques. Figure 4-3 shows the structure of the collection of sample HTML documents that you will use, including a Home page, Table of Contents page, Site Map page, and individual Chapter pages.

4

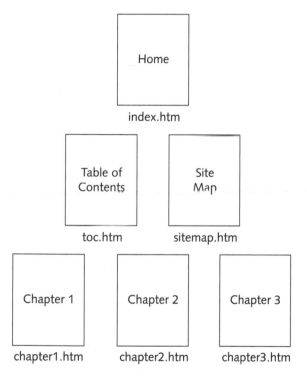

Figure 4-3 Sample file structure

In the hypertext environment, the user should be able to select links in the table of contents to jump to any document in the collection. In the following steps, you will add a variety of linking options that will produce different paths through the information. The focus for these steps is the Table of Contents page, toc.htm, and how it relates to the rest of the content in the collection. You will also add navigation options to the individual chapter pages. The Index and Site Map pages are included to complete the sample Web site, and will be target destinations for some of the links you will build.

To complete the steps in this chapter, you need to work on a computer with a browser and an HTML editor or a simple text editor, such as Notepad or SimpleText.

To prepare for linking the Web pages:

1. Copy the following files from the Chapter04 folder on your Data Disk:
   - index.htm
   - toc.htm
   - sitemap.htm
   - chapter1.htm
   - chapter2.htm
   - chapter3.htm

2. Save the files in a Chapter04 folder in your work folder using the same file-names. Make sure you save all the files in the same folder.

LINKING WITH A TEXT NAVIGATION BAR

The Table of Contents page must link to the other main pages of the Web site, allowing users to go directly to the pages they want. You can achieve this by adding a simple text-based navigation bar.

To build the navigation bar:

1. From the Chapter04 folder in your work folder, open the file **toc.htm** in your browser. It should look like Figure 4-4.

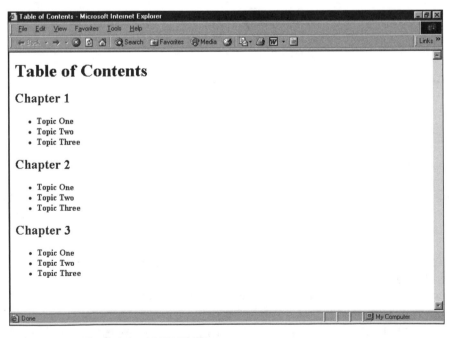

Figure 4-4   The original HTML file

2. Open the file in your HTML editor and examine the code. Notice that this file contains no hypertext links. The complete code for the page follows:

```
<html>
<head>
<title>Table of Contents</title>
</head>
<body>
<h1>Table of Contents</h1>

<h2>Chapter 1</h2>
     <ul>
           <li><b>Topic One</b></li>
           <li><b>Topic Two</b></li>
           <li><b>Topic Three</b></li>
     </ul>
<h2>Chapter 2</h2>
     <ul>
           <li><b>Topic One</b></li>
           <li><b>Topic Two</b></li>
           <li><b>Topic Three</b></li>
     </ul>
<h2>Chapter 3</h2>
     <ul>
           <li><b>Topic One</b></li>
           <li><b>Topic Two</b></li>
           <li><b>Topic Three</b></li>
     </ul>
</body>
</html>
```

3. Add a <div> element to place the navigation bar immediately following the opening <body> tag. Set the align attribute to "center," as shown in the following code. (The new code you should add is shaded in this step and the following steps):

```
<body>
<div align="center"> </div>
```

4. Add text within the new <div> element as shown in the following code.

```
<div align="center">Home | Table of Contents | Site Map
</div>
```

5. Add <a> tags that link to the home page and the site map.

```
<div align="center"><a href="index.htm">Home</a> | Table
of Contents | <a href="sitemap.htm">Site Map</a></div>
```

6. Add <b> tags around the Table of Contents text. Because this is the Table of Contents page, the text "Table of Contents" is not a hypertext link but is bold to designate the user's location. The code looks like this:

```
<div align="center"><a href="index.htm">Home</a> |
<b>Table of Contents</b> | <a href="sitemap.htm">Site Map
</a></div>
```

7. View the finished Table of Contents page in your browser. It should look like Figure 4-5. Test your hypertext links to make sure they point to the correct page.

8. Add this navigation bar to all of the sample pages. Remember to change the links and <b> text to reflect the current page. For example, the Site Map page would have the text "Site Map" in bold and a link to the Table of Contents page. Save **toc.htm** in the Chapter04 folder of your work folder, and leave it open in your HTML editor for the next steps.

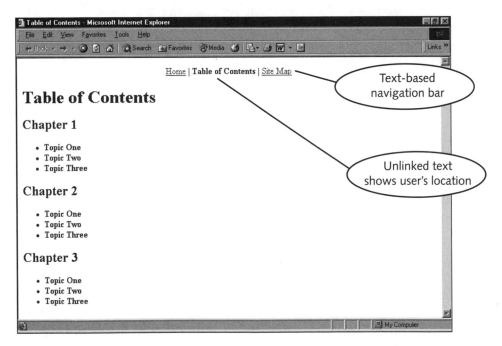

Figure 4-5   Adding a text-based navigation bar

Linking to Individual Files

While the navigation bar lets users access the main pages in the Web site, the table of contents lets users access the exact content they want. The Table of Contents page therefore needs links to the individual chapter files in the Web site. In this set of steps, you will add links to the individual chapter files listed in the table of contents.

To build individual file links:

1. Continue working in the file **toc.htm**. Add the following <a> element around the <h2> text "Chapter 1":

```
<h2><a href="chapter1.htm">Chapter 1</a></h2>
```

2. Add similar <a> elements around the text "Chapter 2" and "Chapter 3" that point to the files chapter2.htm and chapter3.htm, respectively.

3. Save **toc.htm** and view the finished Table of Contents page in your browser. It should look like Figure 4-6. Test your hypertext links to make sure they point to the correct page.

4

```
Table of Contents - Microsoft Internet Explorer

File   Edit   View   Favorites   Tools   Help

Back  →      Search   Favorites   Media                    Links »

                    Home | Table of Contents | Site Map

Table of Contents

Chapter 1

    • Topic One
    • Topic Two
    • Topic Three

Chapter 2

    • Topic One
    • Topic Two
    • Topic Three

Chapter 3

    • Topic One
    • Topic Two
    • Topic Three

Done                                              My Computer
```

Figure 4-6   Adding individual file links

As this example shows, remember always to make <a> the innermost set of tags to avoid extra space in the hypertext link.

This linking method lets the users scroll through the table of contents to scan the chapters and topics and then jump to the chapter they want. The link colors—by default, blue for new and purple for visited—allow users to keep track of which chapters they already have visited.

Adding Internal Linking

In addition to linking to external documents, you also can add links for navigating within the table of contents itself. In the Table of Contents page illustrated in Figure 4-6 you will add a "back to top" link that lets users return to the top of the page from many points within the file.

This requires two <a> anchor elements: one uses the name attribute to name a **fragment identifier** in the document; the other targets the fragment name in the href attribute.

To add an internal link:

1. Continue working with the file **toc.htm** in your HTML editor. Add the name attribute to the first <a> tag in the text-based navigation bar at the top of the page as shown.

```
<div align="center"><a href="index.htm" name="top">
Home</a> | <b>Table of Contents</b> |
<a href="sitemap.htm">Site Map</a></div>
```

This name attribute identifies the navigation bar text as a fragment of the document named "top." You can then refer to this name as an href target elsewhere in the document. The value of the name attribute can be any combination of alphanumeric characters that you choose.

2. Add an <a> element at the bottom of the page, after the listing for Chapter 3 and just before the closing </body> tag. Reference the target fragment "top" by using the number sign (#) in the href attribute, as shown in the following code.

```
<h2><a href="chapter3.htm">Chapter 3</a></h2>
    <ul>
        <li><b>Topic One</a></b></li>
        <li><b>Topic Two</a></b></li>
        <li><b>Topic Three</a></b></li>
    </ul>

<a href="#top">Back to Top</a>

</body>
```

3. Add a <div> element around the <a> element and set the align attribute to "right." This code aligns the Back to Top link to the right side of the page.

```
<div align="right"><a href="#top">Back to Top</a></div>
```

4. Save the **toc.htm** file and view the Table of Contents page in your browser. Resize your browser to show only a portion of the page, as shown in Figure 4-7.

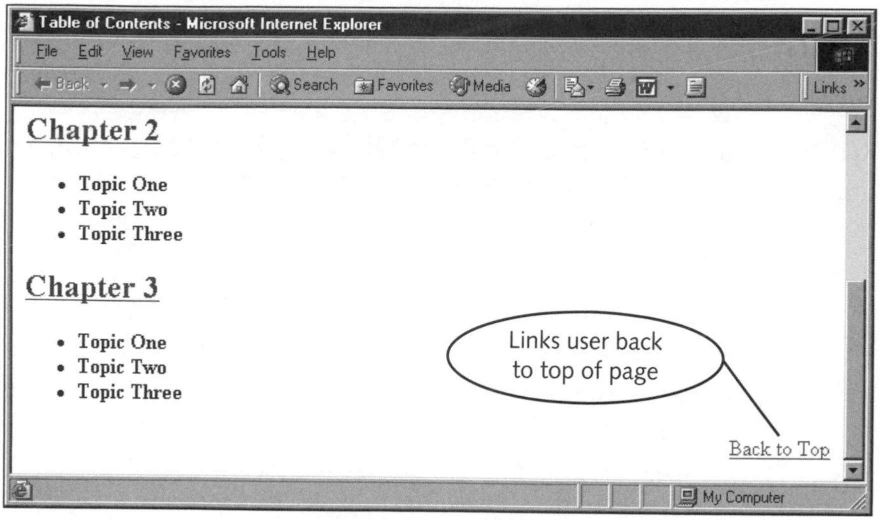

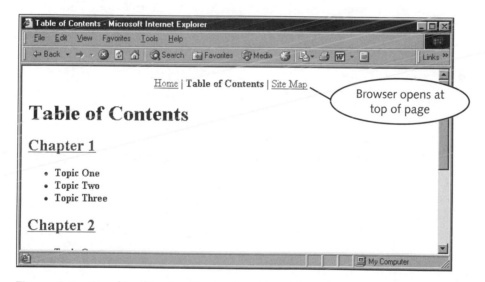

Figure 4-7   Adding a Back to Top link

> 5. Test the link to make sure it opens the browser window at the top of the page, as shown in Figure 4-8.

Figure 4-8   Results of testing the Back to Top link

Adding an Internal Navigation Bar

You can use additional fragment identifiers in the table of contents to add more user-focused navigation choices. Figure 4-9 shows the addition of an internal navigation bar.

When users click one of the linked chapter numbers, they jump to the specific chapter information they want to view within the table of contents.

To add an internal navigation bar:

1. Continue working with the file **toc.htm** in your HTML editor. Add a `<div>` element immediately after the `<h1>` element as shown. Set the align attribute to center.

```
<h1>Table of Contents</h1>
<div align="center"> </div>
```

2. Add text to the `<div>` element as shown in the following code.

```
<div align="center">Jump down this page to Chapter... 1 | 2
| 3</div>
```

3. Add `<a>` elements around each chapter number within the `<div>`. The href attributes point to a named fragment for each chapter.

```
<div align="center">Jump down this page to Chapter...
<a href="#chapter1">1</a> | <a href="#chapter2">2</a> |
<a href="#chapter3">3</a></div>
```

4. Add the name attribute to each chapter's existing `<a>` element. These are the fragment names you referred to in Step 3. The following code shows the new name attributes in the `<a>` element for each chapter.

```
<h2><a href="chapter1.htm" name="chapter1">Chapter 1</a>
</h2>
    <ul>
        <li><b>Topic One</b></li>
        <li><b>Topic Two</b></li>
        <li><b>Topic Three</b></li>
    </ul>
<h2><a href="chapter2.htm" name="chapter2">Chapter 2</a>
</h2>
    <ul>
        <li><b>Topic One</b></li>
        <li><b>Topic Two</b></li>
        <li><b>Topic Three</b></li>
    </ul>
<h2><a href="chapter3.htm" name="chapter3">Chapter 3</a>
</h2>
    <ul>
        <li><b>Topic One</b></li>
        <li><b>Topic Two</b></li>
        <li><b>Topic Three</b></li>
    </ul>
```

5. Save the **toc.htm** file in the Chapter04 folder in your work folder, and then close the file. View the Table of Contents page in your browser. Resize your browser to show only a portion of the page, as shown in Figure 4-9.

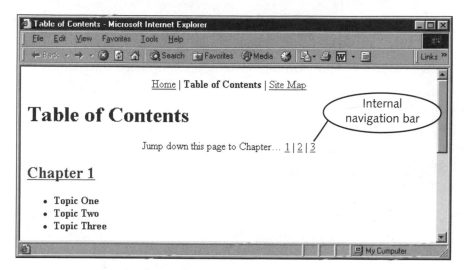

Figure 4-9   Adding an internal navigation bar

6. Test the navigation bar links by selecting a chapter number and making sure the browser window opens to the correct place in the file. Figure 4-10 shows the result of selecting the Chapter 2 link.

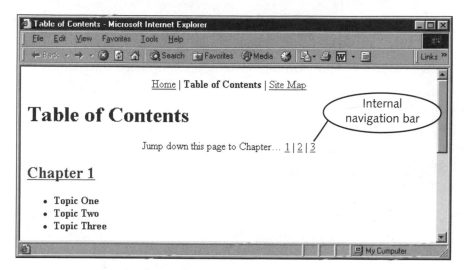

Figure 4-10   Results of testing the internal Chapter 2 link

Linking to External Document Fragments

Now that you have completed internal linking in the table of contents, re-examine how the table of contents is linked to each chapter file. Currently, each chapter has one link in the table of contents; users click the chapter link and the browser opens the chapter file at the top. However, each chapter also contains multiple topics. You can let users jump from the table of contents to the exact topic they want within each chapter. This will require adding code to both the Table of Contents page and each individual chapter page.

To add links to external fragments:

1. In your HTML editor, open the file **chapter1.htm** from the Chapter04 folder in your work folder.

2. Find the topic headings within the file. For example, the following code produces the topic heading for Topic 1:

```
<h2>Topic 1</h2>
```

3. Add an <a> element around the text "Topic1." Set the name attribute to **topic1** for this heading, as shown in the following code.

```
<h2><a name="topic1">Topic 1</a></h2>
```

4. Now add the same code to each of the other topic headings in the file, using **topic2** and **topic3** as the name attribute values for the Topic 2 and Topic 3 headings, respectively.

5. Save **chapter1.htm** in the Chapter04 folder of your work folder, and then close the file.

6. In your HTML editor, open the files **chapter2.htm** and **chapter3.htm** from the Chapter04 folder of your work folder. Repeat Steps 2 through 5 for both files, adding appropriate name attribute values for each topic in each file.

7. In your HTML editor, open the file **toc.htm** from the Chapter04 folder of your work folder. (This is the toc.htm file you saved in the last set of steps.)

8. Find the topic links for each chapter within the file. For example, the following code produces the topic link for Chapter 1:

```
<h2><a href="chapter1.htm" name="chapter1">Chapter 1</a>
</h2>
        <ul>
              <li><b>Topic One</b></li>
              <li><b>Topic Two</b></li>
              <li><b>Topic Three</b></li>
        </ul>
```

9. Add <a> elements for each topic. The href value is the filename combined with the fragment name. The following code shows the <a> element for the Chapter 1, Topic 1 link.

```
<h2><a href="chapter1.htm" name="chapter1">Chapter 1</a>
</h2>
        <ul>
<li><b><a href="chapter1.htm#topic1">Topic One</a></b>
</li>
            <li><b>Topic Two</b></li>
            <li><b>Topic Three</b></li>
        </ul>
```

10. Continue to add similar links for each topic listed in the table of contents. When you are finished your complete page code should look like the following example.

```
<html>
<head>
<title>Table of Contents</title>
</head>
<body>
<div align="center"><a href="index.htm" name="top">Home
</a> | <b>Table of Contents</b> | <a href="sitemap.htm">
Site Map</a></div>

<h1>Table of Contents</h1>

<div align="center">Jump down this page to Chapter...
<a href="#chapter1">1</a> | <a href="#chapter2">2</a> |
<a href="#chapter3">3</a></div>

<h2><a href="chapter1.htm" name="chapter1">Chapter 1</a>
</h2>
        <ul>
        <li><b><a href="chapter1.htm#topic1">Topic
One</a></b></li>
            <li><b><a href="chapter1.htm#topic2">Topic
Two</a></b></li>
            <li><b><a href="chapter1.htm#topic3">Topic
Three</a></b></li>
        </ul>
<h2><a href="chapter2.htm" name="chapter2">Chapter 2</a>
</h2>
        <ul>
        <li><b><a href="chapter2.htm#topic1">Topic
One</a></b></li>
            <li><b><a href="chapter2.htm#topic2">Topic
Two</a></b></li>
            <li><b><a href="chapter2.htm#topic3">Topic
Three</a></b></li>
        </ul>
```

4

```
<h2><a href="chapter3.htm" name="chapter3">Chapter 3</a>
</h2>
     <ul>
     <li><b><a href="chapter3.htm#topic1">Topic
One</a></b></li>
     <li><b><a href="chapter3.htm#topic2">Topic
Two</a></b></li>
     <li><b><a href="chapter3.htm#topic3">Topic
Three</a></b></li>
     </ul>

<div align="right"><a href="#top">Back to Top</a></div>

</body>
</html>
```

11. Save the **toc.htm** file in the Chapter04 folder of your work folder, and view it in your browser. Test the topic links by selecting a chapter topic and making sure the browser window opens to the correct place in the correct file. Figure 4-11 shows the result of selecting the Chapter 2, Topic Two link.

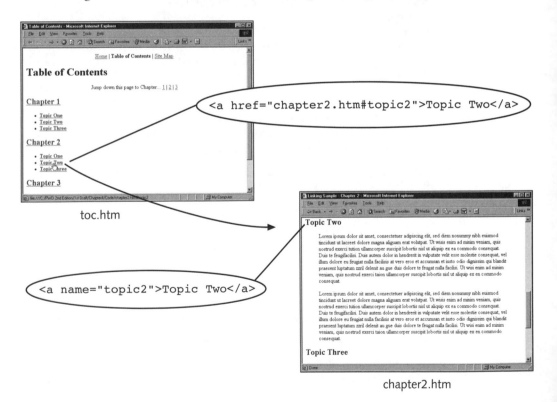

Figure 4-11   Linking to an external fragment

When users click the topic links in the table of contents, the browser opens the destination file and displays the fragment (Figure 4-11).

Adding Page Turners

Each chapter file currently contains a navigation bar and fragment identifiers for each topic within the chapter. In this page collection, the user can jump to any file and topic within a file, though some users may want to read the pages sequentially. You can enhance the functions of the navigation bar in the chapter pages by adding page-turner links. Page turners let you move either to the previous or next page in the collection. These work well in a linear structure of pages, as shown in Figure 4-12.

Note that Chapter 1 includes the table of contents as the previous page, while Chapter 6 uses the index as the next page.

To add page-turner links:

1. In your HTML editor, open the file **chapter1.htm** from the Chapter04 folder of your work folder. If you previously added the text-based navigation bar to the file, it looks like Figure 4-13. (Note that the Latin text is placeholder text, a common design technique that lets you focus on layout instead of content.)

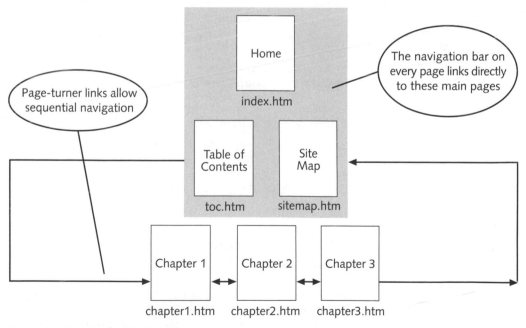

Figure 4-12   Sequential page turning

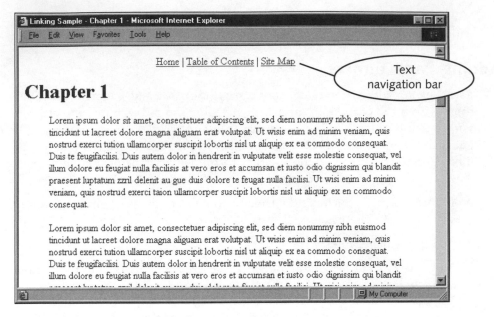

Figure 4-13   Text navigation bar

2. If you have not added the text navigation bar, add it now. Insert the following code immediately after the opening <body> tag.

```
<div align="center"><a href="index.htm" name="top">Home
</a>
| <a href="index.htm">Table of Contents</a> | <a href=
"sitemap.htm">Site Map</a></div>
```

3. Add the page turner for the previous page. Because this is Chapter 1, make the previous page destination **toc.htm**, as shown in the following code.

```
<div align="center"><a href="index.htm" name="top">Home
</a>
| <a href="index.htm">Table of Contents</a> | <a href=
"toc.htm">Previous</a> | <a href="sitemap.htm">Site Map
</a></div>
```

4. Add the page turner for the next page. Because this is Chapter 1, make the next page destination **chapter2.htm**, as shown in the following code.

```
<div align="center"><a href="index.htm" name="top">Home
</a>
| <a href="index.htm">Table of Contents</a> | <a href=
"toc.htm">Previous</a> | <a href="chapter2.htm">Next</a>
| <a href="sitemap.htm">Site Map</a></div>
```

5. Save the **chapter1.htm** file in the Chapter04 folder of your work folder, and then view it in your browser. Your file should now look like Figure 4-14. Test the page-turner links to make sure they point to the correct file.

6. Add the page-turner links to chapter2.htm and chapter3.htm, changing the Previous and Next links to point to the correct files. Test all your links to make sure they work properly. When you are finished, save and close all the .htm files in the Chapter04 folder of your work folder.

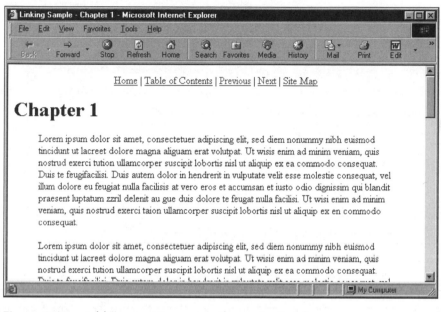

Figure 4-14   Adding page turners in the navigation bar

ADDING CONTEXTUAL LINKING

Many Web sites fail to use one of the most powerful hypertext capabilities—the contextual link. **Contextual links** allow users to jump to related ideas or cross-references by clicking the word or item that interests them. These are links that you can embed directly in the flow of your content by choosing the key terms and concepts you anticipate your users will want to follow. Figure 4-15 shows a page from the World Wide Web Consortium HTML specification that contains contextual linking.

Note the links within the lines of text, which let the user view related information in context. For example, as users read the first bulleted item, "May leave white space intact," they can click the "white space" link to see a definition of that term. Including the link within a line of text is more effective than including a list of keywords, because users can see related information within the context of the sentence they are reading. Users also can see that repeated words are linked no matter how many times they appear within the browser window, offering users the opportunity to access additional information at any time.

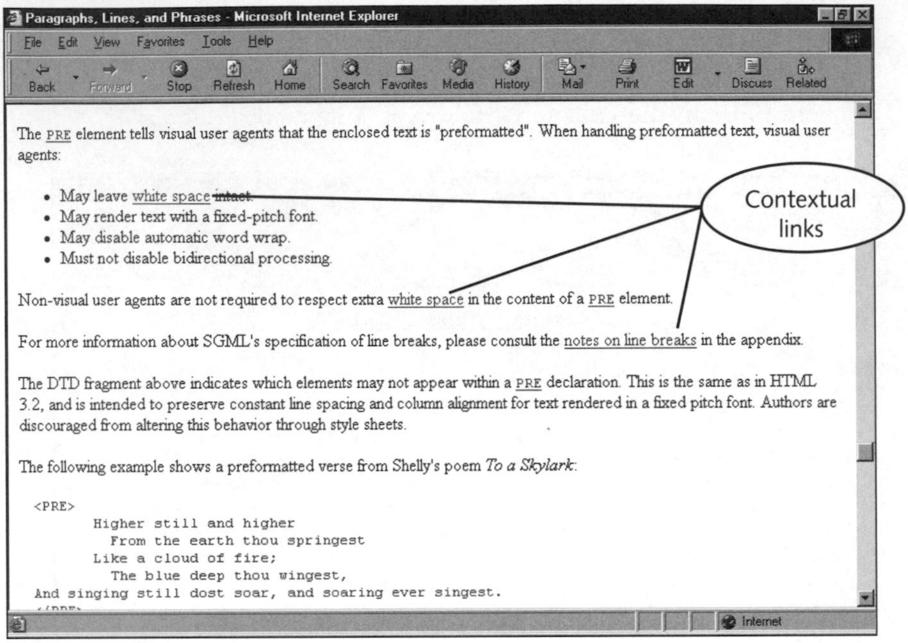

Figure 4-15   Contextual linking

You can choose from a variety of navigation options to link a collection of pages. The sample Web pages in this section demonstrate the following text-based linking actions:

- To main pages (home, table of contents, index)

- To the top of each chapter

- Within the Table of Contents page to chapter descriptions

- From the Table of Contents page to specific topics within each chapter

- Between previous and next chapters

- To related information by using contextual links

Use as many of these options as necessary, but remember to view your content from the user's perspective. Use enough navigation options to allow easy and clear access to your content.

Using Graphics for Navigation and Linking

Like most Web site designers, you probably want to use graphics for some of your navigation cues. The ability to use graphics is one of the most appealing aspects of the Web, but too many graphics used inconsistently confuse the users. To make sure your navigation graphics help rather than hinder your users, use the same graphics consistently throughout your Web site, for the following reasons:

- *To provide predictable navigation cues for the user*—Once users learn where to find navigation icons and how to use them, they expect them on every page. Consistent placement and design also build user trust and help them feel confident that they can find the information they want.

- *To minimize download time*—Once the graphic is downloaded, the browser retrieves it from the cache for subsequent pages rather than downloading it every time it appears.

Using Text Images for Navigation

Navigation graphics on the Web come in every imaginable style. Many sites use text images, rather than HTML text, for navigation graphics. Text images are text created as graphics, usually as labels within the graphic. Many Web designers prefer text images because they offer more typeface and design choices.

Figure 4-16 shows the top navigation bar from a page of The Guardian Web site (*www.guardian.co.uk/*). The navigation bar builds the page name, Web site name, and main section links into a unified graphic that serves as the banner for the top of the page. The banner gives all of the content a consistent look while providing a variety of useful navigation choices. Note that what appears to be a single graphic actually is composed of different graphics held together by a table, a very common technique that you will learn more about in Chapter 7.

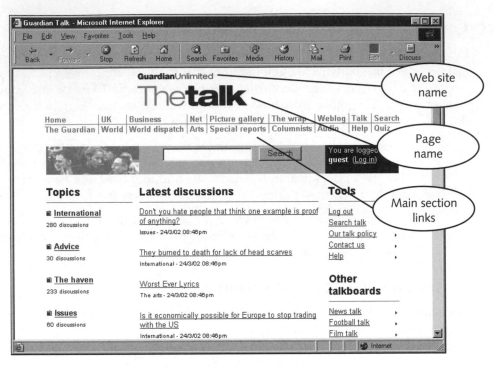

Figure 4-16   The Guardian Web site navigation bar

Using Icons for Navigation

Figure 4-17 shows the navigation icons from the MapQuest Web site (*www.mapquest.com*). The text labeling on the icons points out one of the main problems with icons—not everyone agrees on their meaning. Especially with a worldwide audience, you never can be sure exactly how your audience will interpret your iconic graphics. This is why so many Web sites choose text-based links, even if they are text as graphics.

If you do use navigation icons, be sure to define them. One way is to use a table that lists each icon and describes its meaning. Figure 4-18 shows a page from a student project Web site that clearly explains the Web site's navigation icons.

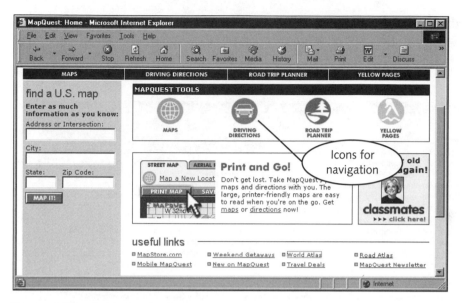

Figure 4-17   Icons for navigation

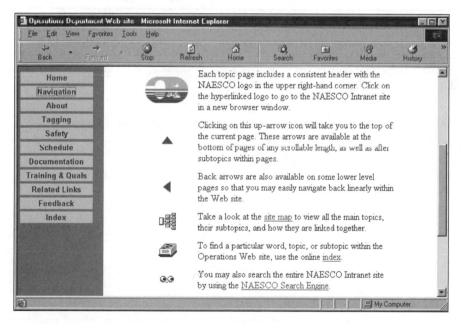

Figure 4-18   Clear definition of navigation icons

No matter what type of graphics you choose as icons, make sure that your users understand their meaning. Test your navigation graphics on users in your target audience and ask them to interpret the icons and directional graphics you want to use. The most obvious type of graphics to avoid are symbols that are culturally specific, especially hand gestures (such as thumbs–up) that may be misinterpreted in other cultures. Other graphics, such as directional arrows, are more likely to be interpreted correctly. Figure 4–19 shows an icon-based navigation bar that includes universal previous, top, and next links.

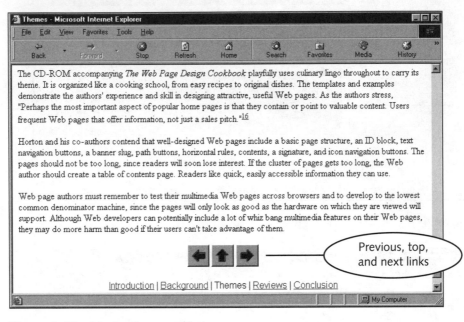

Figure 4-19   Navigation graphics

You also can use navigation graphics to indicate location within a site. For example, you can change the color or shading to indicate which page the user currently is viewing. At the F. A. Cleveland Elementary School Web site, illustrated in Figure 4-20, the navigation graphic includes an arrow to indicate which section of the site the user currently is viewing.

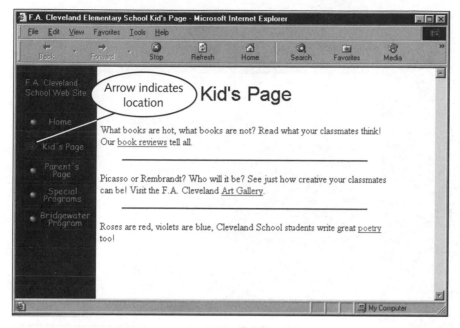

Figure 4-20   Navigation graphic indicates location

Using the alt Attribute

As you read earlier, you should provide alternate text-based links in addition to graphical links. You can do so by including an alt attribute in the <img> tag of the HTML code for the graphic. Repeating navigation options ensures that you meet the needs of a wide range of users. Some sites choose not to offer a text-based alternative, and this makes it difficult for users who cannot view graphics in their browsers. Figure 4-21 shows the main page of the F. A. Cleveland Elementary School Web site, which consists almost entirely of graphics.

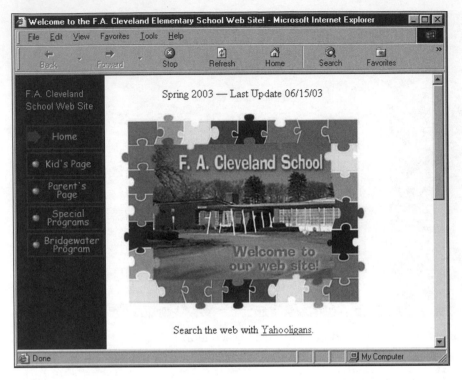

Figure 4-21   Graphics-only navigation

The navigation images in the left column are the only way to navigate the site. Users cannot leave the main page if graphics are turned off or do not download. Figure 4-22 shows the same Web page with images turned off.

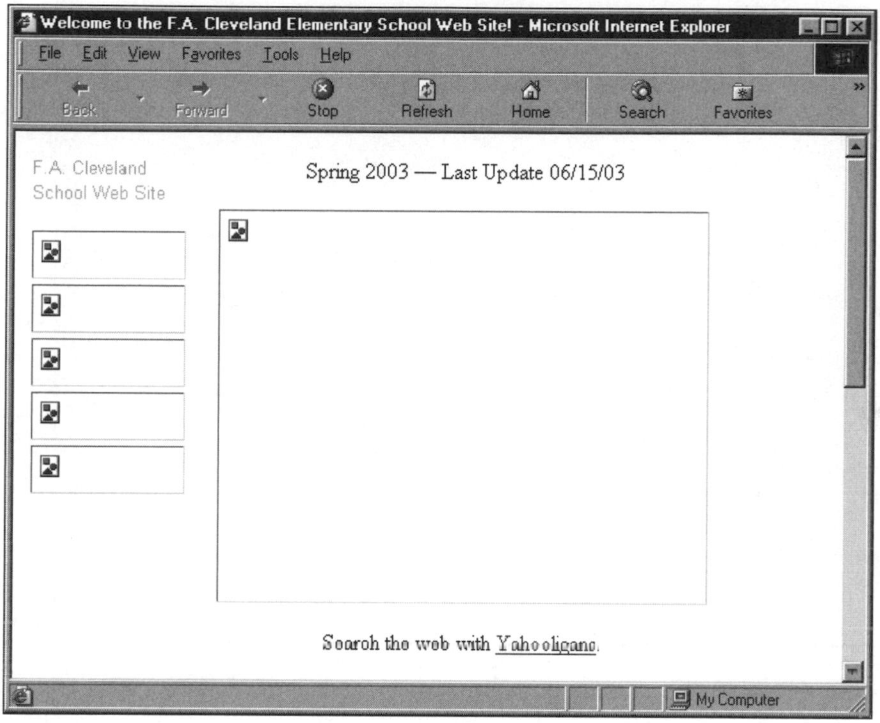

Figure 4-22   No alt valucs in thc <img> tags

Without the graphics, this site offers no navigation information. If you omit alt attributes and make users rely on graphics for navigation, they may be unable to navigate the site effectively.

When you add descriptive alt text, non-graphical browser users can navigate your site. Figure 4-23 shows the F. A. Cleveland Elementary School Web site with the alt attributes added.

Figure 4-23   alt values in the <img> tags

With the graphics turned off, users still can navigate the Web site because the alt attribute values appear in the image space. The user finds navigation cues by reading the alt text and pointing to the image areas to find the clickable spots. The inclusion of alt attributes is of prime importance to the accessibility of your Web site.

The code for one of these navigation buttons looks like this:

```
<a href="parent.htm"><img border=0 height=35 src="smpar-
ent.gif" width=113 ALT="Parent's Page"></a>
```

Note that you must specify the image width and height in the <img> tag to reserve the image space in the browser.

CHAPTER SUMMARY

Usable navigation is the result of working with the power of hypertext and designing for your users' needs. Keep the following points in mind:

❑ Work from the users' point of view. Think about where users want to go within your Web site and make it easy for them to get there.

❏ Add plenty of links to make all areas of your Web site quickly accessible to your users. Link to fragments as well as whole pages. Make it easy to get back to your navigation options.

❏ In addition to providing links, make sure you provide plenty of location cues to let users know where they are.

❏ Use text-based navigation bars to link users to other pages in your site. Use other text-based links to help users move through a long page of information or through a table of contents.

❏ Consider text as an alternative to graphical links. Every additional graphic adds to download time. When using graphics and icons as navigational links, make sure users can interpret these links correctly by including text as part of the images. Also, be sure to use navigation icons consistently throughout your Web site to provide predictable cues for users and to minimize download time.

❏ Include alt values to your <img> tags to provide alternate navigation options for users.

REVIEW QUESTIONS

1. List three advantages of linking by using text instead of graphics.
2. What four navigation questions should the user be able to answer?
3. List three types of navigation cues.
4. List three ways to control information overload.
5. Explain why you would include both graphic and text-based links on a Web page.
6. List two navigation cues you can add to a text-based navigation bar.
7. Why is it best to make <a> the innermost element to a piece of text?
8. What <a> tag attribute is associated with fragment identifiers?
9. List two ways to break up lengthy HTML pages.
10. What character entity is useful as an invisible link destination?
11. What attribute do you use to make an <a> tag both a source and destination anchor?
12. What HTML 4.0 attribute allows you to create fragment identifiers?
13. How do you link to a fragment in an external file?
14. Page turners work best in what type of structure?
15. What are the benefits of contextual linking?
16. List two reasons for standardizing graphics.
17. What are the benefits of using navigation graphics?
18. What are the drawbacks of using navigation icons?
19. What are the benefits of using the ALT attribute?

HANDS-ON PROJECTS

1. Browse the Web and find a Web site that has a successful navigation design. Write a short summary of why the navigation is effective and how it fits the user's needs. Consider the following criteria:

    a. Are the linking text and images meaningful?

    b. Is it easy to access the site's features?

    c. Can you easily search for content?

    d. Is there a site map or other site-orienting feature?

2. Find an online shopping Web site.

    a. Examine the navigation options and indicate whether you think the navigation adds to or detracts from the online shopping experience.

    b. Describe how to change the navigation to increase its effectiveness.

3. Find an online information resource likely to be used for research. Examine the navigation options and describe how the navigation helps or hinders the user's information searching process. Consider the following:

    a. How cluttered is the user interface? Does it deter finding information?

    b. Is navigation prominent or secondary to the page design? Does the user always know his or her location in the site? Is the linking text concise and easy to understand? Is the link destination easy to determine from the linking text?

    c. How deep is the structure of the site? How many clicks does it take to get to the desired information?

4. Use your favorite Web search engine to search for navigation icons.

    a. Assemble a set of icons that would be suitable for international audiences.

    b. Assemble a second set of icons that only would be understood by a local population.

5. Browse the Web to find examples of Web sites that need better navigation options. Using examples from the Web site, describe how you would improve the navigation choices.

6. Browse the Web to find a Web site that uses more than one navigation method and describe whether this benefits the Web site and why.

7. Find a site that illustrates a navigation method different from the ones described in the chapter. Describe the navigation method and state whether this benefits the Web site and why.

8. Take an existing paper-based project and turn it into a hypertext document.

    a. Use a term paper or report from a previous class that you prepared using a word processor and is available in electronic format. Preferably, the document should contain a table of contents and bibliography.

  b. Convert the document to HTML if the program allows, or save the document as ASCII text and paste it into Notepad or an HTML editor.

  c. Mark up the document for Web presentation. Include a linked table of contents, topic links, content links, footnote links, and top links. You may find it best to break the single document into a few HTML files and then link them together.

  d. Test your document in multiple browsers to ensure its portability.

9. This book's companion Web site contains all the HTML files for the sample Web site illustrated in Figure 4-3. Use these sample HTML files to build an alternate navigation scheme. Refer to the information structure illustrations in Chapter 3 (Figures 3-8 to 3-23) for examples of different navigation models. Choose a structure and code examples of usable navigation for the model.

4

CASE PROJECTS

Examine the flowchart you created for your Web site. Consider the requirements of both internal and external navigation. Create a revised flowchart that shows the variety of navigation options you are planning for the Web site.

Using your HTML editor, mark up examples of navigation bars for your content. Make sure your filenames are intact before you start coding. Save the various navigation bars as separate HTML files for later inclusion in your Web pages.

Plan the types of navigation graphics you want to create. Sketch page banners, navigation buttons, and related graphics. Find sources for navigation graphics. For example, you can use public domain (non-copyrighted) clip art collections on the Web for basic navigation arrows and other graphics.

5

CREATING PAGE TEMPLATES

> **When you complete this chapter, you will be able to:**
> ♦ Understand table basics
> ♦ Format tables
> ♦ Follow table pointers to create well-designed tables
> ♦ Create a page template
> ♦ Evaluate examples of page templates

HTML table elements allow Web designers to create grid-based layouts. You can use tables to create templates and to solve design problems. This chapter explains how to create templates by manipulating the most commonly used table elements and attributes. Creating and using templates gives you more control over how content displays in the browser while building more visually interesting pages.

UNDERSTANDING TABLE BASICS

To build effective page templates, you must be familiar with the HTML table elements and attributes. This section describes the most commonly used table elements and attributes.

When HTML was introduced, tables were used only for tabular data, as shown in Figure 5-1.

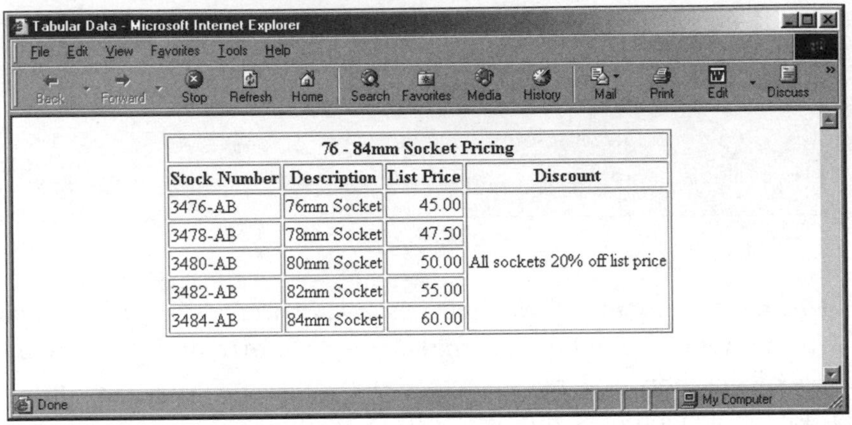

Figure 5-1   The intended use for tables—tabular data

Web designers realized they could use tables to build print-like design structures that allowed them to break away from the left-alignment constraints of basic HTML. With tables, Web designers had the control and the tools to build columnar layouts, align text, add white space, and structure pages. Tables currently are used as the primary design tool throughout the Web. Although Cascading Style Sheets (CSS) provide an alternate method of controlling page display, they will not replace tables until the majority of users have started using the newer browsers, which offer more complete CSS support. There are some discrepancies in table support across browsers, especially with the HTML 4.0 table enhancements, but tables currently are the page design method of choice for most Web sites.

Using Table Elements

The HTML <table> element contains the table information, which consists of table row elements <tr> and individual table data cells <td>. These are the three elements used most frequently when you are building tables, as shown in Figure 5-2.

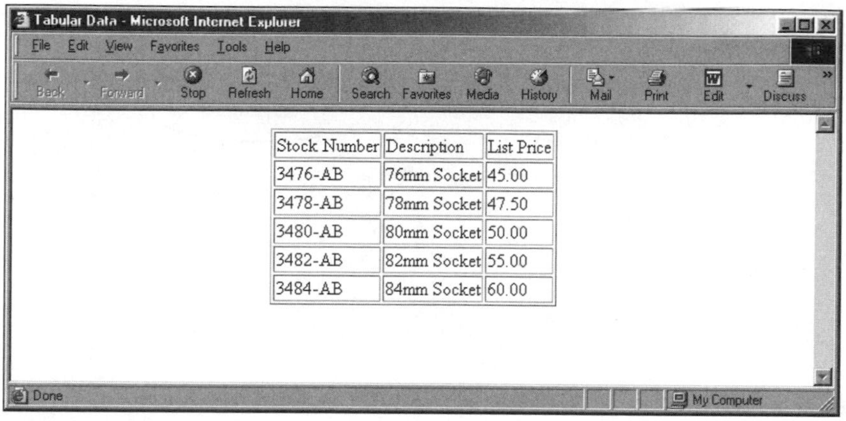

Figure 5-2   Basic data table

The basic table is the result of the following code:

```
<table border>
<tr><td>Stock Number</td><td>Description</td><td>
List Price</td></tr>
<tr><td>3476-AB</td><td>76mm Socket</td><td>45.00
</td></tr>
<tr><td>3478-AB</td><td>78mm Socket</td><td>47.50
</td></tr>
<tr><td>3480-AB</td><td>80mm Socket</td><td>50.00
</td></tr>
<tr><td>3482-AB</td><td>82mm Socket</td><td>55.00
</td></tr>
<tr><td>3484-AB</td><td>84mm Socket</td><td>60.00
</td></tr>
</table>
```

The <table> element contains the rows and cells that make up the table. The <tr> tag marks the beginning and end of each of the six rows of the table. Notice that the <tr> tag contains the table cells, but no content of its own. The border attribute displays the default border around the table and between each cell.

You may occasionally use the <caption> and <th> elements when creating tables. The <caption> tag lets you add a caption to the top or bottom of the table. By default, captions display at the top of the table. You can use the align="bottom" attribute to place the caption at the bottom of the table.

The <th> tag lets you create a table header cell that presents the cell content as bold and centered by default. Figure 5-3 shows the table in Figure 5-2 with a caption and table header cells.

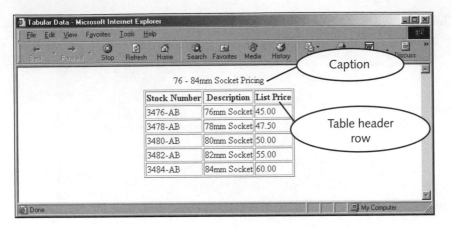

Figure 5-3   Table with caption and table header row

The following code shows the table syntax:

```
<table border>
<caption>76 - 84mm Socket Pricing</caption>
<tr><th>Stock Number</th><th>Description</th><th>List
Price</th></tr>
<tr><td>3476-AB</td><td>76mm Socket</td><td>45.00
</td></tr>
<tr><td>3478-AB</td><td>78mm Socket</td><td>47.50
</td></tr>
<tr><td>3480-AB</td><td>80mm Socket</td><td>50.00
</td></tr>
<tr><td>3482-AB</td><td>82mm Socket</td><td>55.00
</td></tr>
<tr><td>3484-AB</td><td>84mm Socket</td><td>60.00
</td></tr>
</table>
```

The HTML 4.0 table model contains a number of table elements that may not be supported in all browsers. Internet Explorer is the only browser that consistently supports the following elements:

- col - Specifies column properties
- colgroup - Specifies multiple column properties
- thead - Signifies table header
- tbody - Signifies table body
- tfoot - Signifies table footer

Defining Table Attributes

Table attributes let you further define a number of table characteristics. You can apply attributes at three levels of table structure: global, row-level, or cell-level. Notice that some attributes are marked as deprecated, meaning that they will not be included in future releases of HTML.

Using Global Attributes

Global attributes affect the entire table (see Table 5-1). Place these attributes in the initial <table> tag.

Table 5-1   Global table attributes

Attribute	Description
align	Floats the table to the left or right of text. This is a deprecated attribute in HTML 4.0.
background	Specifies a background image that tiles the background of the cell. This is a deprecated attribute in HTML 4.0.
bgcolor	Specifies a color for the table background. This is a deprecated attribute in HTML 4.0.
border	Displays a border around the table and each cell within the table.
cellpadding	Inserts spacing within the table cells on all four sides. The value for this attribute is a pixel count.
cellspacing	Inserts spacing between the table cells, on all four sides. The value for this attribute is a pixel count.
height	Adjusts the height of the table. The value can be either a percentage relative to the browser window size or a fixed pixel amount. This is a deprecated attribute in HTML 4.0.
width	Adjusts the width of the table. The value can be either a percentage relative to the browser window size or a fixed pixel amount.

Using Row-Level Attributes

Row-level attributes affect an entire row (see Table 5-2). Place these attributes in the beginning <tr> tag.

Table 5-2   Row-level table attributes

Attribute	Description
align	Horizontally aligns the contents of the cells within the row. Use left, center, or right values. Left is the default. This is a deprecated attribute in HTML 4.0.
bgcolor	Specifies a background color for the cells within the row. This is a deprecated attribute in HTML 4.0.
valign	Vertically aligns the contents of the cells within the row. Use top, middle, or bottom values. Middle is the default.

Using Cell-Level Attributes

Cell-level attributes affect only the contents of one cell (see Table 5-3). Place these attributes in the beginning <td> tag.

Table 5-3   Cell-level table attributes

Attribute	Description
align	Horizontally aligns the contents of the cell. Use left, center, or right values. Left is the default.
bgcolor	Specifies a background color for the cell. This is a deprecated attribute in HTML 4.0.
colspan	Specifies the number of columns a cell spans.
height	Adjusts the height of the cell. The value can be either a percentage relative to the table size or a fixed pixel amount. This is a deprecated attribute in HTML 4.0.
rowspan	Specifies the number of rows a cell spans.
valign	Vertically aligns the contents of the cell. Use top, middle, or bottom values. Middle is the default.
width	Adjusts the width of the cell. The value can be either a percentage relative to the table size or a fixed pixel amount. This is a deprecated attribute in HTML 4.0 at the cell level.

Cell-level attributes take precedence over row-level attributes. Even though the following code for a single table row has conflicting align attributes, the align="right" value in the <td> tag overrides the align="center" value in the <tr> tag.

```
<tr align="center"><td>Center-
aligned text </td><td align="right">Right-
aligned text </td></tr>
```

Spanning Columns

The colspan attribute lets you create cells that span multiple columns of a table. Column cells always span to the right. Figure 5-4 shows a table with a column span in the first row.

The following code shows the colspan attribute:

```
<table border>
<!-- Row 1 contains the column span -->
<tr><th colspan="3">76 - 84mm Socket Pricing</th></tr>
<tr><th>Stock Number</th><th>Description</th><th>List
Price</th></tr>
<tr><td>3476-AB</td><td>76mm Socket</td><td>45.00
</td></tr>
<tr><td>3478-AB</td><td>78mm Socket</td><td>47.50
</td></tr>
<tr><td>3480-AB</td><td>80mm Socket</td><td>50.00
</td></tr>
<tr><td>3482-AB</td><td>82mm Socket</td><td>55.00
</td></tr>
<tr><td>3484-AB</td><td>84mm Socket</td><td>60.00
</td></tr>
</table>
```

When you build column spans, make sure that all of your columns add up to the correct number of cells. In this code, because each row has three cells, the colspan attribute is set to three to span all columns of the table, as shown in Figure 5-4.

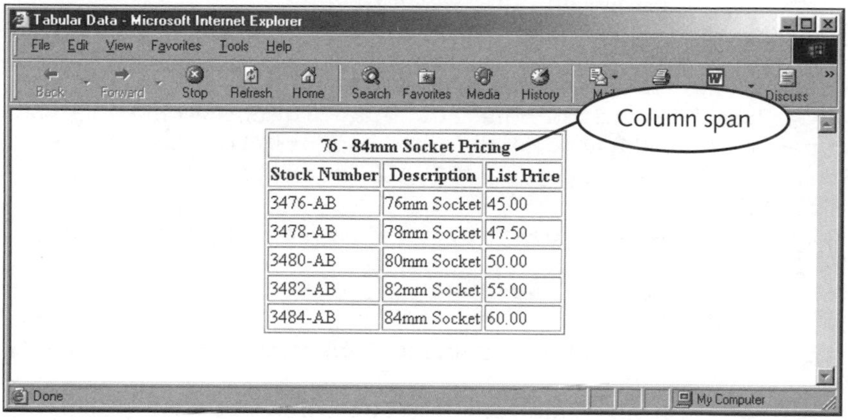

Figure 5-4   Table with a column span

Spanning Rows

The rowspan attribute lets you create cells that span multiple rows of a table. Rows always span down. Figure 5-5 shows the table in Figure 5-4 with a row span added to the right column.

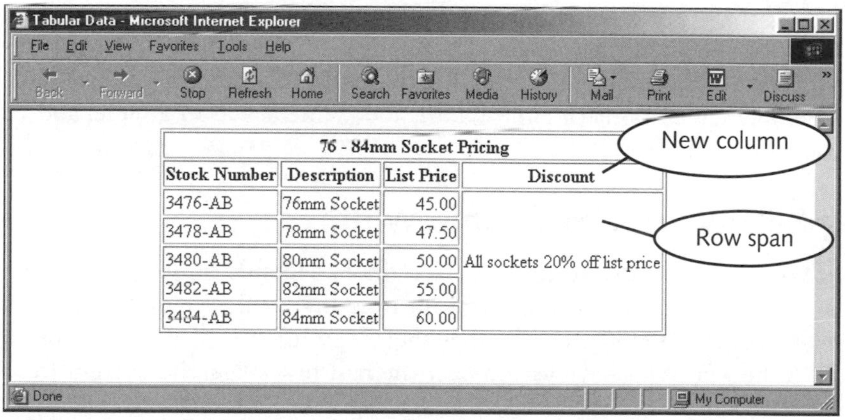

Figure 5-5   Table with new "Discount" column and row span

The following code shows the new cell that contains the rowspan attribute and the extra column cell in the table header row:

```
<table  border>
<!-- Row 1 contains the column span -->
<tr><th colspan="4">76 - 84mm Socket Pricing</th></tr>
<tr><th>Stock Number</th><th>Description</th><th>List
Price</th><th>Discount</th></tr>
<!-- Row 3 contains the row span in the 4th cell -->
<tr><td>3476-AB</td><td>76mm Socket</td><td align="right">
45.00</td> <td rowspan="5">All sockets 20% off list price
</td></tr>
<tr><td>3478-AB</td><td>78mm Socket</td><td align="right">
47.50</td></tr>
<tr><td>3480-AB</td><td>80mm Socket</td><td align="right">
50.00</td></tr>
<tr><td>3482-AB</td><td>82mm Socket</td><td align="right">
55.00</td></tr>
<tr><td>3484-AB</td><td>84mm Socket</td><td align="right">
60.00</td></tr>
</table>
```

The row span cell is the fourth cell in the third row. It spans down across five rows of the table. Notice also that to accommodate the new column, the colspan attribute value in the first row must be changed to four.

FORMATTING TABLES

Now that you understand how to build the basic structure of a table, you can enhance the visual design with a variety of table attributes. In this section you will learn to build fixed or flexible tables, control table width, add white space in a table, and build table-based navigation bars.

Choosing Relative or Fixed Table Widths

Whether you choose to use relative or fixed tables depends on your content, your user's needs, and the amount of control you want over the result. Many Web designers prefer fixed tables because they can ensure that their view of the content will be the same as the user's. Although styles have varied over the past few years, the current trend for most mainstream Web sites is to build fixed-width designs.

You can set relative table widths as percentages in the table width attribute. If you choose relative table widths, your tables resize based on the size of the browser window. Figure 5-6 shows a table with the width attribute set to 100 percent at 800 × 600 resolution.

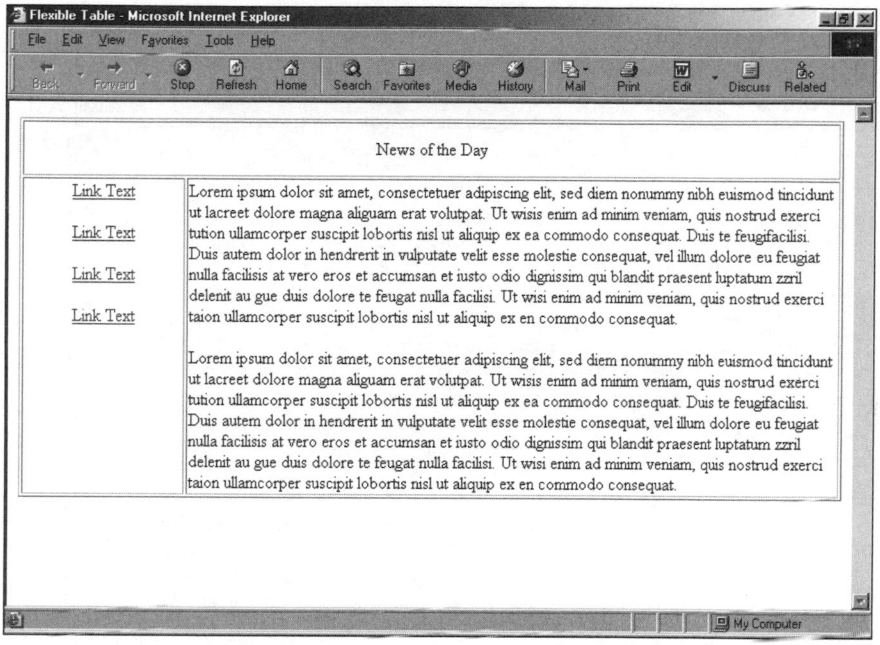

Figure 5-6   A flexible table at 800 × 600 resolution

Figure 5-7 shows the same table at 640 × 480 resolution. The browser fits the content into the window, wrapping text as necessary. Notice that the user must scroll to read the remainder of the content. The advantage to using a relative width is that the resulting table is more compatible across different browser window sizes and screen resolutions. The disadvantage is that you have little control over the way the user sees the result, because your content can shift based on browser window size.

You can set absolute table widths as pixel values in the table width attribute. Fixed tables remain constant regardless of the browser window size, giving the designer greater control over what the user sees. The user's browser size and screen resolution have no effect on the display of the page. The disadvantage is that users may not see all of the content on the page without horizontal scrolling. Figure 5-8 shows a table with the width attribute set to a fixed width of 750 pixels. Notice that at 640 × 480 resolution the table extends beyond the browser window and both horizontal and vertical scroll bars appear.

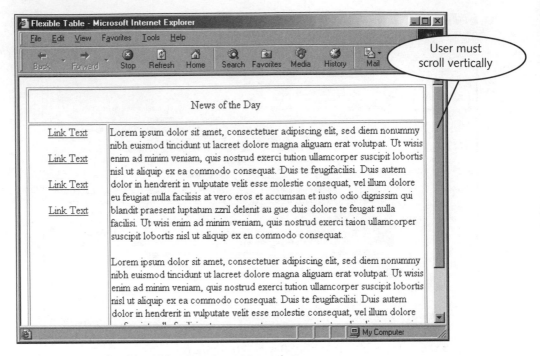

Figure 5-7   A flexible table at 640 × 480 resolution

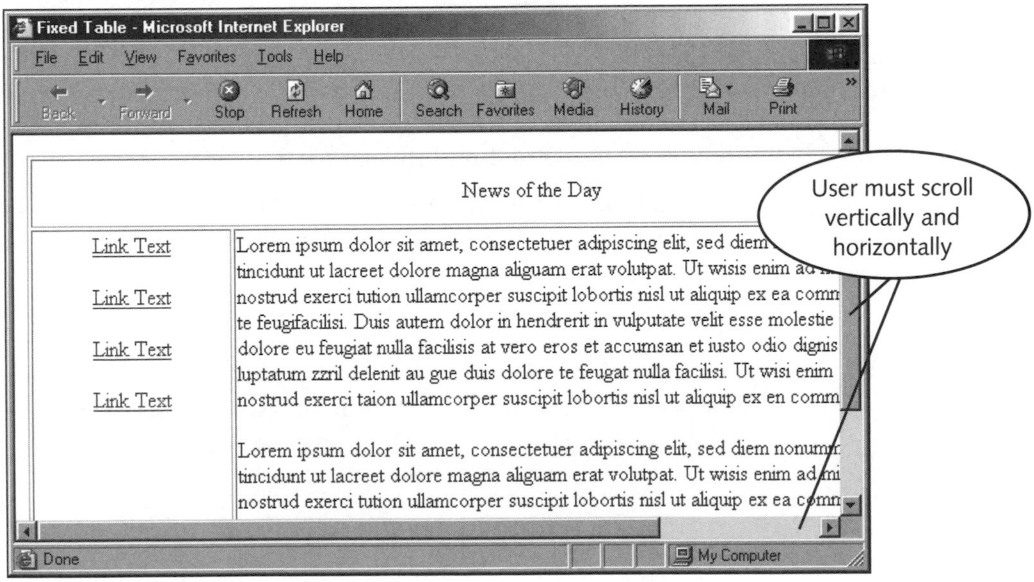

Figure 5-8   A fixed 750 pixel-width table at 640 × 480 resolution

Determining the Correct Fixed Width for a Table

If you decide to build fixed tables, you must choose a pixel width value. You can determine the value to use based on your user's most common screen resolution size. Currently 800 × 600 is the screen resolution favored by most users. A small percentage still use 640 × 480, with the remainder using 1024 × 768 and higher. The fixed width of your tables must be less than the horizontal measurement of the screen resolution. For example, 750 pixels is the optimum width for an 800 × 600 screen resolution. Figure 5-9 shows the areas to account for when calculating table width.

Notice the page margin on the left of the screen. The width of this margin is approximately 10 pixels and is built into the browser. The scroll bar on the right of the screen is approximately 20 pixels. Avoid having your table extend into this area, which will cause the horizontal scroll bar to appear. Finally, allow approximately 20 more pixels for a right page margin. Subtracting all of these values from 800 leaves an approximate table width of 750 pixels. These values vary slightly based on the browser and operating system, so test the results of your work in multiple situations.

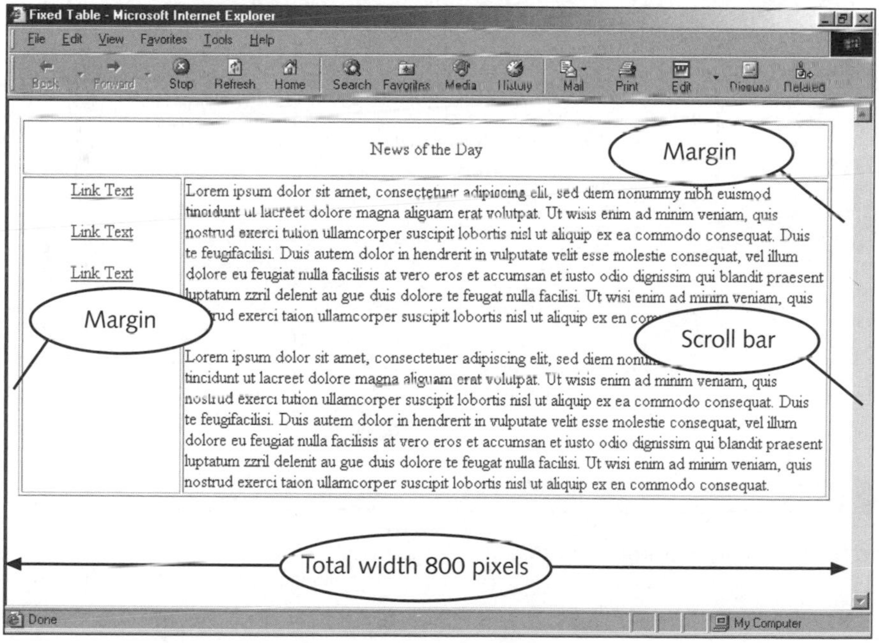

Figure 5-9   Areas to account for when calculating table width

Adding White Space in a Table

You can add white space into a table with the cellpadding and cellspacing attributes. These are global attributes (refer to Table 5-1) that affect every cell in the table. The cellpadding and cellspacing attribute values are always pixel amounts. In Figure 5-10 the cellpadding value is set to 10 pixels, which adds 10 pixels of white space on all four sides of the content within each cell.

The cellspacing attribute adds white space between the cells on all four sides rather than within the cells. Figure 5-11 shows the same table with cellspacing set to 10 pixels. Compare Figures 5-10 and 5-11 to see the difference between the two attributes. There is no definite rule to help you determine which of the attributes you should use. You will have to experiment with each of your table layouts to decide which attribute works best for the particular situation.

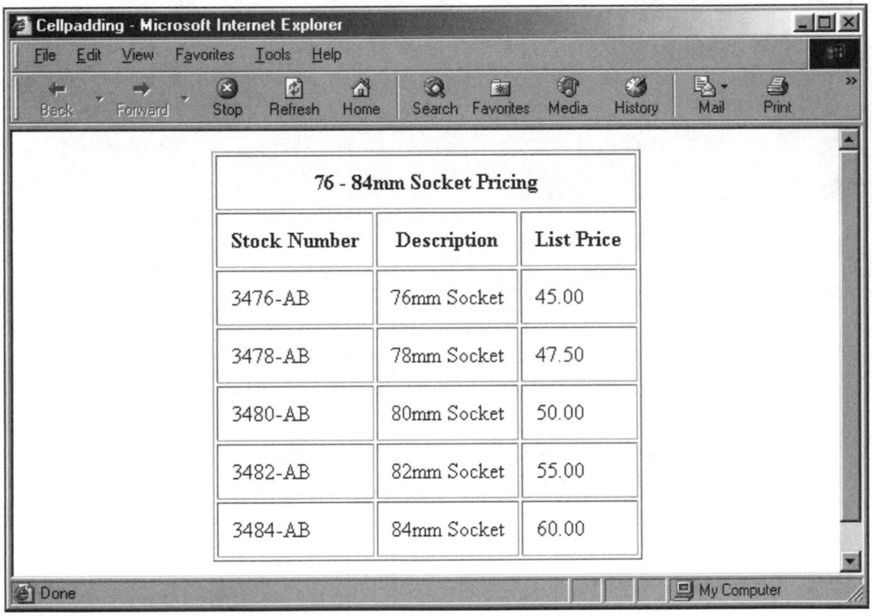

Figure 5-10   Cell padding in a table

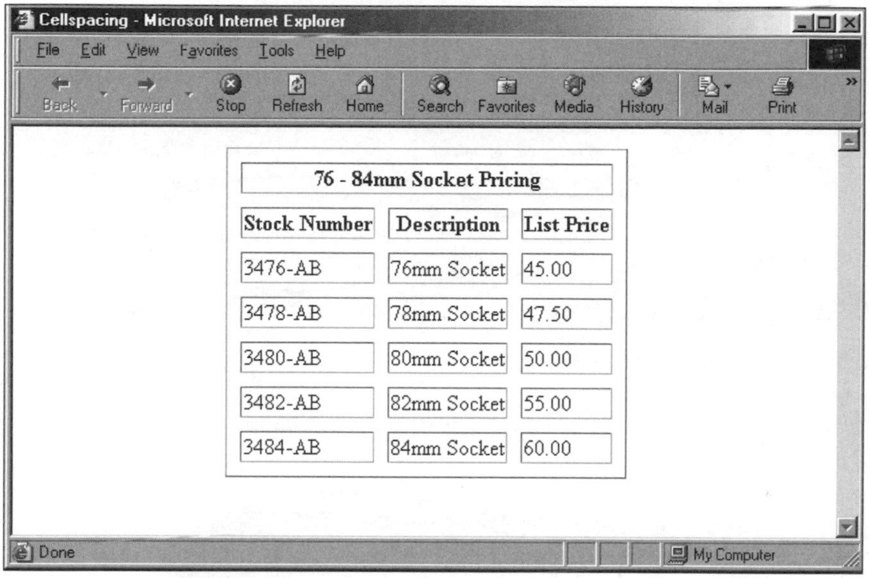

Figure 5-11   Cell spacing in a table

Removing Default Table Spacing

Default spacing values are included in the table even when you do not specify values for the table's border, cellpadding, or cellspacing attributes. Without the default spacing values, the table cells would have no built-in white space between them, and the contents of adjoining cells would run together. Depending on the browser, approximately two pixels are reserved for each of these values. You can remove the default spacing by explicitly stating a zero value for each attribute. The code looks like this:

```
<table border="0" cellpadding="0" cellspacing="0">
```

This very useful technique lets you join the contents of adjacent cells. You can take an image, break it into separate pieces, and then rejoin the pieces in a table by removing the default spacing. Because the image is now composed of separate parts, you can link individual parts of the image to different destinations on your site.

Figure 5-12 shows six images assembled in a table with the default spacing. The background color on this page is set to gray so you can see the images more clearly. Even though borders are turned off, their default space remains in the table. The default cell padding and cell spacing also add to the white space between the images.

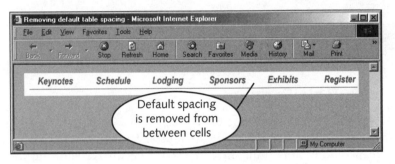

Figure 5-12   Default table spacing

Figure 5-13 shows the same image with border, cellpadding, and cellspacing attributes set to zero.

Figure 5-13   Default table spacing removed

TABLE POINTERS FOR WELL-DESIGNED TABLES

To create effective HTML tables, observe the following guidelines:

- Write easy-to-read code.
- Remove extra white spaces.
- Center tables to adapt to different resolutions.
- Stack tables for quicker downloading.
- Nest tables for more complex designs.

Writing Easy-to-Read Table Code

The HTML table code can get complicated when you add content to your tables. You have to manage not only the table tags and attributes, but also the text, images, and links in your cells. One small error in your code can cause unpredictable results in the browser.

You can simplify your table creation and maintenance tasks by writing clean, commented code. If you use plenty of white space in the code, you will find your tables easier to access and change. Adding comments helps you quickly find the code you want. The various code samples in this chapter demonstrate the use of comments and white space in table code.

Removing Extra Spaces

Always remove any leading or trailing spaces in your table cell content. These spaces cause problems when you try to join the contents of adjacent cells. In some browsers the extra spaces create white space or misalignment in the table cells. Figure 5-14 shows code with one extra trailing space in the second cell after the <img> element. This extra trailing white space causes the misalignment of the images shown in Figure 5-15.

```
<table border="0" cellpadding="0" cellspacing="0">
<tr>
<td><img width="101" height="40" src="tpkeynt.gif"></td>
<td><img width="101" height="40" src="tpsched.gif"> </td>
<td><img width="101" height="40" src="tplodg.gif"></td>
<td><img width="101" height="40" src="tpspons.gif"></td>
<td><img width="101" height="40" src="tpexhib.gif"></td>
<td><img width="88" height="40" src="tpreg.gif"></td>
</tr>
</table>
```

Extra trailing space in code

Figure 5-14   Extra trailing white space in code

Misalignment caused by extra trailing space

Figure 5-15   Extra white space causes misalignment

Centering Tables

You can center tables on the page using the <div> element. Centering a fixed table makes it independent of resolution changes, because the table always is centered in the browser window. Use the align="center" attribute to set the table alignment. Figure 5-16 shows a centered table at 800 × 600 resolution. As the browser size changes the table will always remain centered.

The following code shows the use of the <div> element to center the table.

```
<div align="center">
<table width="750" border>
<tr><td colspan="2" height="50">banner</td></tr>
<tr><td height="250" width="20%">column 1</td><td>
column 2</td></tr>
</table>
</div>
```

Although the <center> element works in most browsers, it is a deprecated element and its use should be avoided. Use <div align="center"> instead.

Stacking Tables

Browsers must read the entire table code before displaying the table. Any text outside of a table displays first. If you build long tables, they increase the time the user has to wait before the tables appear in the browser. Because of the way browsers display tables, it is better to build several small tables rather than one large one. This technique also can simplify your table design task, because smaller tables are easier to work with. Figure 5-17 shows a page template built with two stacked tables.

Another benefit of stacking tables is that they display in the same order in which they appear in the code. This means the user can be reading the contents of your first table while the next one downloads. Also, more complex layouts are easier to build if you break them into multiple tables. Notice that the top table in Figure 5-17 has five columns, while the second has three. It would be impossible to build this layout using a single table.

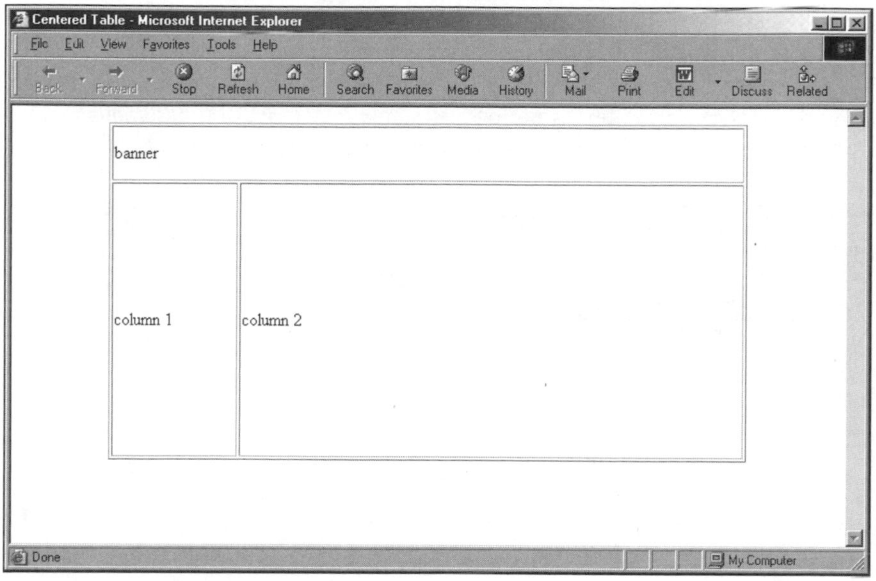

Figure 5-16   Centered table

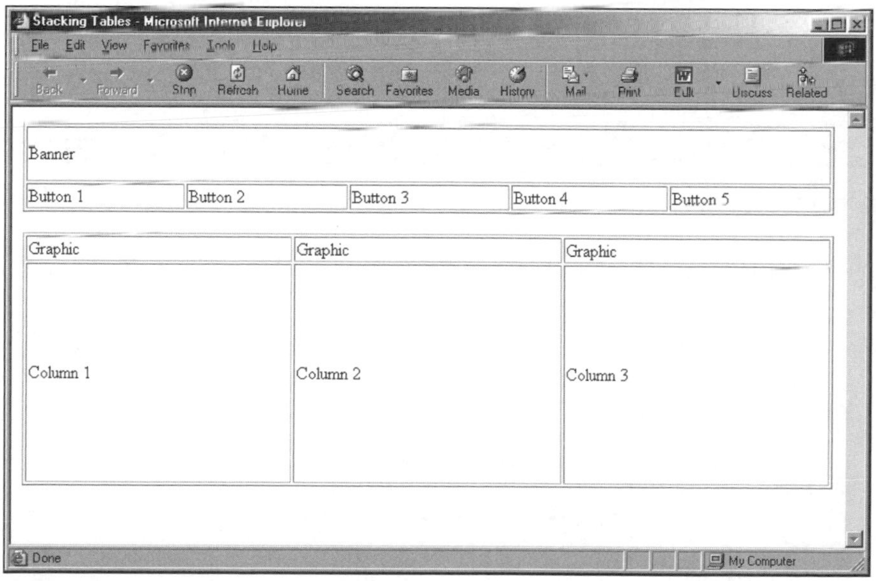

Figure 5-17   Stacked tables

Nesting Tables

You can nest tables by placing an entire table within a table cell. Figure 5-18 shows an example of a table with a second table nested in the right column.

In some of the design samples you will notice the use of Latin text. This is a traditional design technique from the printing layout world, commonly called "greeking." It lets you easily create text areas when you are testing a design. Also, because the text is not understandable to most, the designer's focus is on the content areas rather than on the actual content.

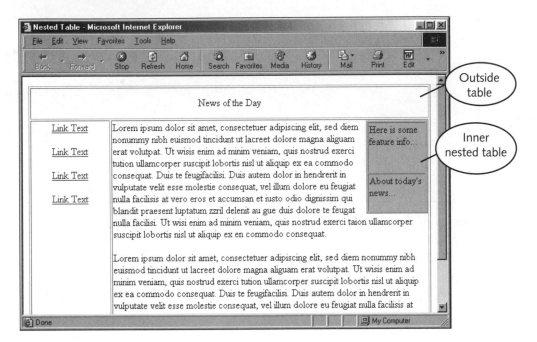

Figure 5-18   Nesting tables

The code for the nested tables follows. The nested table in the right column is shaded.

```
<table width="100%" border>
<tr><td colspan="2" height="50" align="center">News of the
 Day</td></tr>
<tr valign="top">

<td width="20%" align="center">
<p><a href=" ">Link Text</a></p>
<p><a href=" ">Link Text</a></p>
<p><a href=" ">Link Text</a></p>
<p><a href=" ">Link Text</a></p>
</td>

<td>
<table align="right" width="100" border bgcolor="#cccccc">
<tr><td>Here is some feature info...<br><br><br></td></tr>
<tr><td>About today's news...<br><br></td></tr>
</table>
```

```
<p>Lorem ipsum dolor sit amet, consectetuer adipiscing
elit, sed diem nonummy nibh euismod tincidunt ut lacreet
dolore magna aliguam erat volutpat. Ut wisis enim ad minim
veniam, quis nostrud exerci tution ullamcorper suscipit
lobortis nisl ut aliquip ex ea commodo consequat. Duis te
feugifacilisi. Duis autem dolor in hendrerit in vulpu-
tate velit esse molestie consequat, vel illum dolore eu
feugiat nulla facilisis at vero eros et accumsan et iusto
odio dignissim qui blandit praesent luptatum zzril delent
au gue duis dolore te feugat nulla facilisi. Ut wisi enim
ad minim veniam, quis nostrud exerci taion ullamcorper
suscipit lobortis nisl ut aliquip ex en commodo consequat.
</p>
```

5

```
<p>Lorem ipsum dolor sit amet, consectetuer adipiscing
elit, sed diem nonummy nibh euismod tincidunt ut lacreet
dolore magna aliguam erat volutpat. Ut wisis enim ad minim
veniam, quis nostrud exerci tution ullamcorper suscipit
lobortis nisl ut aliquip ex ea commodo consequat. Duis te
feugifacilisi. Duis autem dolor in hendrerit in vulpu-
tate velit esse molestie consequat, vel illum dolore eu
feugiat nulla facilisis at vero eros et accumsan et iusto
odio dignissim qui blandit praesent luptatum zzril delenit
au gue duis dolore te feugat nulla facilisi. Ut wisi enim
ad minim veniam, quis nostrud exerci taion ullamcorper
suscipit lobortis nisl ut aliquip ex en commodo consequat.
</p></td>
</tr>
</table>
```

CREATING A PAGE TEMPLATE

Now that you understand the mechanics of building tables, you can apply your knowledge to the creation of a page template. This hands-on example demonstrates how to take a design sketch for a Web page and build a template for the page layout. Figure 5-19 shows a sketch of the desired Web page layout. This layout is designed for a base screen resolution of 800 × 600, so the table will be fixed at a width of 750 pixels.

Notice that the basic structure of the table is three rows by four columns. Each column uses 25 percent of the total width of the template. Row spans and column spans break across the layout to provide visual interest.

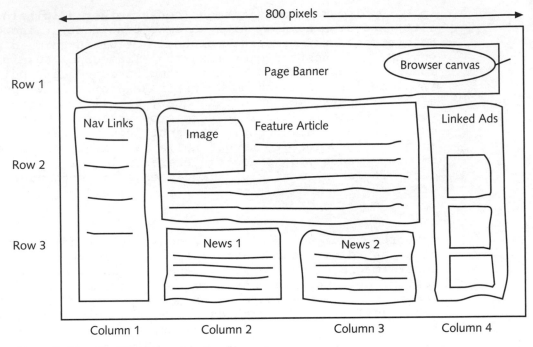

Figure 5-19   Sketch of the visualized layout

Building the Basic Table Structure

Start by building the basic table structure, including all the cells and rows of the table. As you customize the table, you can remove extraneous cells. The basic structure is a three-row by four-column table, as shown in Figure 5-20.

To begin building the page template:

1. Copy the **template.htm** file from the Chapter05 folder on your Data Disk.

2. Save the file to your work folder using the same filename.

3. Open the file in your HTML editor and add the following code to the page between the existing <body> tags:

```
<table border>
<tr><td>R1C1</td><td>R1C2</td><td>R1C3</td><td>R1C4</td>
</tr>
<tr><td>R2C1</td><td>R2C2</td><td>R2C3</td><td>R2C4</td>
</tr>
<tr><td>R3C1</td><td>R3C2</td><td>R3C3</td><td>R3C4</td>
</tr>
</table>
```

Notice the use of row and cell placeholders such as R1C1, which stands for Row One, Cell One. These placeholders are visible in the browser and provide helpful reference points as you build a table. Making the borders visible with the border attribute provides another visual reference to the structure of the table. When you complete your design, you can turn borders off by removing the border attribute from the <table> element.

    4. Save template.htm and leave it open for the next set of steps. Then view the file in the browser. It should look like Figure 5-20. 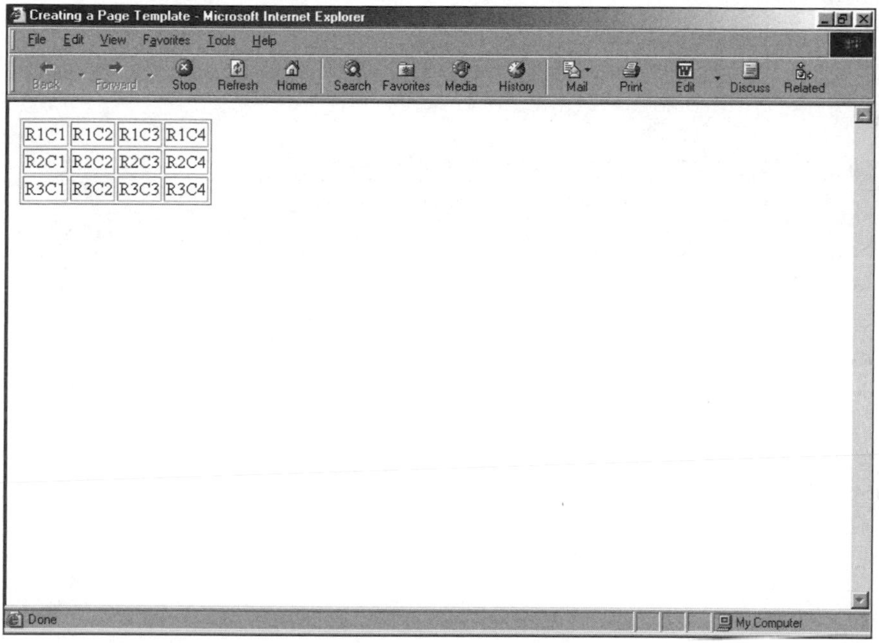

Figure 5-20   Basic three-row by four-column table

Setting a Fixed Width

One of the design characteristics of the template is a fixed width that is not dependent on the user's browser size or screen resolution. To create this characteristic, use a pixel value in the table width attribute.

To set the fixed width:

    1. Continue working in the file **template.htm**.

    2. Add the width attribute to the opening <table> tag.

3. Set the width attribute value to 750 as shown in the following code. (Insert the shaded code):

```
<table border width="750">
<tr><td>R1C1</td><td>R1C2</td><td>R1C3</td><td>R1C4</td>
</tr>
<tr><td>R2C1</td><td>R2C2</td><td>R2C3</td><td>R2C4</td>
</tr>
<tr><td>R3C1</td><td>R3C2</td><td>R3C3</td><td>R3C4</td>
</tr>
</table>
```

4. Save template.htm and leave it open for the next set of steps. Then view the file in the browser. It should look like Figure 5-21.

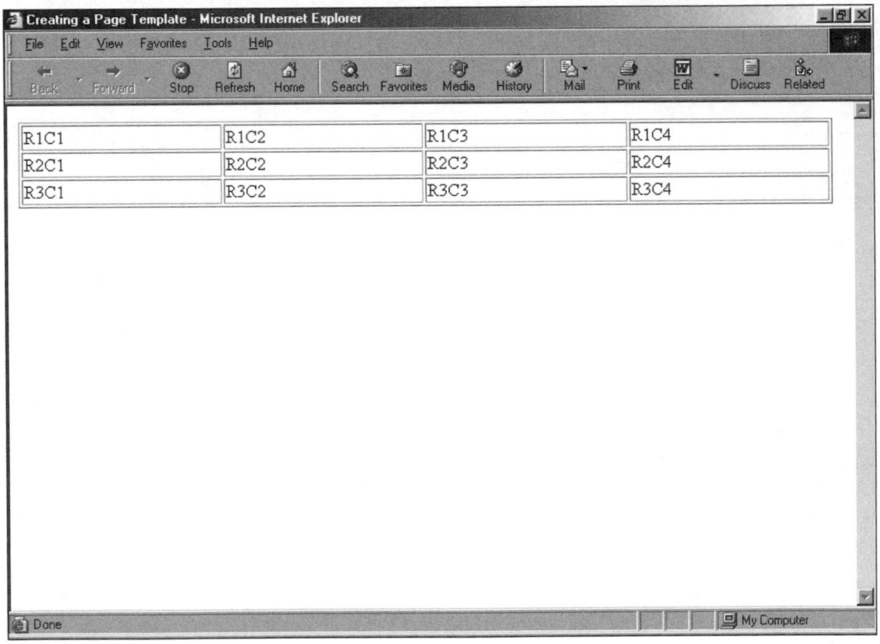

Figure 5-21 Width set to 750 pixels

Creating the Page Banner Cell

The page banner cell is R1C1, which spans the four columns of the table using the colspan attribute. To create the column span successfully, you must remove all but one cell in the first row of the table.

To create the page banner cell:

1. Continue working in the file **template.htm**.

2. Remove the cells shown as shaded text in the following code fragment.

```
<tr><td>R1C1</td><td>R1C2</td><td>R1C3</td><td>R1C4</td>
</tr>
```

3. Add the **colspan** attribute to the R1C1 cell and set it to a value of **4**.

4. Add the align attribute and set it to **center**.

5. Change the R1C1 text to **Page Banner**. Your complete table code should now look like the following.

```
<table border width="750">
<tr><td colspan="4" align="center">Page Banner</td></tr>
<tr><td>R2C1</td><td>R2C2</td><td>R2C3</td><td>R2C4</td>
</tr>
<tr><td>R3C1</td><td>R3C2</td><td>R3C3</td><td>R3C4</td>
</tr>
</table>
```

6. Save template.htm and leave it open for the next set of steps. Then view the file in the browser. It should look like Figure 5-22.

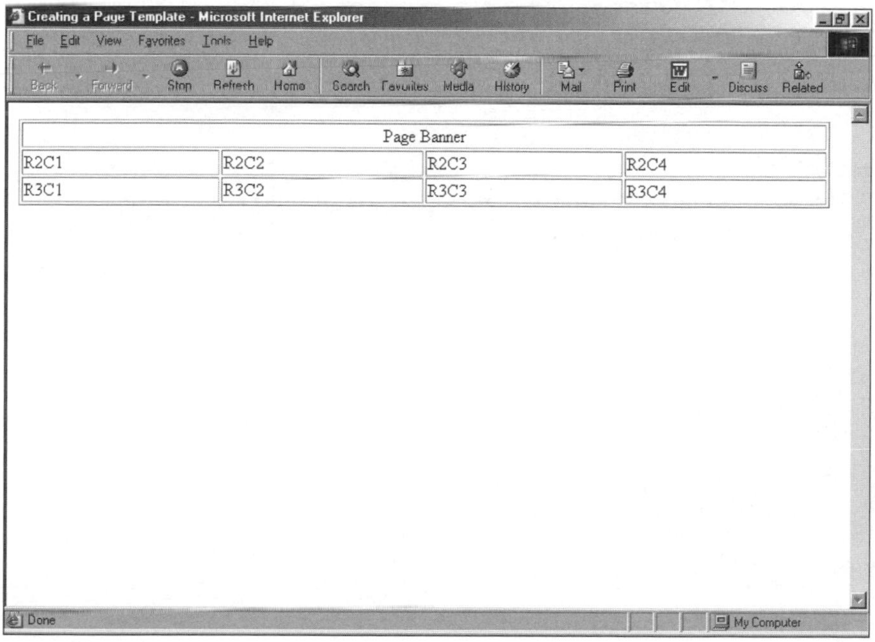

Figure 5-22   The Page Banner cell

Creating the Feature Article Cell

The Feature Article cell in the layout is cell R2C2, which spans two columns. This column span requires the removal of one cell in row 2 to make room for the span.

To create the feature article cell:

1. Continue working in the file **template.htm**.

2. Remove the cell shown as shaded text in the following code.

```
<table border width="750">
<tr><td colspan="4" align="center">Page Banner</td></tr>
<tr><td>R2C1</td><td>R2C2</td><td>R2C3</td><td>R2C4</td>
</tr>
<tr><td>R3C1</td><td>R3C2</td><td>R3C3</td><td>R3C4</td>
</tr>
</table>
```

3. Add the **colspan** attribute to the R2C2 cell and set it to a value of **2**.

4. Change the R2C2 text to **Feature Article**. Your complete table code should now look like the following. The shaded text shows the code you just added.

```
<table border width="750">
<tr><td colspan="4" align="center">Page Banner</td></tr>
<tr><td>R2C1</td><td colspan="2">Feature Article</td>
<td>R2C4</td></tr>
<tr><td>R3C1</td><td>R3C2</td><td>R3C3</td><td>R3C4</td>
</tr>
</table>
```

5. Save template.htm and leave it open for the next set of steps. Then view the file in the browser. It should look like Figure 5-23.

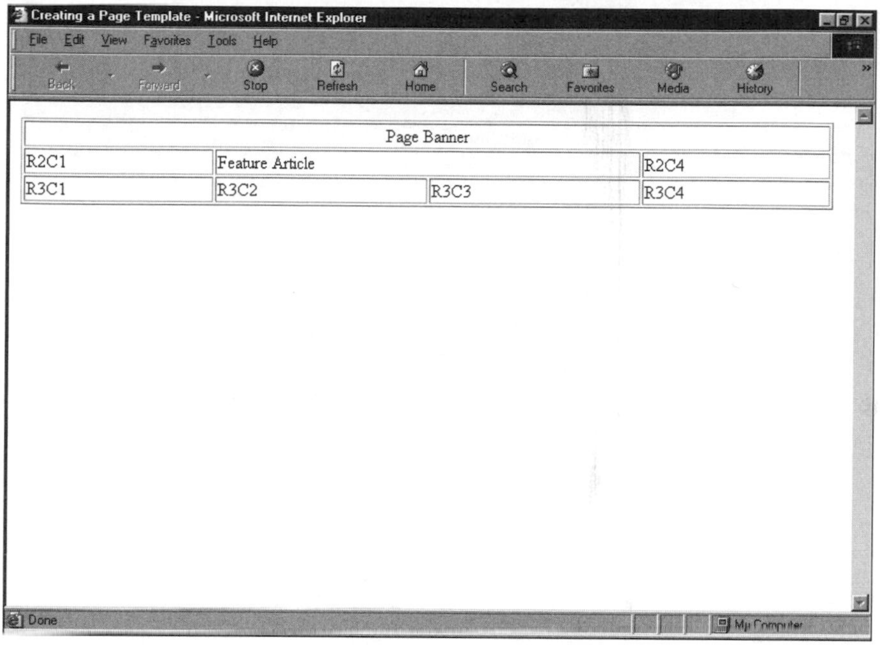

Figure 5-23   The Feature Article cell

Creating the Link Column Cells

The Nav Links and Linked Ads columns in the layout reside in cells R2C1 and R2C4, respectively. These cells span rows 2 and 3 of the table. The row spans require the removal of cells R3C1 and R3C4, as illustrated in Figure 5-24.

To create the link column cells:

1. Continue working in the file **template.htm**.

2. Remove the cells shown as shaded text in the following code fragment.

```
<table border width="750">
<tr><td colspan="4" align="center">Page Banner</td></tr>
<tr><td>R2C1</td><td colspan="2">Feature Article</td>
<td> R2C4</td></tr>
<tr><td>R3C1</td><td>R3C2</td><td>R3C3</td><td>R3C4</td>
</tr>
</table>
```

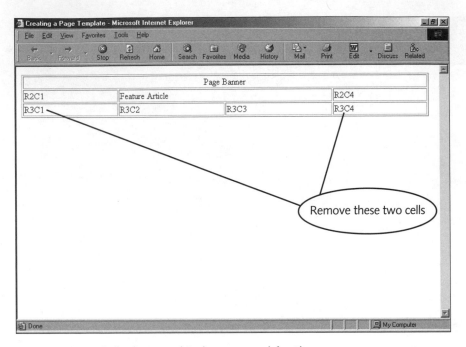

Figure 5-24   Cells that need to be removed for the row spans

3. Add the **rowspan** attribute to cells R2C1 and R2C4. Set the value to **2**. The shaded text in the following excerpt shows the code you should add.

```
<table border width="750">
<tr><td colspan="4" align="center">Page Banner</td></tr>
<tr><td rowspan="2">R2C1</td><td colspan="2">Feature
Article</td><td rowspan="2">R2C4</td></tr>
<tr><td>R3C2</td><td>R3C3</td></tr>
</table>
```

4. Change the R2C1 text to **Nav Links**.

5. Change the R2C4 text to **Linked Ads**.

6. Save template.htm and leave it open for the next set of steps. Then view the file in the browser. It should look like Figure 5-25.

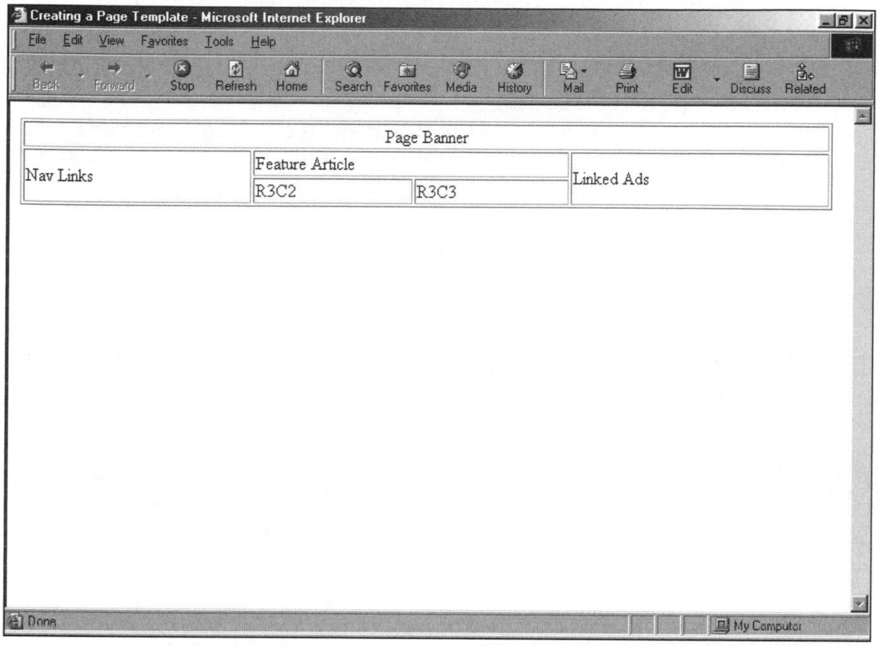

Figure 5-25   The Link columns

Setting the Column Widths

You can set column widths by using the width attribute at the cell level. Column widths must be set in only one cell per column. Setting the column widths ensures that the text will wrap properly without skewing the evenly distributed four-column layout.

To set the column widths:

1. Continue working in the file **template.htm**.

2. Add the **width** attribute and set it to a value of **25%** in both the "Nav Links" and "Linked Ads" cells, as shown in the following code.

```
<table border width="750">
<tr><td colspan="4" align="center">Page Banner</td></tr>
<tr><td rowspan="2" width="25%">Nav Links</td><td
colspan="2">Feature Article</td><td rowspan="2" width=
"25%">Linked Ads</td></tr>
<tr><td>R3C2</td><td>R3C3</td></tr>
</table>
```

3. Change the R3C2 text to **News Column 1**.

4. Change the R3C3 text to **News Column 2**.

5. Add the **width** attribute to the News Column 1 and News Column 2 cells and set it to a value of **25%**, as shown in the following code.

```
<table border width="750">
<tr><td colspan="4" align="center">Page Banner</td></tr>
<tr><td rowspan="2" width="25%">Nav Links</td><td
colspan="2">Feature Article</td><td rowspan="2" width="
25%">Linked Ads</td></tr>
<tr><td width="25%">News Column 1</td><td width="25%">
News Column 2</td></tr>
</table>
```

6. Save template.htm and leave it open for the next set of steps. Then view the file in the browser. It should look like Figure 5-26.

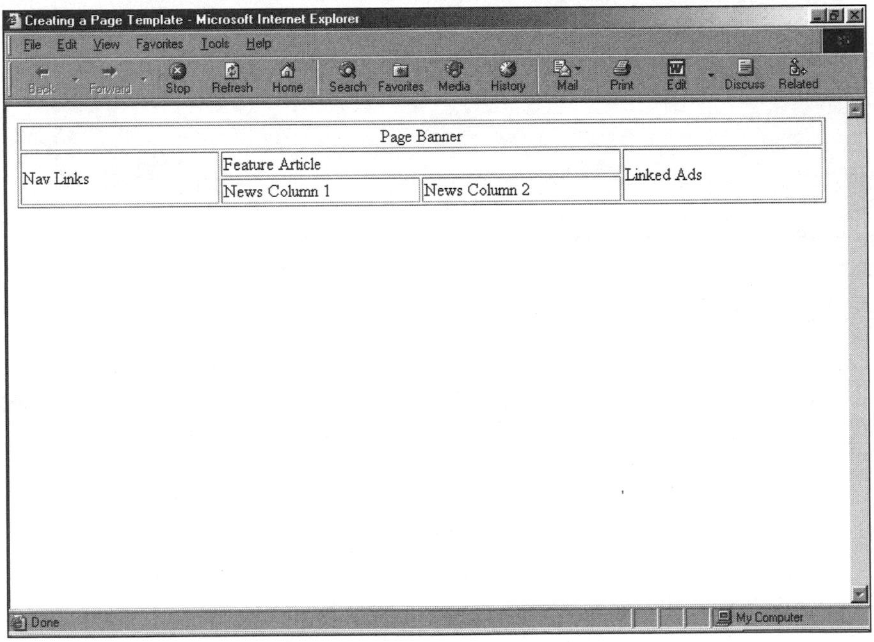

Figure 5-26   Column widths set to 25%

You can set widths at the cell level to either a pixel or percentage amount. Test carefully to make sure that the layout is browser-compatible, as column widths can be troublesome.

 You can define column widths precisely if you use a graphic within the cell. Because the browser cannot wrap or truncate a graphic, the cell always will be at least as wide as the graphic.

Completing and Testing the Template

To prepare the table for content, add the valign attribute to top-align all of the content in the table. To verify that your template works properly, populate it with test content. Finally, remove the borders from the table and test it in different browsers.

To complete the template:

1. Continue working in the file **template.htm**.

2. Add the **valign** attribute to each of the three <tr> elements in the table. Set the value to **"top"**. This forces all of the content in the table to align to the top of each row. Refer to the following code to see the changes.

```
<table border width="750">
<tr valign="top"><td colspan="4" align="center">Page
Banner</td></tr>
<tr valign="top"><td rowspan="2" width="25%">Nav Links
</td><td colspan="2">Feature Article</td><td
rowspan="2" width="25%">Linked Ads</td></tr>
<tr valign="top"><td width="25%">News Column 1</td><td
width="25%">News Column 2</td></tr>
</table>
```

3. Add test content to the page to verify that it works properly. Start by placing a dummy **<img>** element in the Page Banner cell. The <img> has width, height, and alt attributes but no src value. This allows you to create empty image placeholders, as shown in the following code.

```
<table border width="750">
<tr valign="top"><td colspan="4" align="center"><img
width="740" height="50" alt="Page Banner"></td></tr>
<tr valign="top"><td rowspan="2" width="25%">Nav Links
</td><td colspan="2">Feature Article</td><td
rowspan="2" width="25%">Linked Ads</td></tr>
<tr valign="top"><td width="25%">News Column 1</td><td
width="25%">News Column 2</td></tr>
</table>
```

4. Add <b> tags around the Nav Links text to make it bold. Add five dummy test links to the Nav Links column. The links look like this:

```
<p><a href="dummy link">link one</a></p>
<p><a href="dummy link">link two</a></p>
<p><a href="dummy link">link three</a></p>
<p><a href="dummy link">link four</a></p>
<p><a href="dummy link">link five</a></p>
```

5. Add the **align** attribute to the opening <td> tag in the Nav Links column to center the links within the column. The shaded text indicates the code you should add:

```
<table border width="750">
<tr valign="top"><td colspan="4" align="center"><img
width="740" height="50" alt="Page Banner"></td></tr>
<tr valign="top">
<td rowspan="2" width="25%" align="center">
<p><b>Nav Links</b></p>
<p><a href="dummy link">link one</a></p>
<p><a href="dummy link">link two</a></p>
<p><a href="dummy link">link three</a></p>
<p><a href="dummy link">link four</a></p>
<p><a href="dummy link">link five</a></p>
</td><td colspan="2">Feature Article</td><td
rowspan="2" width="25%">Linked Ads</td></tr>
<tr valign="top"><td width="25%">News Column 1</td><td
width="25%">News Column 2</td></tr>
</table>
```

6. Save template.htm and leave it open for the next steps. Then test your work in the browser. The file should look like Figure 5-27.

7. Continue to add test content to the remaining cells of the table. In the Feature Article cell, add a dummy <img> element with the following values.

```
<img width="180" height="140" align="left" alt="Feature
Img">
```

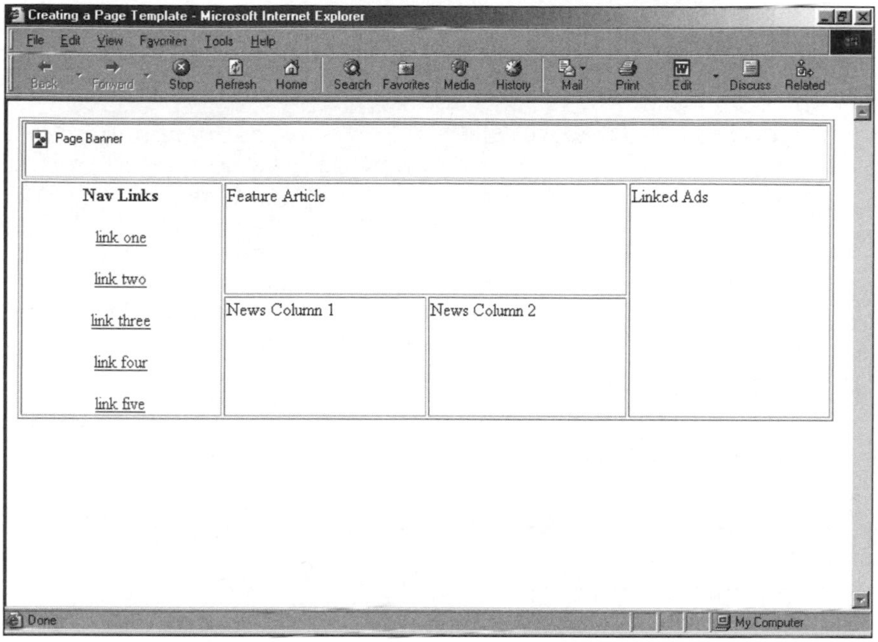

Figure 5-27   Testing content in the Nav Links cell

8. Add bold tags around the Feature Article text, and add some body copy text to the cell as well. The shaded text indicates the code you should add along with sample dummy text:

```
<table border width="750">
<tr valign="top"><td colspan="4" align="center"><img
width="740" height="50" alt="Page Banner"></td></tr>
<tr valign="top">
<td rowspan="2" width="25%" align="center">
<p><b>Nav Links</b></p>
<p><a href="dummy link">link one</a></p>
<p><a href="dummy link">link two</a></p>
<p><a href="dummy link">link three</a></p>
<p><a href="dummy link">link four</a></p>
<p><a href="dummy link">link five</a></p>
</td>
<td colspan="2"><img width="180" height="140"
align="left" alt="Feature Img"><b>Feature
Article</b><p>Lorem ipsum dolor sit amet, consectetuer
adipiscing elit, sed diem nonummy nibh euismod tincidunt
```

```
ut lacreet dolore magna aliguam erat volutpat. Ut wisis
enim ad minim veniam, quis nostrud exerci tution
ullam  corper suscipit lobortis nisl ut aliquip ex ea
commodo consequat. Lorem ipsum dolor sit amet,
consectetuer adipiscing elit, sed diem nonummy nibh
euismod tincidunt ut lacreet dolore magna aliguam erat
volutpat. Ut wisis enim ad minim veniam, quis nostrud
exerci tution ullamcorper suscipit lobortis nisl ut
aliquip ex ea commodo consequat.</p></td><td
rowspan="2" width="25%">Linked Ads</td></tr>
<tr valign="top"><td width="25%">News Column 1</td><td
width="25%">News Column 2</td></tr>
</table>
```

9. Save template.htm and leave it open for the next steps. Then test your work in the browser. When you view the file it looks like Figure 5-28.

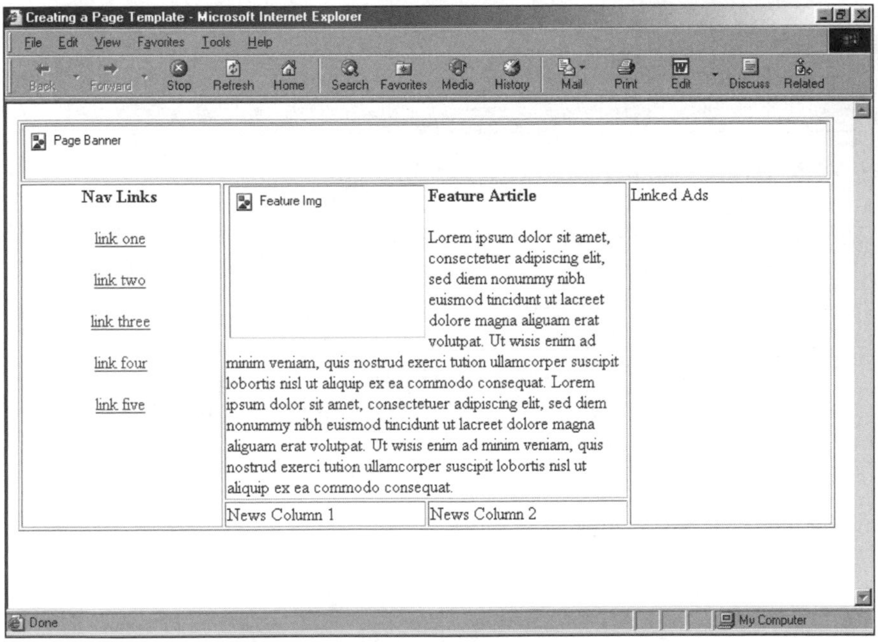

Figure 5-28   Testing content in the Feature Article cell

10. In the Linked Ads cell, add <b> tags around the Linked Ads text and add test images. Place each <img> element within a set of <p> tags to provide white space around each image. Add the **align="center"** attribute to the cell's opening <td> tag to center-align the content. The shaded text indicates the code you should add:

```
<table border width="750">
<tr valign="top"><td colspan="4" align="center"><img
width="740" height="50" alt="Page Banner"></td></tr>
<tr valign="top">
<td rowspan="2" width="25%" align="center">
<p><b>Nav Links</b></p>
<p><a href="dummy link">link one</a></p>
<p><a href="dummy link">link two</a></p>
<p><a href="dummy link">link three</a></p>
<p><a href="dummy link">link four</a></p>
<p><a href="dummy link">link five</a></p>
</td>
<td colspan="2"><img width="180" height="140" align=
"left" alt="Feature Img"><b>Feature Article</b><p>
Lorem ipsum dolor sit amet, consectetuer adipiscing
elit, sed diem nonummy nibh euismod tincidunt ut lacreet
dolore magna aliguam erat volutpat. Ut wisis enim ad
minim veniam, quis nostrud exerci tution ullamcorper
suscipit lobortis nisl ut aliquip ex ea commodo
consequat. Lorem ipsum dolor sit amet, consectetuer
adipiscing elit, sed diem nonummy nibh euismod
tincidunt ut lacreet dolore magna aliguam erat
volutpat. Ut wisis enim ad minim veniam, quis nostrud
exerci tution ullamcorper suscipit lobortis nisl ut
aliquip ex ea commodo consequat.</p></td>
<td rowspan="2" width="25%" align="center">
<b>Linked Ads</b>
<p><img  width="80" height="80" alt="ad 1"></p>
<p><img  width="80" height="80" alt="ad 2"></p>
<p><img  width="80" height="80" alt="ad 3"></p>
</td></tr>
<tr valign="top"><td width="25%">News Column 1</td><td
width="25%">News Column 2</td></tr>
</table>
```

11. Save template.htm and leave it open for the next steps. Then test your work in the browser. It should look like Figure 5-29.

12. Add some test content to the News Column 1 and News Column 2 cells. Use <b> tags to bold the heading in each cell.

13. Remove the border attribute from the opening <table> element to turn off the table borders. Save template.htm and close your HTML editor. Then test your work in the browser. The completed test page template should look like Figure 5-30.

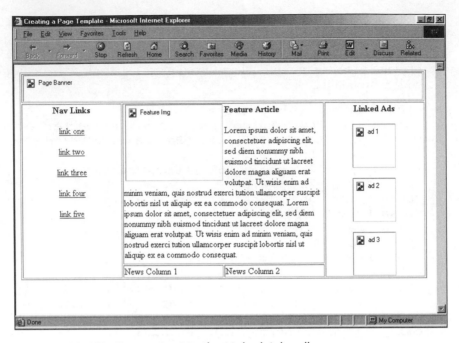

Figure 5-29   Testing content in the Linked Ads cell

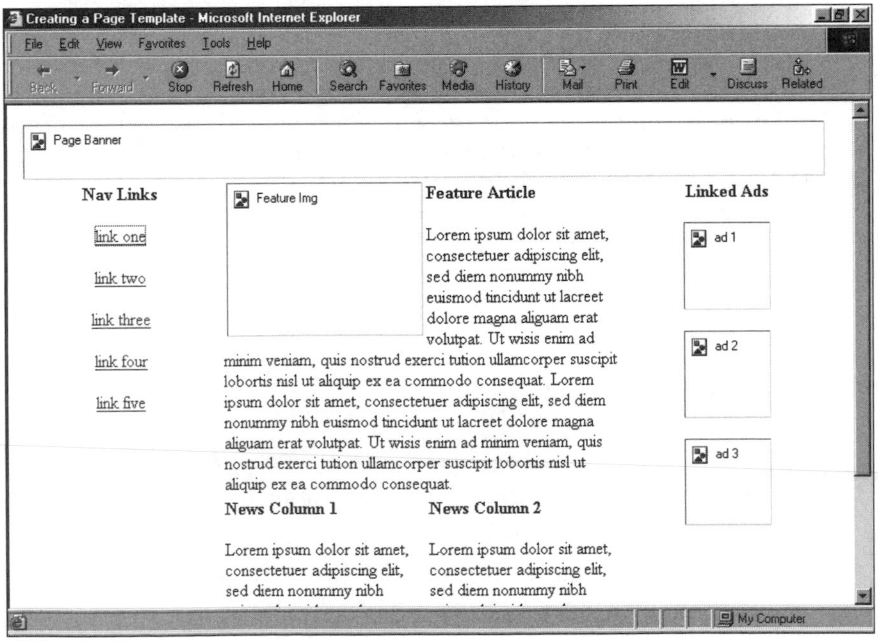

Figure 5-30   The completed page template in Internet Explorer 6

14. Test the page template in multiple browsers. For example, Figure 5-31 shows the page template in Netscape 6.2.

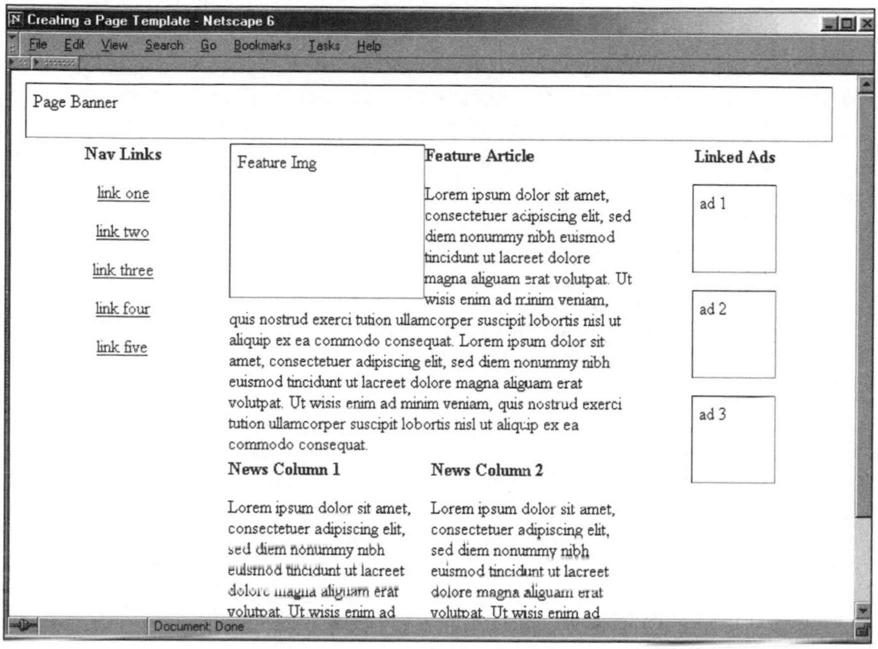

Figure 5-31   The completed page template in Netscape 6.2

The complete code for the page follows.

```
<html>
<head>
<title>Creating a Page Template</title>
</head>

<body>

<table  width="750">
<tr valign="top"><td colspan="4" align="center"><img width
="740" height="50" alt="Page Banner"></td></tr>
<tr valign="top">
<td rowspan="2" width="25%" align="center">
<p><b>Nav Links</b></p>
<p><a href="dummy link">link one</a></p>
<p><a href="dummy link">link two</a></p>
<p><a href="dummy link">link three</a></p>
<p><a href="dummy link">link four</a></p>
<p><a href="dummy link">link five</a></p>
</td>
```

```
<td colspan="2"><img width="180" height="140" align="left"
alt="Feature Img"><b>Feature Article</b><p>Lorem ipsum dol
or sit amet, consectetuer adipiscing elit, sed diem non-
ummy nibh euismod tincidunt ut lacreet dolore magna aligua
m erat volutpat. Ut wisis enim ad minim veniam, quis nos-
trud exerci tution ullamcorper suscipit lobortis nisl ut a
liquip ex ea commodo consequat. Lorem ipsum dolor sit amet
, consectetuer adipiscing elit, sed diem nonummy nibh euis
mod tincidunt ut lacreet dolore magna aliguam erat volut-
pat. Ut wisis enim ad minim veniam, quis nostrud exerci tu
tion ullamcorper suscipit lobortis nisl ut aliquip ex ea c
ommodo consequat.</p></td><td rowspan="2" width="25%" alig
n="center">
<b>Linked Ads</b>
<p><img  width="80" height="80" alt="ad 1"></p>
<p><img  width="80" height="80" alt="ad 2"></p>
<p><img  width="80" height="80" alt="ad 3"></p>
</td></tr>
<tr valign="top"><td width="25%"><b>News Column 1</b><p>Lo
rem ipsum dolor sit amet, consectetuer adipiscing elit, se
d diem nonummy nibh euismod tincidunt ut lacreet dolore ma
gna aliguam erat volutpat. Ut wisis enim ad minim veniam,
quis nostrud exerci tution ullamcorper suscipit lobortis n
isl ut aliquip ex ea commodo consequat.</p></td>
<td width="25%"><b>News Column 2</b><p>Lorem ipsum dolor s
it amet, consectetuer adipiscing elit, sed diem nonummy ni
bh euismod tincidunt ut lacreet dolore magna aliguam erat
volutpat. Ut wisis enim ad minim veniam, quis nostrud exer
ci tution ullamcorper suscipit lobortis nisl ut aliquip ex
ea commodo consequat.</p></td></tr>
</table>
</body>
</html>
```

EVALUATING EXAMPLES OF PAGE TEMPLATES

The following templates cover a variety of page layout needs. You may choose to stack different templates on top of each other for more complex layouts. Remember that in these examples, the height attribute gives the blank tables some vertical height. Normally you would remove this attribute and let the content determine the height of the table.

Two-Column Template

Figure 5-32 shows a typical two-column template. The left cell is for navigation, the right cell for content. This template is well-suited for lengthier text content. You can adjust the width of the table to constrain the text width.

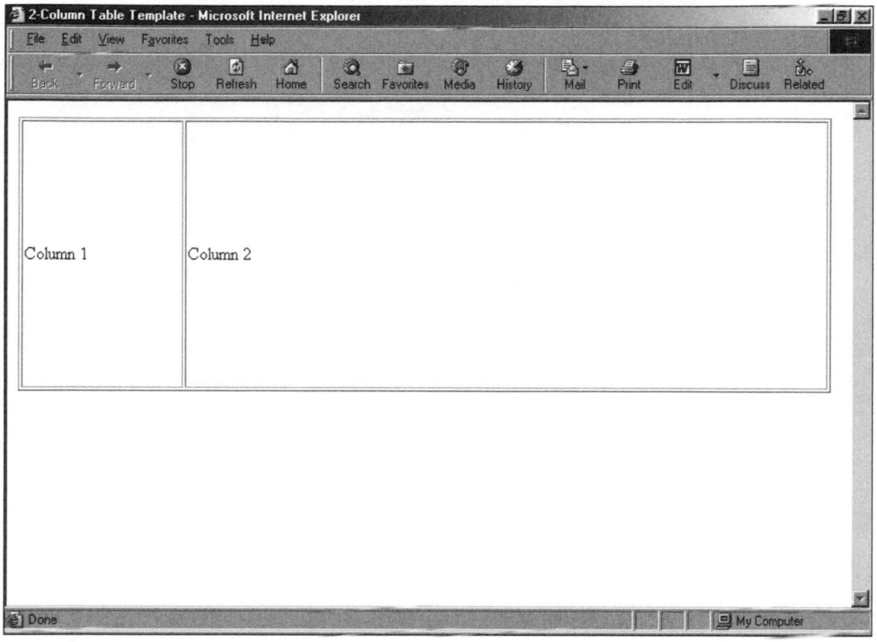

Figure 5-32 Two-column template

```
<table width="750" height="250" border>
<tr>
<td width="20%">Column 1</td>
<td>Column 2</td>
</tr>
</table>
```

Two-Column with Banner Template

Figure 5-33 shows a basic two-column template with an additional column span in the first row. You can use the banner row for logos, navigation graphics, or banner ads.

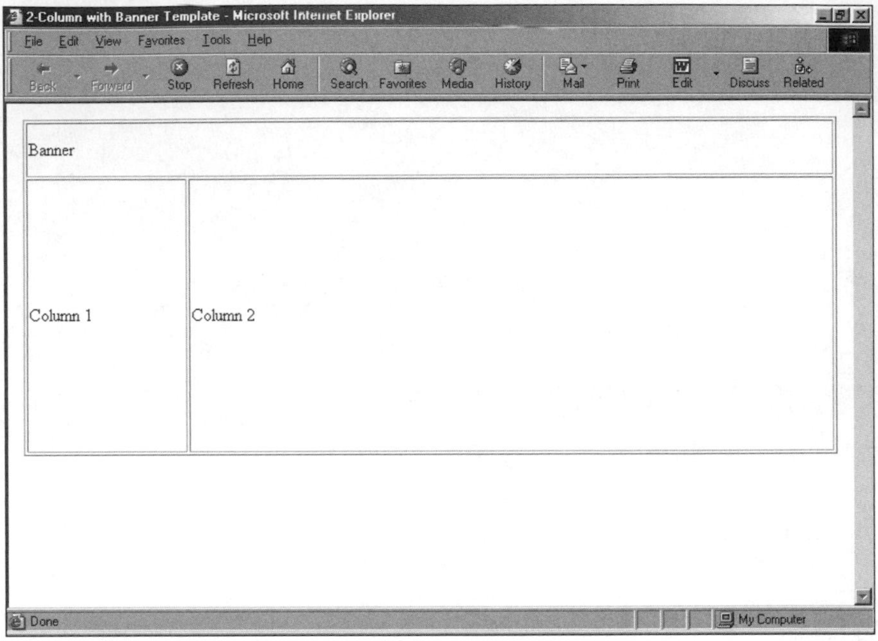

Figure 5-33   Two-column with banner template

```
<table width="750" border>
<tr><td colspan="2" height="50">Banner</td></tr>
<tr><td height="250" width="20%">Column 1</td><td>Column 2
</td></tr>
</table>
```

Three-Column Template

Figure 5-34 shows a three-column template, which can be used to contain plain text or a variety of mixed content. The outer columns can be used for links, advertising, or related content. You can adjust the width of the cells to suit your content.

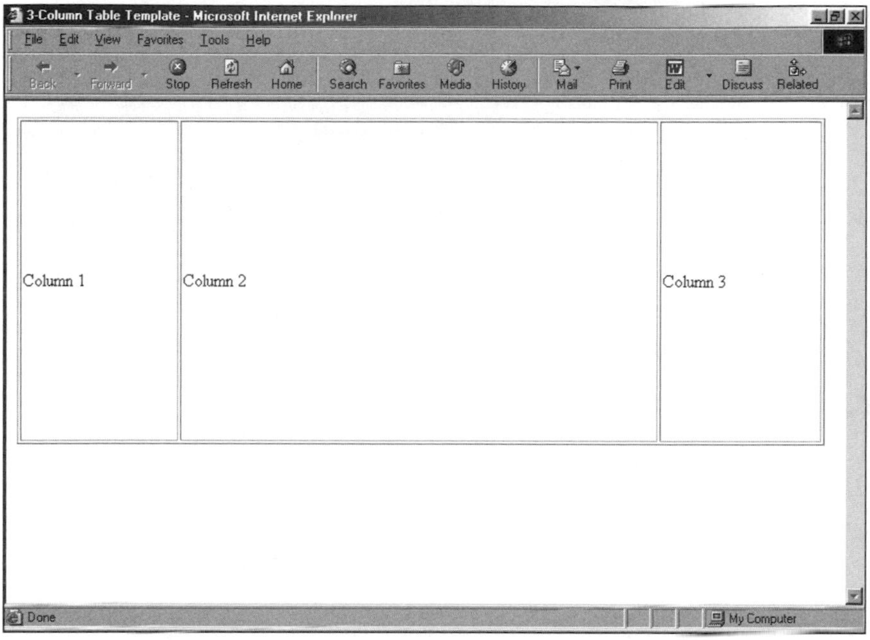

Figure 5-34   Three-column template

```
<table width="750" height="300" border>
<tr>
<td width="20%">Column 1</td>
<td width="60%">Column 2</td>
<td width="20%">Column 3</td>
</tr>
</table>
```

Three-Column with Banner Template

Figure 5-35 shows the addition of a banner to the three-column layout. This layout works well as a top-level page of a section or an entire Web site. The columnar structure lends itself to scanning rather than reading.

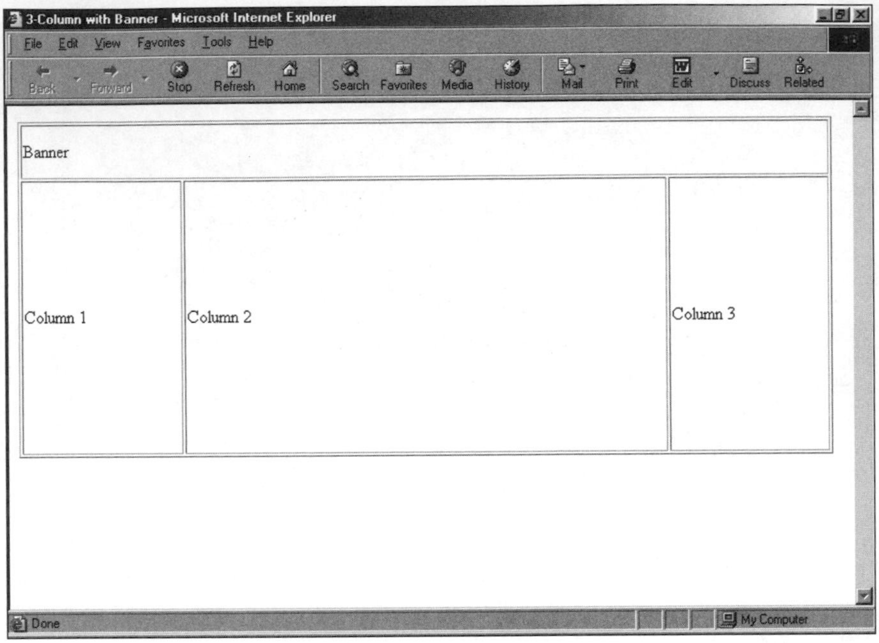

Figure 5-35   Three-column with banner template

```
<table width="750" border>
<tr><td height="50" colspan="3">Banner</td></tr>
<tr><td height="250" width="20%">Column 1</td>
<td width="60%">Column 2</td>
<td width="20%">Column 3</td>
</tr>
</table>
```

Three-Column Sectioned Template

Figure 5-36 shows the right and center columns divided into four content areas. Use this template when you want to provide the user a choice between a variety of topics or sections. You can place navigation information in the left column. You most likely would use this template as a top-level page.

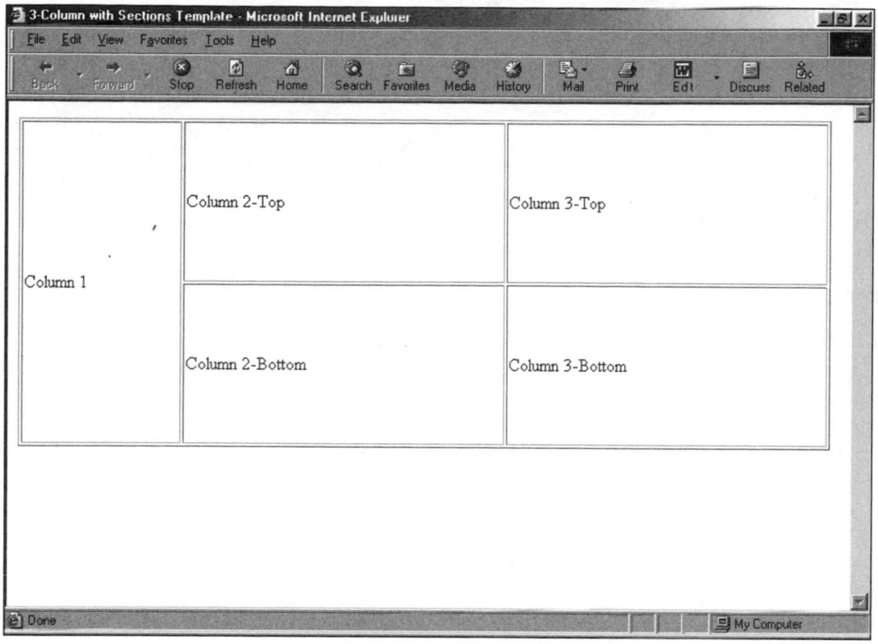

Figure 5-36   Three-column sectioned template

```
<table width="750" height="300" border>
<tr>
<td rowspan="2" width="20%">Column 1</td>
<td>Column 2-Top</td>
<td>Column 3-Top</td>
</tr>
<tr>
<td>Column 2-Bottom</td>
<td>Column 3-Bottom</td>
</tr>
</table>
```

Three-Column Main Sectioned Template

Figure 5-37 shows the center column divided into two content areas. Another variety of a top-level page, this one lets you break up the primary area of the screen into two sections. Left and right columns can be used for navigation or associated links.

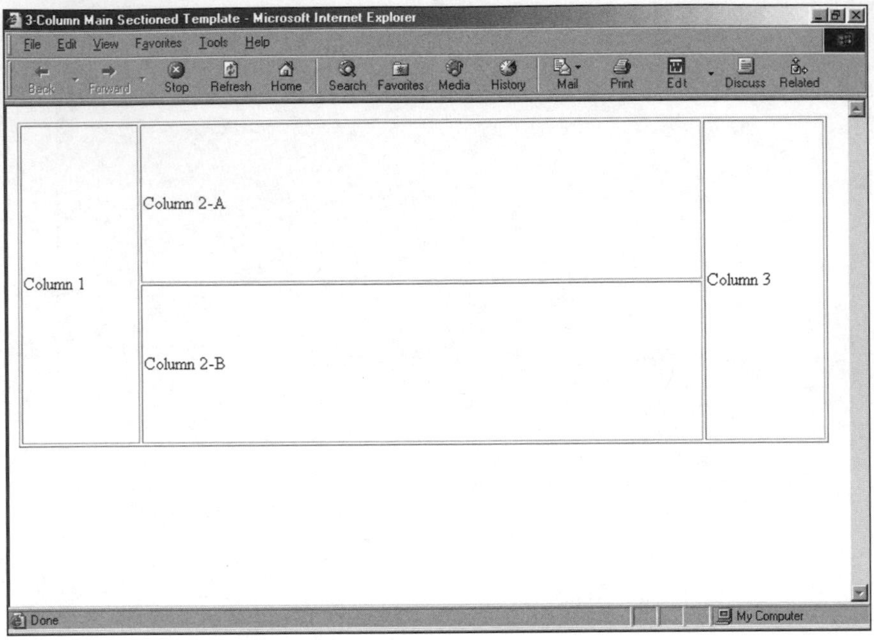

Figure 5-37   Three-column main sectioned template

```
<table width="750" height="300" border>
<tr>
<td width="15%" rowspan="2">Column 1</td>
<td width="70%">Column 2-A</td>
<td width="15%" rowspan="2">Column 3</td>
</tr>
<tr>
<td>Column 2-B</td>
</tr>
</table>
```

CHAPTER SUMMARY

Tables are one of the Web designer's best design tools. Once you master tables, you can build page templates and position content anywhere on a Web page. Tables can be tricky, so remember the following points:

- ❑ To build effective page templates, you must be familiar with the HTML table elements and attributes, including the <table>, <caption>, and <th> elements and global, row-level, and cell-level attributes.

- ❑ Plan your tables by sketching them out on paper first. Then create a page template that includes a design for tables.

❑ When designing HTML tables, write easy-to-read table code, remove extra spaces, and choose whether to center, stack, or nest tables.

❑ Use fixed table widths if you want to determine the size of your page rather than letting the browser determine the width.

❑ Use relative widths if you want to build tables that resize with the browser window, wrapping your content to fit.

❑ Work on your pages with the table borders turned on, which display the cell boundaries. When you are finished with your layout, turn the borders off.

❑ Size your tables based on the page size you want to create. Use 800 × 600 as your base screen resolution. In most cases you set the width but not the height of your tables, allowing the content to flow down the page.

❑ Test your work. Table settings, especially cell widths and heights, can vary based on the user's browser.

REVIEW QUESTIONS

1. Name three print-based design structures that Web designers can duplicate with tables.
2. What are the three basic table elements?
3. What table element presents its content as bold and centered?
4. What attribute can you use with the <caption> element?
5. What are the three levels of table structure?
6. What attribute would you use to adjust spacing between table cells?
7. What attribute would you use to adjust spacing within table cells?
8. In the following code, which attribute takes precedence?

   ```
   <tr valign="top"><td valign="middle">Cell 1</td><td>Cell 2
   </td></tr>
   ```

9. Which attribute lets you color the background of a cell?
10. What value should colspan equal in the following code?

    ```
    <tr><td>R1C1</td><td>R1C2</td><td>R1C3</td></tr>
    <tr><td>R2C1</td><td colspan= >R2C2</td></tr>
    ```

11. Write the code for a table that fills 75 percent of the browser window.
12. What is the major disadvantage of relative-width tables?
13. Write the code to remove the default spacing from a table.
14. Why would you want to remove the default spacing from a table?
15. How do extra character spaces affect a table?

16. What is the best way to center a table?

17. What are the benefits of stacking tables?

18. What are two rules for setting column widths in a table?

19. What attribute lets you align content to the top of a cell?

20. What is the difference between removing the border attribute and setting border="0"?

HANDS-ON PROJECTS

1. Browse the Web and find Web sites that use page templates. You will see the use of templates in Web sites that have a consistent page design across multiple pages of the site.

   a. Create a sketch of a page from the Web site that depicts your idea of the page template.

   b. Examine the code to see how the template actually was built.

   c. Compare and contrast your method with the designer's method of building the template.

2. Practice building test pages.

   a. Using one of the template examples from this chapter, build a mock-up of a finished page using test content.

   b. Test the page in multiple browsers and note any differences in the way the content is displayed.

3. Surf the Web and find examples of Web sites that use fixed tables. Describe why you think the designers chose a fixed layout for the content.

4. Surf the Web and find examples of Web sites that use relative tables. Describe why you think the designers chose a relative layout for the content.

5. Choose an example template from the Principles of Web Design Companion Web site and fill it with test content.

   a. Set the width to 100 percent.

   b. Test the results in multiple browsers and at multiple resolutions.

   c. Note any display problems and suggest how you might solve the problems.

6. Create a seamless navigation bar using a table to hold the graphics together. Use the navigation graphics from the Principles of Web Design Companion Web site, or choose your own graphics.

7. Describe two ways that multiple tables can affect the way your pages download.

8. Build a template that meets the following criteria:

- ❐ Fills the screen at 800 × 600 resolution without showing a horizontal scroll bar
- ❐ Builds a three-column layout
- ❐ Contains a banner cell that spans the layout
- ❐ Fixes content independent of browser size

CASE PROJECT

Design the page templates for the different information levels of your Web site. Create sketches for each template, and describe why the templates fit your content.

You will find all of the page templates shown in this chapter on the Companion Web site. Use these templates as starting points for your Web pages. Adapt the page templates to your own needs or build your page templates from scratch. Test the page templates with content in different browsers to make sure that they display properly.

Once your templates test properly, start to build the files for your Web site by copying the templates to individual files and naming them to match your flowchart from Chapter 3.

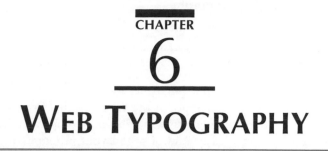

6

WEB TYPOGRAPHY

When you complete this chapter, you will be able to:

♦ Understand principles for type design on a Web site

♦ Control typography with the <font> element

♦ Control typography with Cascading Style Sheets (CSS)

♦ Understand the basics of CSS and its selection techniques

♦ Specify CSS font properties and block-level space values

♦ Build a style sheet

Everyone visiting your Web site is a reader and responds instinctively to words set in type. The consistent use of type provides valuable information cues to the reader, and recent innovations provide powerful tools for working with type. Until recently, Web typography meant having to use too many <font> tags and lots of text as graphics. Today, Cascading Style Sheets offer a potent style language, allowing you to manipulate a variety of text properties to achieve professional, effective results, all without resorting to graphics that add download time.

TYPE DESIGN PRINCIPLES

Type can flexibly express emotion, tone, and structure. Most of the type principles that apply to paper-based design apply to the Web as well. However, it is possible to go overboard by using too many typefaces and sizes, ending up with the "ransom note" look that was characteristic of the early days of page layout programs. Just because you have many typefaces at your disposal does not mean you should use them all. Designing for the Web actually restricts your font choices to those your users have installed on their computers. If you specify a font that is not available, the browser substitutes the default font.

As you work with type, consider the following principles for creating an effective design:

- Choose fewer fonts and sizes

- Use available fonts

- Design for legibility

- Avoid using text as graphics

 In strict typography terms, a **typeface** is the name of the type, such as Times New Roman or Futura Condensed. A **font** is the typeface in a particular size, such as Times Roman 24 point. For the most part, in HTML the two terms are interchangeable.

Choose Fewer Fonts and Sizes

Your pages will look cleaner when you choose fewer fonts and sizes of type. Decide on a font for each different level of topic importance, such as page headings, section headings, and body text. Communicate the hierarchy of information with changes in the size, weight, or color of the typeface. For example, a page heading should have a larger, bolder type, while a section heading would appear in the same typeface, only lighter or smaller.

Pick a few sizes and weights in a type family. For example, you might choose three sizes, such as 24 point for headings, 18 point for subheadings, and 12 point for body text (CSS lets you specify point sizes). You can vary these styles by changing the weight; for example, 12-point bold type can be used for topic headings within text. Avoid making random changes in your use of type conventions. Consistently apply the same fonts and the same combination of styles throughout your Web site; consistency develops a strong visual identity. The Web Style Guide Web site (*www.webstyleguide.com*) is a good example of effective type usage. The site has a strong typographic identity, yet uses only two typefaces. The designers of this site built a visually interesting page simply by varying the weight, size, white space, and color of the text.

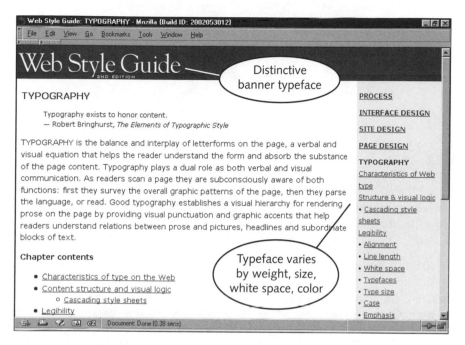

Figure 6-1   Effective typographic design

Use Available Fonts

Fonts often are a problem in HTML because font information is client-based. The user's browser and operating system determine how a font is displayed, or if it is displayed at all. If you design your pages using a font that your user does not have installed, the browser defaults to Times on a Macintosh or Times New Roman on a PC. To make matters worse, even the most widely available fonts appear in different sizes on different operating systems. Unfortunately, the best you can do about this is to test on multiple platforms to judge the effect on your pages.

To control more effectively how text appears on your pages, think in terms of font families, such as serif and sans-serif typefaces (see Figure 6-2), rather than specific styles. Notice that serif fonts have strokes (or serifs) that finish the top and bottom of the letter. Sans-serif fonts consist of block letters without serifs.

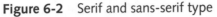

Serif   Sans-serif

Figure 6-2   Serif and sans-serif type

Because of the variable nature of fonts installed on different computers, you never can be sure the user will see the exact font you have specified. You can, however, specify font substitution attributes (described later in this chapter), which let you specify a variety of fonts within a font family, such as the common sans-serif fonts, Arial or Helvetica.

Table 6-1 lists the most common fonts on the PC, UNIX, and Macintosh systems.

Table 6-1   Common installed fonts

Common PC Fonts	Common UNIX Fonts	Common Macintosh Fonts
Arial	Helvetica	Helvetica
Courier New	Times	Courier
Times New Roman		Palatino
Trebuchet MS		Times
Verdana		Verdana
		Arial

The table shows that Times (or Times New Roman) is available on all three operating systems; it is the default browser font. Courier is the default monospace font, and Arial or Helvetica is the default sans-serif font. Arial, Trebuchet, and Verdana come with Internet Explorer, so many Macintosh and PC users have these fonts installed. Some Macintosh users only have Helvetica, so it is a good idea to specify this font as an alternate choice when you are using sans-serif fonts.

 You can download a package of Web fonts from Microsoft at *www.microsoft.com/typography/fontpack/default.htm*. The core fonts package includes Arial, Verdana, and a number of other fonts designed specifically for the Web.

Design for Legibility

Figure 6-3 shows the same paragraph in Times, Trebuchet, Arial, and Verdana at the default browser size.

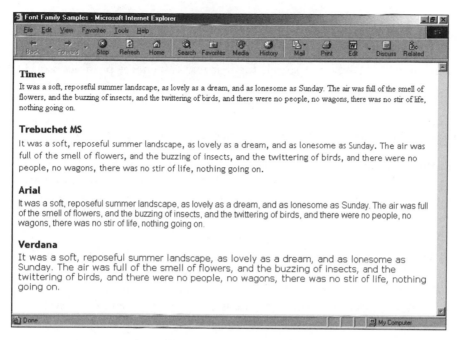

Figure 6-3   Common Web font families

In these examples, where the text wraps at the end of each line depends on the font. Because its x-height (the height of the letter x in the font) is smaller than that of other fonts, Times can be hard to read, even though it is a serif typeface. This makes it a bad choice for a default font. Trebuchet is a sans-serif face that has a large x-height and rounded letterforms for easy screen legibility. Arial is widely available and is the most commonly used sans-serif font. Verdana is an expanded font—each letter takes up more horizontal space than letters in the other font families. This makes the text easier to read online, but takes much more space on the page.

The size and face of the type you use on your pages determine the legibility of your text. The computer screen has a lower resolution than the printed page, making fonts that are legible on paper more difficult to read on screen. Keep fonts big enough to be legible and avoid specialty fonts that degrade when viewed online. To aid the reader, consider adding more white space to the page around your blocks of text and between lines as well. Test your content with both serif and sans-serif body text. Finally, make sure that you provide enough contrast between your text color and the background color; in general, darker text on a light background is easiest to read.

Avoid Using Text as Graphics

If you must use a specific font, create text as a graphic. Using Adobe Photoshop or another graphics program, create text and save it as either a GIF or JPG file. (See Chapter 7 for more information on these file formats.) This technique allows you to add drop shadows and other effects to your text. However, because you also are adding download overhead with every additional graphic, save text graphics for important purposes, such as the main logo for your page or for reusable navigation graphics. Remember that including text as graphics means users cannot search for that text. Whenever possible, use HTML-styled text on your pages.

CONTROLLING TYPOGRAPHY WITH THE <FONT> ELEMENT

Until the addition of the <font> element in HTML 3.2, an HTML author could do little to control type display on a Web page. This is because HTML is intended to express document structure only, not document style. The <font> element, although simplistic in its control over text display, allows HTML authors to choose the font, color, and size of their type.

With HTML 4.0 and XHTML, the <font> element has been deprecated (made obsolete by the W3) in favor of CSS. To ensure forward compatibility with all browsers, move to CSS and limit or remove the <font> element from your code. Designers need to understand the <font> element because it is still widely used on the Web and supported by browsers. You can use it to set font size, font color, and to specify font substitution.

Setting Font Size

Use the size attribute to set the font size. The range of sizes is one to seven (smallest to largest), with three being the default. The sizes are relative to the default browser size. The following code sets the font size to six:

```
<font size="6">Some text</font>
```

You also can set sizes relative to the default base font using the plus (+) or minus (−) signs. Setting size="+2" would produce a font two sizes larger than the default. If the default is size three, the following code sets the size to six:

```
<font size="+3">Some text</font>
```

This size attribute expresses default size three plus three.

Specifying Font Alternates

You can include a list of alternate fonts to force the browser to look for matching fonts installed on the user's machine. Specify alternate fonts in the <font> element by listing a string of fonts within quotes in the face attribute. For example, the following statement tells the browser to display the text in Arial; if Arial is not available, the browser attempts to use Helvetica. If neither is available, the text appears in the browser default font, usually Times New Roman.

```
<font size="6" face="arial, helvetica">some text</font>
```

Setting Font Color

You can set font color with the color attribute, using either a color name or hexadecimal color code. (See Chapter 7 for more information on hexadecimal color codes.)

```
<font size="6" face="arial, helvetica" color="red">some
text</font>
```

Using the <font> Element

Figure 6-4 shows how the <font> element formats the type size, face, and color of text on the Web page.

6

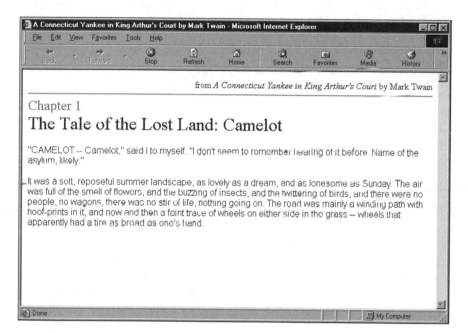

Figure 6-4 Text formatted with the <font> element

The following shaded code shows the syntax of the <font> element.

```
<html>
<head>
<title>A Connecticut Yankee in King Arthur's Court by
 Mark Twain</title>
</head>
<body>
<div align="right">
from <i>A Connecticut Yankee in King Arthur's Court</i> by
 Mark Twain</div>
<hr>
```

```
<p><font size="5" color="gray">Chapter 1</font><br>
<font size="6">The Tale of the Lost Land: Camelot</font>
</p>
<p><font face="arial">
"CAMELOT -- Camelot," said I to myself. "I don't seem to
remember hearing of it before. Name of the asylum, likely."
</font></p>
<p><font face="arial">
It was a soft, reposeful summer landscape, as lovely as a
dream, and as lonesome as Sunday. The air was full of the
smell of flowers, and the buzzing of insects, and the
twittering of birds, and there were no people, no wagons,
there was no stir of life, nothing going on. The road was
mainly a winding path with hoof-prints in it, and now and
then a faint trace of wheels on either side in the grass --
wheels that apparently had a tire as broad as one's hand.
</font></p>
</body>
</html>
```

CONTROLLING TYPOGRAPHY WITH CASCADING STYLE SHEETS

This section acquaints you with the CSS properties that affect how type appears in the browser. This is not meant to be a complete CSS lesson, but rather a typography-oriented look at the benefits of using Cascading Style Sheets.

Cascading Style Sheets offers much greater control over type characteristics than the <font> element. You can use standard type conventions, such as point or pixel sizes, leading (the vertical space taken up by a line of type), indents, and alignment. You gain more control but use much less code than was previously necessary. For example, suppose that you want every <h1> element on your Web site to be green and centered. Using the <font> element, you need the following shaded code for every instance of the <h1> element:

```
<h1 align="center"><font color="green">the heading</font>
</h1>
```

With Cascading Style Sheets you can express this style information once as a rule in a style sheet:

```
h1 {color: green; text-align: center;}
```

This style rule affects every <h1> element on any page that uses the Cascading Style Sheet.

CSS Basics

CSS is based on rules that select an HTML element and declare style characteristics for it. You can state sets of rules, known as style sheets, in the head section of an HTML document or in a separate document known as an external style sheet. Use external style sheets to set rules when working with a number of HTML documents.

Understanding Style Rules

Style sheet rules are easy to interpret. The following style sheet shows a simple style rule for the <p> element. Note that the style rules are contained in the <style> element in the document's <head> section:

```
<head>
<title>Sample Document</title>
<style>
p {color: blue; font-size: 24pt;}
</style>
</head>
```

This rule sets all <p> elements in the document to blue 24-point text.

Style rules are composed of two parts: a **selector** and a **declaration**. The selector determines the element to which the rule is applied. The declaration details the exact property values. Figure 6-5 is an example of a simple rule.

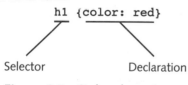

Selector   Declaration

Figure 6-5   Style rule syntax

This rule forces the browser to display all <h1> headings in red.

The declaration contains a property and a value (see Figure 6-6). The property is a quality or characteristic, and its precise specification is contained in the value. CSS includes over 50 properties, each with a specific number of values.

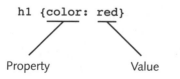

Property   Value

Figure 6-6   Property declaration syntax

You must include all CSS rules within a <style> element or define them using a style attribute. The <style> element always is contained in the <head> section. To add the preceding rule to an entire HTML document, use the following code in the <head> section of the document:

```
<head>
<title>Sample Document</title>
<style type="text/css">
h1 {color: red;}
</style>
</head>
```

In the preceding code, note the type attribute to the <style> element. This defines the style language as Cascading Style Sheets.

Alternately, you can define the style for a single <h1> element using the style attribute:

```
<h1 style="color: blue">Some Text</h1>
```

You generally would use the style attribute to override a style that was set at a higher level in the document.

Linking to an External Style Sheet

Placing style sheets in an external document lets you specify rules for different HTML documents. This is an easy and powerful way to use style sheets. An external style sheet is a text document with a .css extension that contains the style rules. Here is an example of a simple external style sheet named style1.css:

```
/* StyleSheet #1 */
body {color: red;}
h1 {color: green;}
h2 {color: green; border: solid blue;}
```

Notice that the CSS comment line begins with the characters "/*" and ends with the characters "*/". The style sheet file contains no HTML code, only CSS style rules.

To link to this external style sheet, add the <link> element within the head section of any HTML file, as shown in the following code:

```
<head>
<title>Sample Document</title>
<link href="style1.css" rel="stylesheet">
</head>
```

The file containing this code displays with the characteristics specified by the style sheet. The href attribute specifies the URL of the style sheet, and all relative file location rules apply. The rel attribute specifies the relationship between the linked and current documents. All pages that are linked to this style sheet display the style rules. The advantage of the external style sheet is that you have to change the style rules in only one document to affect all the pages on a Web site.

Check out WebReview's CSS master list at *www.webreview.com/style/ css1/charts/mastergrid.shtml*. This site allows you to look up any CSS property quickly and check its support in a variety of browsers.

Solving Problems with Style Sheets

The current browsers, including Netscape 6.0, Opera 5.0, and Internet Explorer 6.0, offer very good CSS support, albeit with some inconsistencies. The main problem with style sheets is older browser support. Strange results can appear when browsers cannot interpret the rules properly. See Figures 2-1 and 2-2 for examples. Finally, older browsers will not be able to interpret your CSS rules at all. Test carefully to make sure your users can still read your content if your style rules are ignored or misinterpreted.

CSS Selection Techniques

Your goal is to apply your style rules to the elements in your document. The power in CSS comes from the different methods of selecting elements. You can choose from a variety of selection methods, including:

- Selecting multiple elements
- Selecting by context
- Selecting with the class attribute

More complex selection involves the creation of artificial divisions, using two elements designed expressly for CSS:

- <div> – Block Division
- <span> – Inline Division

The use of these elements, in combination with the class attribute, effectively allows you to create entirely new HTML elements specific to your working environment. You then can use these techniques in external style sheets to apply your style properties to multiple documents in a Web site or other HTML-based application.

Selecting Multiple Elements

Using multiple selectors lets you use less code to accomplish the same results. For example, to make both <h1> and <h2> headings green, you could use the following rules:

```
<style type="text/css">
h1 {color: green;}
h2 {color: green;}
</style>
```

These two rules can be expressed in a single rule statement using multiple selectors for the same property. Multiple selectors must be separated by commas:

```
<style type="text/css">
h1, h2 {color: green;}
</style>
```

Selecting by Context

A context-based selector lets you specify the exact context in which a style is applied. To specify that <i> elements appear blue only within <p> elements, use the following rule:

```
<style type="text/css">
p i {color: blue;}
</style>
```

Selecting with the class Attribute

The class attribute lets you write rules and then apply them to groups of elements that you have classified. The class attribute lets you define your own tags and then apply them anywhere you want.

To create a class, first declare it within the <style> element. The period (.) flag character indicates that the selector is a class selector. Figure 6-7 is an example of a rule with a class selector.

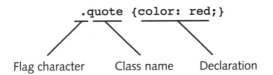

Flag character   Class name   Declaration

Figure 6-7   Class syntax

Place this rule in the <style> element:

```
<style type="text/css">
.quote {color: red;}
</style>
```

Next, use the class attribute in the document. In the following example, the code defines the <p> element as a special class named "quote."

```
<p class="quote">Some text</p>
```

The selected paragraph will display the style properties of the quote class. In this example, the text color of the paragraph is red.

Working with the <div> Element

Within a document, the <div> element lets you specify logical divisions that have their own name and style properties. The <div> element is a block-level element that contains a leading and trailing carriage return. You can use the <div> element with the class attribute to create customized block-level elements.

To create a division, first declare it within the <style> element. The following example specifies a division named "introduction" as the selector for the rule:

```
<style type="text/css">
div.introduction {color: red;}
</style>
```

Next, specify the <div> element in the document, and then use the class attribute to specify the exact type of division. In the following example, the code defines the <div> element as a special class named "introduction."

```
<div class="introduction">some text</div>
```

Working with the <span> Element

Within a document, the <span> element lets you specify inline elements that have their own name and style properties. Place inline elements within a line of text, like the <b> or <i> elements. You can use the <span> element with the class attribute to create customized inline elements and apply styles more accurately.

To create a span, first declare it within the <style> element. The following example specifies a <span> element named "logo" as the selector for the rule:

```
<style type="text/css">
span.logo {color: red;}
</style>
```

Next, specify the <span> element in the document, and then use the class attribute to specify the exact type of <span> element. In the following example the code defines the <span> element as a special class named "logo." Note that <span> is used within the line of text.

```
Welcome to the <span class="logo">Wonder Software</span>
Web site.
```

CSS Font Properties

CSS lets you control over 50 style properties. Support varies widely for these properties, so always test your work carefully. The font properties you will work with most often include:

- Font families and alternates
- Font size
- Font weight
- Line height
- Letter spacing

- Text indent
- Color

Selecting a Specific Font Family and Alternates

The font family property lets you specify any font or generic font family. Users must have the font installed on their computers; otherwise the browser uses the default font. The following rule specifies Arial as the font for the <p> element:

```
<style type="text/css">
p {font-family: arial;}
</style>
```

You can specify a list of alternate fonts, using commas as a separator. The browser attempts to load each successive font in the list. If no fonts match, the browser uses its default font. The following code tells the browser, "Use Arial. If Arial is not present, use Helvetica."

```
<style type="text/css">
p {font-family: arial, helvetica;}
</style>
```

You can add a generic name for greater portability across browsers and operating systems. The following code tells the browser to use a sans-serif font if Arial and Helvetica are not available.

```
<style type="text/css">
p {font-family: arial, helvetica, sans-serif;}
</style>
```

You can use the following generic names for font families:

- Serif
- Sans-serif
- Monospace

If you do not specify any font family, the browser displays the default font.

CSS Measurement Values

CSS offers a variety of measurement units, including absolute units such as points, relative units such as pixels, and percentages of the base font. The measurement values you choose depend on the destination medium for your content. For example, if you are designing a style sheet for printed media, you can use absolute units of measurement such as points or centimeters. When you are designing a style sheet for a Web page, you can use relative measurement values that adapt to the user's display type, such as ems (see Table 6-2) or pixels.

Table 6-2   CSS measurement units

Unit	Unit Abbreviation	Description
Absolute Units		
Centimeter	cm	Standard metric centimeter
Inch	in	Standard U.S. inch
Millimeter	mm	Standard metric millimeter
Pica	pc	Standard publishing unit equal to 12 points
Point	pt	Standard publishing unit, with 72 points in an inch
Relative Units		
Em	em	The width of the capital M in the current font, usually the same as the font size
Ex	ex	The height of the letter x in the current font
Pixel	px	The size of a pixel on the current monitor
Percentage	For example: 150%	Sets a font size relative to the base font size. 150% equals one-and-one-half the base font size.

The relative measurement units are designed to let you build scalable Web pages that adapt to different display types and sizes. The W3C recommends that you always use relative values to set font sizes on your Web pages. This practice ensures that your type sizes will display properly relative to each other or to the default font size set in the user's browser.

Specifying Font Size

The following rule sets the <blockquote> element to 1.5em Arial:

```
<style type="text/css">
blockquote {font-family: arial; font-size: 1.5em;}
</style>
```

Because the em is equivalent to the default font size, this measurement value would create text that is 1.5 times the default. With the default set at 12-point text, this style rule will create 18-point text. Figure 6-8 shows the results of the style rule.

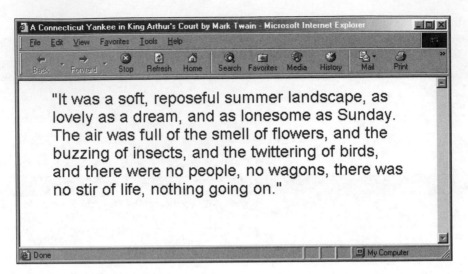

Figure 6-8   1.5em Arial

Specifying Font Weight

CSS allows either a numerical or descriptive value for font weight. Commonly used descriptive values include:

- Normal
- Bold
- Bolder
- Lighter

You should test values other than bold; not all weights are available for all typefaces. Experiment to determine what works.

The following shaded rule shows the addition of the font weight property to the rule:

```
<style type="text/css">
blockquote {font-family: arial; font-size: 1.5em;
font-weight: bold;}
</style>
```

Figure 6-9 shows the result of this rule.

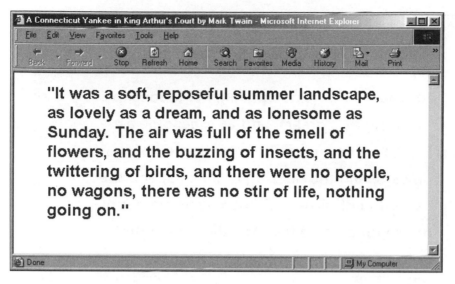

Figure 6-9   1.5em Arial bold

Specifying Line Height

CSS allows you to specify either a percentage or absolute value for the line height, commonly called leading. The percentage is based on the font size. Setting the value to 150% with a 10-point font size results in a line height of 15 points. For absolute values, use any of the standard CSS measurement units. The following shaded rule sets the line height to 30 points:

```
<style type="text/css">
blockquote {font-family: arial; font-size: 1.5em;
font-weight: bold; line-height: 30pt;}
</style>
```

Figure 6-10 shows the adjustment in line height.

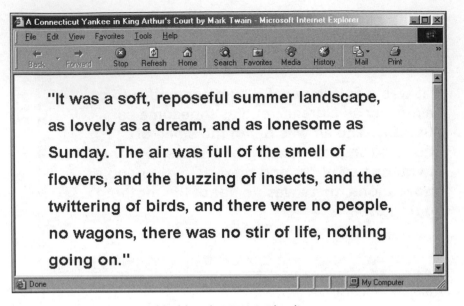

Figure 6-10   1.5em Arial bold with 30-point leading

The font property is a shortcut that lets you specify the most common font properties in a single statement. You must use the following syntax in this exact order, and always include a font size:

```
selector {font: font-weight font-size/line-height font-family;}
```

For example, you can abbreviate the following rule:

```
<style type="text/css">
body {font-weight: bold; font-size: 18pt; line-height: 30pt;
font-family: arial;}
</style>
```

to the following shorter version:

```
<style type="text/css">
{font: bold 18pt/30pt arial;}
</style>
```

Specifying Letter Spacing

Kerning is the printer's term for adjusting the white space between letters.

To adjust kerning use the letter spacing property with any of the CSS measurement units for the value. The following shaded rule sets the letter spacing to 2 points.

```
<style type="text/css">
blockquote {font-family: arial; font-size: 1.5em;
font-weight: bold; line-height: 30pt; letter-spacing: 2pt;}
</style>
```

Figure 6-11 shows the 2-point spacing between letters.

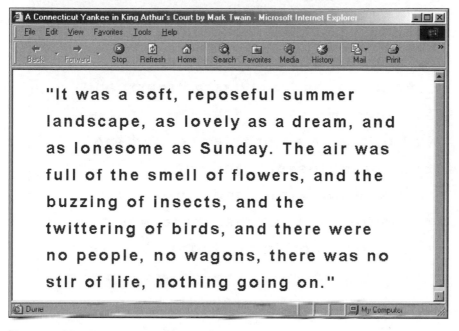

Figure 6-11   Two points of letter spacing

Specifying Text Indents

Use the text indent property to set the amount of indentation for the first line of text in an element, such as a paragraph. Again, use any of the CSS measurement units for the value. You can use a negative value to set a hanging indent. The following rule sets an indent of 24 points:

```
<style type="text/css">
blockquote {font-family: arial; font-size: 1.5em;
font-weight: bold; line-height: 30pt; letter-
spacing: 2pt;
text-indent: 24pt;}
</style>
```

Figure 6-12 shows the result of the text indent property.

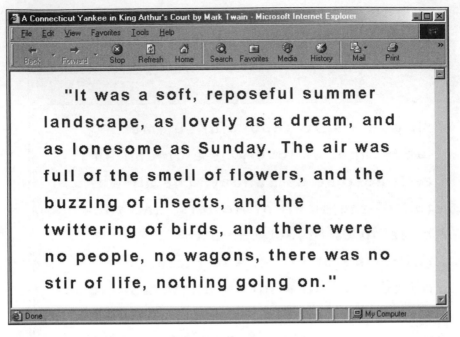

Figure 6-12   24-point text indent

 You can create a hanging indent by using a negative value in the text indent property. For example, the following code creates a paragraph with a 12-point hanging indent:

```
<style type="text/css">
p {text-indent: -12pt;}
</style>
```

Specifying Color

The color attribute sets the color of the text in an element. You also can use the color attribute to set the color of borders. You can use any one of the 16 predefined colors, or specify a hexadecimal value. (See Chapter 7 for more information on hexadecimal color values.) The following rule sets the text color to blue:

```
<style type="text/css">
h1 {color: blue;}
</style>
```

Specifying Text Background Color

You can set the background color—the color behind the text—for any element. Use the following syntax:

```
<style type="text/css">
h2 {color: white; background-color: black;}
</style>
```

The result of this rule is a white text on a black background, often called a reverse in printing jargon. Figure 6-13 shows an <h2> element with this style.

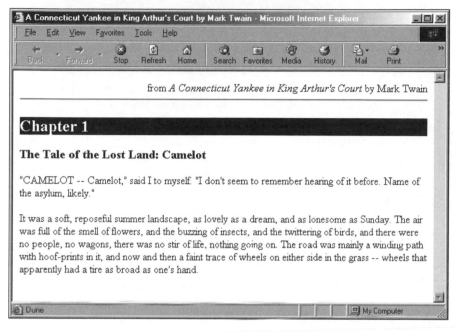

Figure 6-13   Reversed text—white on black

Specifying Block-Level Space Values

Cascading Style Sheets allows you to specify property values for the space around block-level elements. You can set the following three properties:

- Padding: The area between the text and border
- Border: The area separating the padding and margin
- Margin: The area outside the border

Figure 6-14 shows these three areas around a block-level text element.

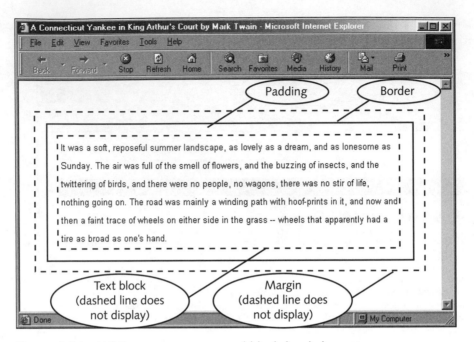

Figure 6-14   White space areas around block-level elements

Specifying Text Padding

You can specify the padding amount with any CSS measurement unit. Use the padding property to set the padding on all four sides, or set individual margins with the following settings:

- padding-top
- padding-bottom
- padding-left
- padding-right

The following rule sets the left and right padding to 24 points:

```
<style type="text/css">
p {padding-left: 24pt; padding-right: 24pt;}
</style>
```

Specifying Text Margins

You can specify the margin amount with any CSS measurement unit. Use the margin attribute to set the text margin on all four sides, or set individual margins with the following settings:

- margin-top
- margin-bottom

- margin-left
- margin-right

The following rule sets the margin to 30 pixels:

```
<style type="text/css">
p {margin: 30px;}
</style>
```

Specifying Text Borders

CSS offers a wide variety of border options, including width, style, and color. You can use the border shortcut property to specify multiple border properties at one time. Use the following syntax:

```
border: {border-style border-width border-color;}
```

For example, the following code sets a solid, 2-point red border around the text:

```
<style type="text/css">
border: {solid 2pt red;}
</style>
```

Coding Easy-to-Read Rules

To the browser, it does not matter how you space and indent your style rules, as long as the syntax is correct. However, many HTML authors indent their style rules to make them easier for humans to read and maintain. It is possible to express the following single-line style rule in a much neater fashion:

```
<style type="text/css">
p {font-family: arial, helvetica, sans-serif; font-
size: 10pt; line-height: 20pt; margin-left: 20px; margin-
right: 20px;}
</style>
```

The same rule is easier to read using indenting and alignment:

```
<style type="text/css">
p       {font-family: arial, helvetica, sans-serif;
        font-size: 10pt;
        line-height: 20pt;
        margin-left: 20px;
        margin-right: 20px;
        }
</style>
```

BUILDING A STYLE SHEET

In this set of steps you will create a style sheet for a document using a variety of font properties. Suppose you have been asked to develop an online library of public domain texts. You want to design a style sheet that you can apply to all the documents in the collection. In this example, the public domain content is the first chapter from Mark Twain's *A Connecticut Yankee in King Arthur's Court*. Figure 6-15 shows the page coded with standard HTML. The code for the page follows the figure.

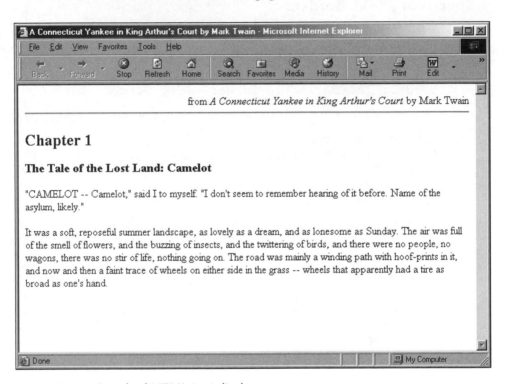

Figure 6-15   Standard HTML text display

```
<html>
<head>
<title>A Connecticut Yankee in King Arthur's Court by
 Mark Twain</title>
</head>
<body>
<div align="right">
from <i>A Connecticut Yankee in King Arthur's Court</i> by
 Mark Twain</div>
<hr>
<h2>Chapter 1</h2>
<h3>The Tale of the Lost Land: Camelot</h3>
```

```
<p>
"CAMELOT -- Camelot," said I to myself. "I don't seem to
remember hearing of it before. Name of the asylum, likely."
</p>
<p>
It was a soft, reposeful summer landscape, as lovely as a
dream, and as lonesome as Sunday. The air was full of the
smell of flowers, and the buzzing of insects, and the
twittering of birds, and there were no people, no wagons,
there was no stir of life, nothing going on. The road was
mainly a winding path with hoof-prints in it, and now and
then a faint trace of wheels on either side in the grass --
wheels that apparently had a tire as broad as one's hand.
</p>
</body>
</html>
```

Setting Up Document Divisions

To set up a style sheet, start by determining the logical divisions for the document. Each division has its own unique type characteristics that can be stated as style rules. Figure 6-16 shows the divisions you could use for this type of document.

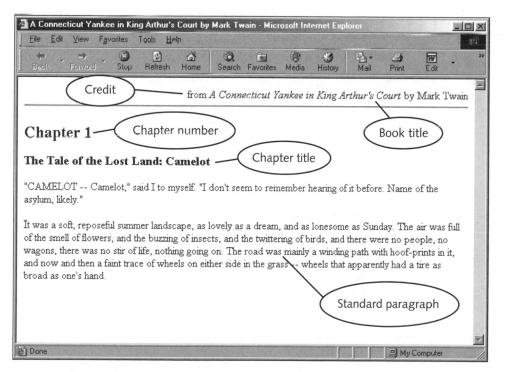

Figure 6-16   Logical document division

Using style sheets, you can create a different set of style rules for each division. For this example, you can build the style sheet internally in the <style> section. Later you can move the rules to an external style sheet for use with multiple documents.

Styling the Standard Paragraph

Start the project by setting up the style for the most basic content division—the standard paragraph. Here are the style requirements for the paragraph:

- Sans-serif font
- .85em type with 26-pixel leading
- 20-pixel left and right margins

To build the style for the standard paragraph:

1. Copy the **camelot.htm** file from the Chapter06 folder on your Data Disk.

2. Save the file to your work folder using the same filename.

3. Open camelot.htm in Notepad or another text editor and add a <style> element within the <head> section, as shown within the following code fragment. (Insert the text that appears bold in the following code.)

```
<head>
<title>A Connecticut Yankee in King Arthur's Court by
 Mark Twain</title>
<style type="text/css">

</style>
</head>
```

4. Leave a few lines of white space between the <style> tags to contain the style rules.

5. Write a style rule that selects the <p> element. Set the font size to .85em, as shown in the following code. This measurement is the equivalent of approximately 10-point text.

```
p      {font-size: .85em;}
```

6. Add the font-family property and use font substitution to ensure that Arial, Helvetica, or the default sans-serif font applies.

```
p      {font-size: .85em;
        font-family: arial, helvetica, sans-serif;
        }
```

7. Add more properties to the rule. Set the line height to 26px and the left and right margins to 20px.

```
p       {font-size: .85em;
        font-family: arial, helvetica, sans-serif;
        line-height: 26px;
        margin-left: 20px;
        margin-right: 20px;
        }
```

8. Save camelot.htm and leave it open in Notepad. Then view camelot.htm in your browser. Figure 6-17 shows the file in Internet Explorer.

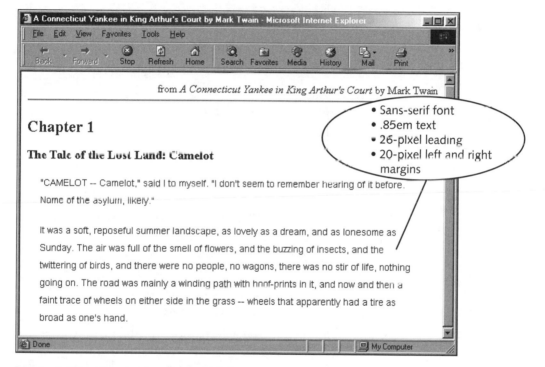

Figure 6-17 Standard paragraph style

Styling the Chapter Number

Continue building the style sheet by setting up a class name and associated style rule for the chapter number. Call this class "chapternumber." Here are the style characteristics for the class:

- Default browser font

- White text on a gray background

- 2em bold text with 48-pixel leading

- 20-pixel margin

To create the chapter number style:

1. Switch to Notepad to continue working with the file **camelot.htm**.

2. Add a style rule to the style sheet that selects the class name "chapternumber." Set the font size to 2em, which is equivalent to 24-point, and set the font weight to bold.

```
div.chapternumber {font-size: 2em;
                   font-weight: bold;}
```

3. Set the line height to 48px.

```
div.chapternumber {font-size: 2em;
                   font-weight: bold;
                   line-height: 48px;}
```

4. Build the reverse for the text by adding a color property set to white and a background-color property set to gray.

```
div.chapternumber {font-size: 2em;
                   font-weight: bold;
                   line-height: 48px;
                   color: white;
                   background-color: gray;}
```

5. Complete the style by adding a margin property and set it to 20px.

```
div.chapternumber {font-size: 2em;
                   font-weight: bold;
                   line-height: 48px;
                   color: white;
                   background-color: gray;
                   margin: 20px;}
```

6. Locate the chapter number text in the body of the document. Currently it is an <h2> element, as shown in the following code fragment.

```
<h2>Chapter 1</h2>
```

7. Change the <h2> tags to <div> tags and add the class attribute with the value set to "chapternumber."

```
<div class="chapternumber">Chapter 1</div>
```

8. Save the file and leave it open in Notepad. Then view and refresh camelot.htm in your browser. Figure 6-18 shows the file in Internet Explorer.

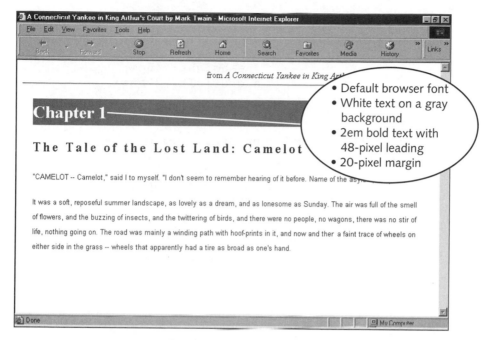

Figure 6-18   Chapter number style

Styling the Chapter Title

Continue building the style sheet by setting up a class name and associated style rule for the chapter title. Call this class "chaptertitle." Here are the style characteristics for the class:

- Default browser font
- 1.5cm bold text with 40-pixel leading
- 4 pixels of spacing between each letter
- 20-pixel left margin

To create the chapter title style:

1. Switch to Notepad to continue working with the file **camelot.htm**.

2. Add a style rule to the style sheet that selects the class name "chaptertitle." Set the font size to 1.5em, which is equivalent to 18-point, and set the font weight to bold.

   ```
   div.chaptertitle   {font-size: 1.5em;
                       font-weight: bold;}
   ```

3. Set the line height to 40 pixels.

   ```
   div.chaptertitle   {font-size: 1.5em;
                       font-weight: bold;
                       line-height: 40px;}
   ```

4. Add the margin property and set it to 20 pixels.

```
div.chaptertitle  {font-size: 1.5em;
                   font-weight: bold;
                   line-height: 40px;
                   margin-left: 20px;}
```

5. Add the letter-spacing property and set it to 4 pixels. This will add 4 pixels of white space between each letter in the chapter title.

```
div.chaptertitle {font-size: 1.5em;
                  font-weight: bold;
                  line-height: 40px;
                  margin-left: 20px;
                  letter-spacing: 4px;}
```

6. Locate the chapter title text in the body of the document. Currently it is an \<h3\> element, as shown in the following code fragment.

```
<h3>The Tale of the Lost Land: Camelot</h3>
```

7. Change the \<h3\> tags to \<div\> tags and add the class attribute with the value set to "chaptertitle."

```
<div class="chaptertitle">The Tale of the Lost Land:
Camelot</div>
```

8. Save the file and leave it open in Notepad. Then view and refresh camelot.htm in your browser. Figure 6-19 shows the file in Internet Explorer.

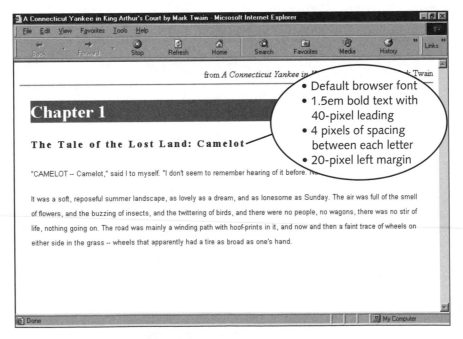

Figure 6-19   Chapter title style

Styling the Credit and Book Title

Finish the document style sheet by setting up classes for the credit and book title. The credit is a block element and, therefore, a <div>. The book title is an inline and will be styled with a <span> element. Here are the style requirements:

- Default font
- .85em type on 26-pixel leading
- Right-aligned
- Black bottom border rule
- 20-pixel left margin

To create the credit and book title styles:

1. Switch to Notepad to continue working with the file **camelot.htm**.

2. Add a style rule to the style sheet that selects the class name credit. Set the font size to .85em and the line height to 26px.

   ```
   div.credit {font-size: .85em;
               line-height: 26px;}
   ```

3. Add a left margin of 20 pixels and align it to the right with the text-align property.

   ```
   div.credit {font-size: .85em;
               line-height: 26px;
               margin-left: 20px;
               text-align: right;}
   ```

4. Use the border-bottom property to add a border. Specify a solid 1-pixel-wide line. The color of the border will appear in the default text color, which is black.

   ```
   div.credit {font-size: .85em;
               line-height: 26px;
               margin-left: 20px;
               text-align: right;
               border-bottom: solid 1px;}
   ```

5. Find the <div> within the code that contains the credit as shown:

   ```
   <div align="right"> from <i>A Connecticut Yankee in King
    Arthur's Court</i> by Mark Twain</div>
   <hr>
   ```

6. Remove the **align="right"** and replace it with **class="credit"**. Also, remove the **<hr>** element that follows the <div>. The code now looks like the following:

   ```
   <div class="credit">from <i>A Connecticut Yankee in King
    Arthur's Court</span> by Mark Twain</i>
   ```

7. The book title is contained within the credit line of text. Use the inline <span> element to apply a style to the book title. The font-style property lets you make the text italicized. Add the following rule to your style sheet:

```
span.booktitle {font-style: italic;}
```

8. Locate the book's title in the <div class="credit"> element, remove the existing **<i>** tags, and add **<span>** tags around it, as shown in the following code fragment:

```
<div class="credit">from <span>A Connecticut Yankee in
   King Arthur's Court</span> by Mark Twain</div>
```

9. Add the class attribute to the opening <span> tag. Set the attribute value to "booktitle."

```
<div class="credit">from <span class="booktitle">
A Connecticut Yankee in King Arthur's Court</span>
by Mark Twain</div>
```

10. Save the file and close Notepad. Then view and refresh camelot.htm in your browser. Figure 6-20 shows the file in Internet Explorer. When you are finished viewing this page, close your browser.

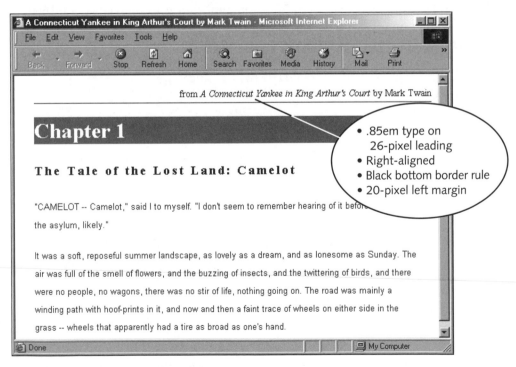

Figure 6-20   Credit and book title styles

The code for the entire document follows:

```
<html>
<head>
<title>A Connecticut Yankee in King Arthur's Court by
 Mark Twain</title>
<style type="text/css">

p        {
         font-size: .85em;
         font-family: arial, helvetica, sans-serif;
         line-height: 26px;
         margin-left: 20px;
         margin-right: 20px;
         }

div.chapternumber
         {
         font-size: 2em;
         font-weight: bold;
         line-height: 48px;
         color: white;
         background-color: gray;
         margin: 20px;
         }
div.chaptertitle
         {
         font-size: 1.5em;
         font-weight: bold;
         line-height: 40px;
         margin-left: 20px;
         letter-spacing: 4px;
         }

div.credit
         {
         font-size: .85em;
         line-height: 26px;
         margin-left: 20px;
         text-align: right;
         border-bottom: solid 1px;
         }

span.booktitle {font-style: italic;}
</style>
</head>


<body>
<div class="credit">from <span class="booktitle">A
 Connecticut Yankee in King Arthur's Court</span> by
 Mark Twain</div>
```

```
<div class="chapternumber">Chapter 1</div>
<div class="chaptertitle">The Tale of the Lost Land:
 Camelot</div>

<p>
"CAMELOT -- Camelot," said I to myself. "I don't seem to
remember hearing of it before. Name of the asylum, likely."
</p>
<p>
It was a soft, reposeful summer landscape, as lovely as a
dream, and as lonesome as Sunday. The air was full of the
smell of flowers, and the buzzing of insects, and the
twittering of birds, and there were no people, no wagons,
there was no stir of life, nothing going on. The road was
mainly a winding path with hoof-prints in it, and now and
then a faint trace of wheels on either side in the grass --
 wheels that apparently had a tire as broad as one's hand.
</p>
</body>
</html>
```

CHAPTER SUMMARY

You can use Cascading Style Sheets to manipulate a variety of text properties and achieve professional-quality typography on your Web site. Keep the following points in mind:

▫ Use type to communicate information structure. Be sparing with your type choices; use fonts consistently and design for legibility.

▫ Remember that HTML text downloads faster than graphics-based text. Use HTML text whenever possible.

▫ Use browser-safe fonts that will appear as consistently as possible across operating systems.

▫ Limit the use of the <font> element because it is deprecated in HTML 4.0.

▫ Experiment with and consider implementing Cascading Style Sheets (CSS). CSS eventually will replace the <font> element; it offers more control and ease of use.

▫ If you use CSS, standardize your styles by building external style sheets and linking them to multiple documents.

▫ Test your work. Different browsers and computing platforms render text in different sizes.

REVIEW QUESTIONS

1. What is the default browser font?
2. What does the browser do if you specify a font that is not stored on a user's computer?
3. What are two drawbacks to the use of graphics-based text?
4. What three attributes can you use with the <font> element?
5. Why would you want to limit use of the <font> element?
6. What are the two ways to set size with the <font> element?
7. Why is face="arial, helvetica" a common font substitution string?
8. Name the two parts of a style rule.
9. Name the two parts of a property declaration.
10. What element contains the style rules?
11. How do you override a style for a specific element?
12. What is the common filename extension for style sheets?
13. Name three ways to select elements.
14. Name two elements designed for use with style sheets.
15. Write a rule specifying that <p> elements appear as 14-point text with 20-point leading.
16. Write a rule specifying that <i> elements display red only when they appear within <p> elements.
17. Write a rule defining a division named NOTE. Specify 12-point bold Arial text on a yellow background.
18. What three white-space areas can you affect with style rules?
19. Write a style rule to create a white-on-black reverse <h1> heading.
20. Write a style rule for a <p> element with a 24-point hanging indent and a 30-pixel margin on the left and right sides.

HANDS-ON PROJECTS

1. Convert an existing HTML document to Cascading Style Sheets.
   a. Build styles using the existing standard HTML elements in the file.
   b. Test the work in multiple browsers to verify that all styles are portable.
   c. Remove the files and place them in an external style sheet.
   d. Link the HTML file to the style sheet. Test to make sure the file displays properly.

2. Convert an existing document to Cascading Style Sheets.

   a. Decide on logical divisions for the document.

   b. Give the divisions class names.

   c. Write style rules for the divisions.

   d. Apply the styles to the divisions using <div> or <span>.

   e. Test your work.

3. Convert an existing document to Cascading Style Sheets. Test your work in an older browser, such as Netscape Navigator 3.0, which does not support style sheets. You can download older versions of browsers from *www.browsers.com*.

4. Browse the Web for examples of good typography. Write a short design critique of whether the type works effectively on the Web sites you find and why.

5. Browse the Web for examples of poor typography. Write a short design critique of why the type is confusing or misleading to the user. Save and print screen shots of the sample Web pages to accompany your critique.

6. Mock up a page for testing body text fonts. Try a variety of fonts at different resolutions to determine which is the most readable. Test your work on a variety of subjects (friends, family, and coworkers, for example) to see if they agree with your choices. Provide the sample pages and a synopsis of user opinions on the legibility of the fonts.

CASE PROJECT

Use Cascading Style Sheets for the case study project. Design the type hierarchy for the information levels in your Web site. Create a type specification page in HTML that shows examples of the different typefaces and sizes and where each of them will be used.

Determine the body copy typeface and size for your Web site. Mock up a couple of test pages with some content. Test for legibility of your text. Try different leading, padding, and margins to see how this affects the clarity of the text.

Once you have decided on your typefaces, start to add actual content to the different pages of the Web site using the styles you have developed to display the text.

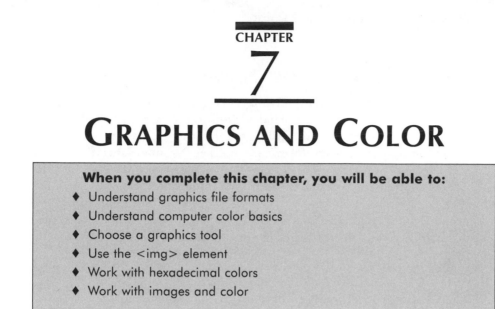

CHAPTER

7

GRAPHICS AND COLOR

When you complete this chapter, you will be able to:

♦ Understand graphics file formats
♦ Understand computer color basics
♦ Choose a graphics tool
♦ Use the <img> element
♦ Work with hexadecimal colors
♦ Work with images and color

The combination of graphics and text is what makes the Web so attractive and popular, but it also can be the undoing of many Web sites. Graphics used wisely produce an attractive and engaging Web site. The use of too many large or complex images or graphics forces users to endure long download times—and they may not wait. Find a good balance between images and text and use the image capabilities of HTML to suit your users' needs. Test your work in a variety of browsers and at a variety of connection speeds to make sure downloading your graphics does not discourage your readers.

The incorrect use of color in many Web sites creates unreadable text or navigation confusion for the user. Use color judiciously to communicate, to guide the reader, or to create branded areas of your site. Test your color choices carefully to make sure they appear properly across different browsers.

UNDERSTANDING GRAPHICS FILE FORMATS

You currently can use only three image file formats on the Web: GIF, JPG, and PNG. A fourth format, SVG, is a new standard from the World Wide Web Consortium (W3C) that is not yet in common use. All these formats compress images to create smaller files, but choosing the right file format for an image is important. If you choose the wrong file type, your image will not compress or appear as you expect. Color depth (described in the "Computer Color Basics" section of this chapter) affects image file format as well. JPG supports 24-bit color, GIF supports 8-bit color, and PNG supports both 8-bit and 24-bit color. The file format's color depth controls the number of colors the image can display; the greater the bit depth, the greater the number of colors that can be displayed.

GIF

The **Graphics Interchange Format (GIF)** is designed for online delivery of graphics. GIF uses a lossless compression technique, meaning that no color information is discarded when the image is compressed.

The color depth of GIF is 8-bit, allowing a palette of no more than 256 colors. The fewer colors you use, the greater the compression and the smaller the file size. The GIF file format excels at compressing and displaying flat color areas, making it the logical choice for line art and color graphics. Because of its limited color depth, GIF is not the best file format for photographs or more complex graphics that have gradations of color, such as shadows and feathering.

GIF Transparency

With GIF files you can choose one color in an image to appear as transparent in the browser. The background color or pattern will show through the areas that you have designated as transparent. Using transparent areas allows you to create graphics that appear to have an irregular outside shape, rather than being bounded by a rectangle. Figure 7-1 shows the same shape with and without transparency.

You can create transparent areas using a graphics editor. When you choose the transparent color, all pixels of that color in the image will let the background color show through. In Figure 7-1, white was chosen as the transparent color.

GIF Animation

The GIF format lets you store multiple images and timing information about the images in a single file. This means that you can build animations consisting of multiple static images that change continuously, creating the illusion of motion. This is exactly the same technique used in cell-based animation. You can create animated GIFs by using a variety of both shareware and commercial software.

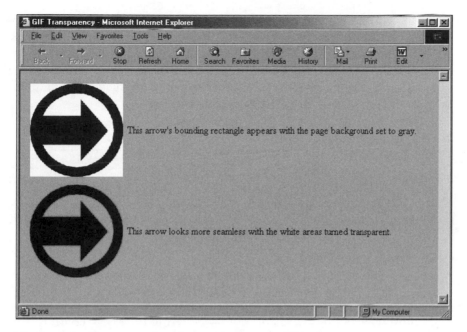

Figure 7-1   Transparent and non-transparent GIFs

When you create a GIF animation, you can determine the time between frames and the number of times the animation plays. With a little imagination, you can create all types of effects, including text scrolls, color changes, animated icons, and slide shows. Figure 7-2 shows a series of individual GIFs that can be combined to play as an animated GIF. The final GIF animation file is a single file whose name ends in the .GIF extension.

Figure 7-2   Individual frames of a GIF animation

GIF animation is somewhat limited when compared with the results of other proprietary animation tools such as Macromedia Shockwave or Flash, which can play synchronized sounds and allow Web users to interact with the animation. Creating animations with these applications, however, requires browser plug-ins, and viewing the animations demands heavy download times. Unlike most proprietary tools, animated GIFs do not require any special plug-ins for viewing; also, if you limit color and motion when creating your animations, you can keep your file sizes small for faster downloads.

Use restraint when adding animated GIFs like blinking icons and scrolling banners to your pages. Users may find them annoying because they are repetitive and distract from the page content. Consider choosing to play an animation a limited number of times rather than letting it loop endlessly. Creating animated images with GIF animation software streamlines the process of setting the timing, color palette, and individual frame effects. See Table 7-1 for a list of GIF animation tools.

Table 7-1   GIF animation tools

Animagic GIF Animator	*rtlsoft.com/animagic/index.html*
GIF Construction Set Professional	*www.mindworkshop.com/alchemy/gifcon.html*
Ulead GIF Animator	*www.ulead.com/ga/runme.htm*
VSE Animation Maker (Macintosh)	*vse-online.com/animation-maker/download.html*

JPG

The **Joint Photographic Experts Group** (**JPG**, sometimes called **JPEG**) format is best for photographs or continuous-tone images. JPGs are 24-bit images that allow millions of colors. Unlike GIFs, JPGs do not use a palette to display color.

JPGs use a "lossy" compression routine specially designed for photographic images: when the image is compressed, some color information is discarded, resulting in a loss of quality from the original image. Since the display device is a low-resolution computer monitor, the loss of quality is not usually noticeable. Furthermore, the resulting faster download time compensates for the loss of image quality.

Using Adobe Photoshop or other imaging software, you can translate photographic images into JPG format. When you create the JPG file, you can balance the amount of compression versus the resulting image quality manually. Figure 7-3 shows the Photoshop Save For Web dialog box.

The Quality list box lets you adjust the quality of the file; the higher the quality, the lower the file compression. You can play with this setting to create good-looking files that are as small as possible. Many photos can sustain quite a bit of compression while still maintaining image integrity. The Preview window shows the result of your changes, allowing you to experiment with the image quality before saving the file. Photoshop displays the estimated download time based on the file size.

Whether you are creating GIFs or JPGs, always remember to save an original copy of your artwork or photo. Both file formats permanently degrade the quality of an image as a result of compression. Once you have converted to GIF or JPG you cannot return to the original image quality.

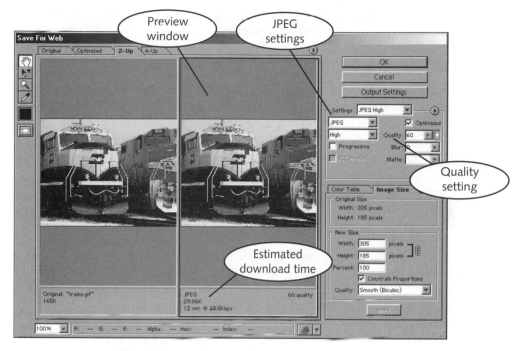

Figure 7-3   Photoshop Save For Web dialog box

PNG

The **Portable Network Graphics (PNG)** format is designed specially for the Web. PNG has been available since 1995 but has been slow to gain popularity because of its lack of browser support. It is a royalty-free file format that is intended to replace GIF. This lossless format compresses 8-bit images to smaller file sizes than GIF. PNG also is intended to work as an image-printing format, so it supports 8-bit indexed-color, 16-bit grayscale, and 24-bit true-color images. Even though PNG supports 24-bit color, its loss-less compression routine does not compress as efficiently as JPG.

PNG supports transparency and interlacing but not animation, although the W3C has created a draft specification for a Multiple-image Network Graphics format (MNG) that will support animation. One useful feature of PNG is its built-in text capabilities for image indexing, allowing you to store a string of identifying text within the file itself. Now that browser support is improving for PNG, designers can start to use it more often.

SVG

The **Scalable Vector Graphics (SVG)** format is a new standard from the W3C. SVG is not yet supported by all browsers, but it is expected to be widely used on the Web. SVG is a language for describing two-dimensional graphics using XML. SVG files can contain shapes such as lines and curves, images, text, animation, and interactive events. SVG is compatible with common Web technologies such as HTML, XML, JavaScript, and Cascading Style Sheets. For more information on SVG, visit the W3C SVG page at *www.w3.org/Graphics/SVG/*.

SVG graphics are scalable to different display resolutions or to allow printed output on a high-resolution printer. The same SVG graphic can be re-used at different sizes throughout a Web site without downloading multiple files to the user. SVG graphics can be viewed at different sizes based on user needs, allowing magnification of an image to see fine detail or to increase legibility.

SVG is a vector graphics file format. **Vector graphics** represent images as geometrical formulas, as compared with **raster graphics** format, which represents images pixel-by-pixel for the entire image. GIFs and JPGs are raster formats. The vector graphics format allows SVG graphics to be scalable and cross-platform compatible.

All computer displays, whether desktop or handheld, are raster-type devices. The vector-based SVG files will eventually be displayed on a raster device, so why use SVG? SVG's conversion to pixels is based on the individual display type and settings, resulting in images that reproduce more faithfully for the greatest number of users.

Adobe offers an SVG plug-in for Windows and Macintosh browsers at *www.adobe.com/svg/viewer/install/main.html*. JASC software offers WebDraw, an SVG graphics program, at *www.jasc.com*.

Using Interlacing and Progressive Display

Most Web-capable graphics editors let you save images in an interlaced (progressive) format. You can choose this display option when creating GIF, PNG, and JPG files. GIF and PNG files use an interlacing format, while JPG files use a progressive format. Interlacing and progressive formats generally are the same thing—the gradual display of a graphic in a series of passes as the data arrives in the browser. Each additional pass of data creates a clearer view of the image until the complete image is displayed. Figure 7-4 shows three rendering passes to display a complete image.

The only real advantage to displaying graphics in the interlaced or progressive method is that users immediately see at least a blurred view of the complete image, giving them something to look at while waiting for the entire graphic to download. The disadvantage of choosing this display method is that older browsers may not display the graphic properly, and more processing power is needed on the user's machine to render the image.

Figure 7-4   Three passes complete this progressive JPG image

Where You Can Find Images

You can acquire images from a variety of sources, including from a graphics professional you hire to create and prepare your images. If your budget does not allow for funding this service, consider one of the following resources:

- *Stock photo collections*—Stock photo collections can cost anywhere from thousands of dollars for a few images to under $20 for thousands of images at your local computer discount store or mail-order retailer. These collections contain royalty-free images that you can use for any Web site. You can manipulate the graphics to add or delete text or images, change the color, or make any other modifications. Most stock photo collections include a built-in browsing program that lets you search for a particular image, and some also provide basic image-editing software.

- *Digital camera*—A digital camera lets you take your own photos and use them on the Web. These cameras store photos in JPG format, so you do not have to convert them. Most also provide image-cataloguing software, and some include basic image-editing software. The price of digital cameras continues to drop, while the quality of the images remains quite good.

- *Scanner*—Good scanners are available for under $150. You can scan your own photos or images and save them as GIF, JPG, or PNG files for use on your Web site. Remember to set the scanner resolution to 72 dpi to match the computer display resolution.

- *Public domain Web sites*—Many Web sites maintain online catalogs of images that are available for download. Some of these sites charge a small membership fee, so you can download as many images as you want. Other public domain Web sites are completely free.

- *Create your own*—If you need a basic image or if you have graphic design skills, you can download a shareware graphics tool and learn to use it. Keep your custom image simple, such as text on colored backgrounds, and use fundamental shapes and lines. Look at graphics on other Web sites; many are simple but effective and may provide a useful model for your own images.

- *Clip art*—Clip art is a viable alternative for the Web, especially as more polished collections become available for sale on CD-ROM. Price generally corresponds to quality for clip art—if you pay $9.95 for 20,000 images, do not expect excellent quality. You also can use a graphics program to customize clip art to meet your particular needs.

 Do not borrow images from other Web sites. Although your browser allows you to copy graphics, you should never use someone else's work unless it is from a public domain Web site and freely available for use. Digital watermarking technology lets artists copyright their work with an invisible signature; if you use someone else's graphics, you may find yourself in a cyber-lawsuit.

Choosing the Right Format

The following list summarizes the advantages and disadvantages of each graphic file format for the Web.

- *GIF*—The everyday file format for all types of simple colored graphics and line art. Use GIF sparingly for its animation capabilities to add visual interest to your pages. GIF's transparency feature lets you seamlessly integrate graphics into your Web site.

- *JPG*—Use JPG for all 24-bit full-color photographic images, as well as more complicated graphics that contain color gradients, shadows, and feathering.

- *PNG*—If most browsers are supporting it, use PNG as a substitute for GIF. Because PNG does not compress your 24-bit images as well as JPG does, do not use it for photos.

COMPUTER COLOR BASICS

Before you create or gather graphics for your Web site, you need a basic understanding of how color works on computer monitors.

Your computer monitor displays color by mixing the three basic colors of light: red, green, and blue, often called RGB colors. Each of these three basic colors is called a color channel. Your monitor can express a range of intensity for each color channel, from 0 (absence of color) to 255 (full intensity of color). Colors vary widely between monitors based on both the user's preferences and brand of equipment.

Color Depth

As mentioned earlier in the chapter, the amount of data used to create color on a display is called the **color depth**. If your monitor can display 8 bits of data in each of the three color channels, it has a 24-bit color depth ($8 \times 3 = 24$). 24-bit images can contain almost 17 million different colors and are called true-color images. Both JPG and PNG support 24-bit color. If your users have a 24-bit color display, they can appreciate the full color depth of your images. But many monitors cannot display 24-bit images; some have only 16-bit color depth (called high color) and some have only 8-bit color depth. If your monitor does not support the full color depth of an image, the browser must resort to mixing colors in an attempt to match the original colors in the image.

Dithering

The browser must mix its own colors when you display a 24-bit image on an 8-bit monitor, or when you use a file format that does not support 24-bit color. Since the 8-bit monitor has fewer colors to work with (256, to be exact), the browser must try to approximate the missing colors by creating colors from the ones the browser already has. This type of color mixing is called dithering. **Dithering** occurs when the browser encounters a color that it does not support, such as when you try to turn a 24-bit photographic image into an 8-bit, 256-color image. Dithered images often appear grainy and pixelated. The dithering will be most apparent in gradations, feathered edges, or shadows. Figure 7-5 shows the same image in both JPG and GIF format at 8-bit, 256 colors.

The JPG file on the left has a lot of dithering in the sky area of the photo, where the browser was forced to mix colors to approximate the existing colors in the image. The GIF file on the right exhibits a different type of color matching called banding. Unlike dithering, **banding** is an effort to match the closest colors from the GIF's palette to the original colors in the photo. When you create a GIF, you can choose whether or not to use dithering. A non-dithered image will be smaller than one that uses dithering, but the banding may create an unacceptable image. JPGs, when viewed on an 8-bit or 16-bit display, will dither to the closest colors. Photos are best saved as JPGs, even when viewed at a lower color depth, because the dithering creates a more acceptable image.

Using Non-Dithering Colors

One way to control the dithering process is to create images that use non-dithering colors. The 216 non-dithering colors that are shared by PCs and Macintoshes are called the Web palette or browser-safe colors. The non-dithering palette only applies to GIF or 8-bit PNG, not to 24-bit JPG. Most Web-capable graphics programs include the Web palette colors. If you do create graphics for the Web, avoid trouble by using the Web palette as your color palette for all flat-color areas of your graphics.

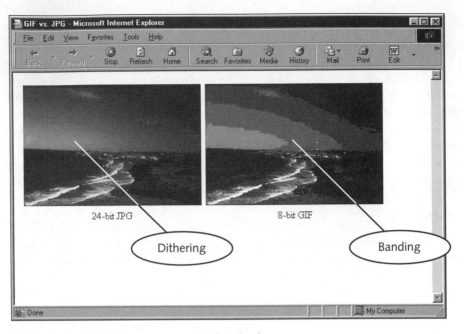

Figure 7-5   24-bit images on an 8-bit display

CHOOSING A GRAPHICS TOOL

As a Web designer, you may be in the enviable position of having a complete staff of graphic design professionals preparing graphics for your site. Most Web designers, however, do not have this luxury. Whether you want to or not, you eventually must use a graphics tool. Most of your graphics tasks will be simple, such as resizing an image or converting an image from one file format to another. More complex tasks could include changing color depth or adding transparency to an image. These are tasks that anyone can learn to do using any of the popular graphics software currently available.

When it comes to creating images, you may want to enlist professional help. Your Web site will not benefit if you choose to create your own graphics and you are really not up to the task. Professional-quality graphics can greatly enhance the look of your Web site. Take an honest look at your skills and remember that the best Web sites usually are the result of collaboration.

You will use graphics software to create or manipulate graphics. Most Web designers use Adobe Photoshop, which is an expensive and full-featured product that takes time to master. Adobe Illustrator, a high-end drawing and painting tool, also is available. Other commercial tools you can consider include Ulead PhotoImpact and Macromedia Fireworks. Most are available as downloadable demos, so you can try before you buy. In general, look for a tool that meets your needs and will not take a long time to learn. Table 7-2 shows a list of Web sites for the graphic tools mentioned in the text.

Table 7-2   Graphic tools Web sites

Graphic tool	URL
Adobe Photoshop and Illustrator	*www.adobe.com*
LView Pro	*www.lview.com*
Macromedia Fireworks	*www.macromedia.com*
Paint Shop Pro 7	*www.jasc.com*
Ulead PhotoImpact 7	*www.ulead.com*

The list in Table 7-2 is not exhaustive, and you may have to try different tools to find the one that suits your needs.

7

Of course, you also can choose from a variety of shareware graphics tools. Two of the more established tools are Paint Shop Pro 7 and LView Pro. These tools are each priced under $100 and contain a full range of image-editing features. Like most other shareware, these tools can be downloaded and used for a trial period.

USING THE <IMG> ELEMENT

By definition, <img> is a replaced element in HTML, meaning that the browser replaces the <img> element with the image file referenced in the src attribute. <img> is also an empty element, so never use a closing tag with it. The browser treats the image as it treats a character; normal image alignment is to the baseline of the text. Images that are within a line of text must have spaces on both sides or the text will touch the image.

The <img> element only needs the src attribute for the image to be displayed in the browser. The following is a valid <img> element that displays a GIF file named logo:

```
<img src="logo.gif">
```

This simplified use of the <img> element, however, does not take advantage of the wide variety of valid attributes. Table 7-3 lists the most commonly used attributes.

Table 7-3   <img> element attributes

Attribute	Use
align	Specifies the position of the image in relation to the surrounding text
alt	Displays an alternate string of text instead of an image if the user has a text-only browser or has graphics turned off
border	Determines whether a border appears on the image. State the border value in pixels. You can use this attribute to turn off the hypertext border if the image is a link.
height	Specifies the height of the image in pixels

Table 7-3   <img> element attributes (continued)

Attribute	Use
hspace	Specifies the amount of horizontal white space on the left and right sides of the image, in pixels
src	The only required attribute, src specifies the URL of the graphic file you want to display. As with any URL, the path must be relative to the HTML file.
title	A string of text that provides information about the image. Visual browsers display the contents of the title attribute as a "tool tip" (a pop-up window that appears when the user pauses the pointing device over an object). An audio browser could speak the title information.
vspace	Specifies the amount of vertical white space on the top and bottom sides of the image, in pixels
width	Specifies the width of the image in pixels

Replacing img Attributes with Style Sheet Properties

Align, border, vspace, and hspace have been deprecated in HTML 4.0 in favor of CSS. Table 7-4 shows the equivalent CSS properties that replace these attributes.

Table 7-4   CSS properties that replace <img> attributes

Deprecated Attribute	Equivalent CSS Property
align	float allows you to flow text around an image or other object; for example: img {float: left;}
border	border lets you set a border on an image or remove the border from a linked image
vspace and hspace	The padding or margin properties set white space around an image. You can control individual sides of the image, or apply white space around the entire image.

Style properties usually are expressed as global rules that specify the characteristics for every occurrence of an element. The variety of uses for graphics on a Web page defy a homogenous rule. For example, the following style rule makes all images left-aligned:

```
img {float: left;}
```

However, this rule may be too restrictive, because every image in the document will be left-aligned. A good alternative is to express the style information using the style attribute in the <img> element. For example, the following code shows two images, one left-aligned and one right-aligned:

```
<img src="logo.gif" style="float: left" width="40"
height="40" alt="Company Logo">
```

```
<img src="product.gif" style="float: right" width="80"
height="60" alt="Our Product">
```

Many of the standard CSS text properties can be used with the <img> element. This chapter includes both standard HTML code and, wherever applicable, the equivalent CSS properties expressed using the style attribute.

Specifying alt and title Attribute Text

In Chapter 4, you learned about the benefits of including alt attribute text, which provides a description of the image if the image does not appear. Proper use of the alt attribute improves Web accessibility by describing the function of each image in your Web site. If you use images for navigation, use the alt attribute to provide descriptive navigation information. For example, Figures 7-6 and 7-7 show the same Web page. In one figure images are visible in the browser; in the other figure, the images are turned off. In Figure 7-7 the navigation bar is still useful because of the descriptive alt text.

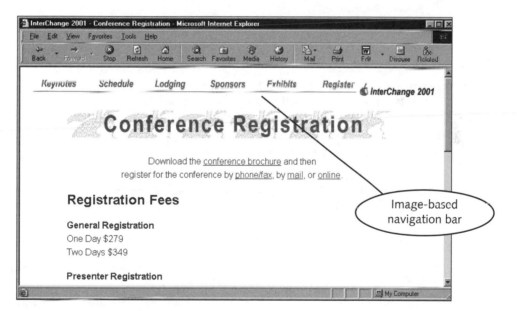

Figure 7-6 Image-based navigation

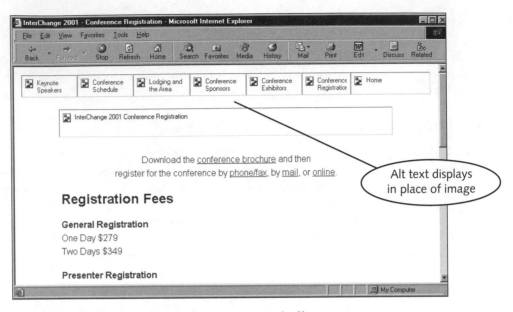

Figure 7-7   Navigation bar with images turned off

In Netscape 4 and Internet Explorer 5 and 6, the value of the alt attribute appears in a pop-up window when the user uses the mouse to point to an image. This behavior, as defined by the W3C, is actually a function of the title attribute. Netscape 6.2 and Opera 5.0 will only display the pop-up text if the title attribute is present. Figure 7-8 shows an example of the title attribute used with an <img> element, as shown in the following code:

```
<img src="trains.jpg" alt="Locomotives Picture"
title="Diesel locomotives from Burlington Northern and
Santa Fe railroads">
```

Specifying Image Width and Height

Every <img> element on your Web site should contain width and height attributes. These attributes provide important information to the browser by specifying the amount of space to reserve for the image. This information dramatically affects the way your pages download, especially at slower connection speeds. If you have included the width and height, the browser knows how much space the image needs. The browser reserves the space on the page without waiting for the image to download, and displays the rest of your text content. If the browser does not know the width and height values, it must download the image before displaying the rest of the page. This means the user will be looking at a blank page while waiting for the image to download. Figure 7-9 shows the result of including the width and height in the <img> element.

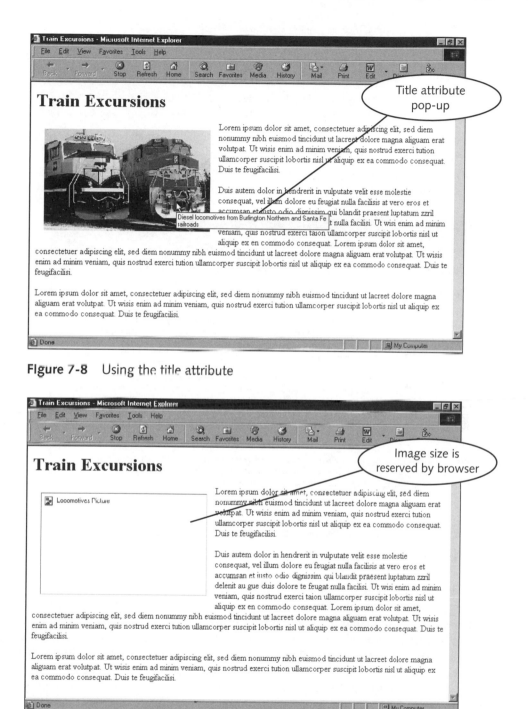

Figure 7-8   Using the title attribute

Figure 7-9   Image size reserved in the browser

The following code shows the width and height attributes for the image. It indicates that the browser should reserve a 305 × 185-pixel space for the trains.jpg image and should display the alternate text "Locomotives Picture" if it cannot display the image.

```
<img src="trains.jpg" width="305" height="185"
alt="Locomotives Picture">
```

If you are not using tables, set the width and height to preserve the look of your layout, whether the images are displayed or not. In Figure 7-10, the width and height have been omitted. Notice that when the browser does not know the width and height, the text wrapping and appearance of the page change dramatically when the image is not displayed.

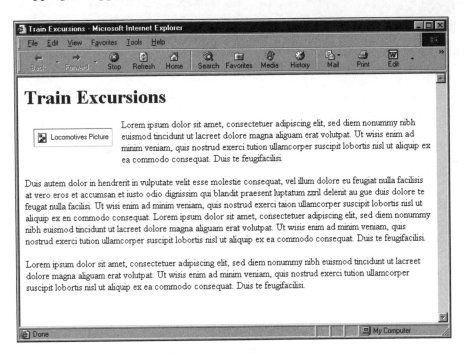

Figure 7-10   Browser unable to reserve image size

You may notice that you can manipulate the width and height of the image itself using the width and height attributes in the <img> element. While it is tempting to use these attributes to change graphic size without using a graphics program, it is not a good idea. If the original graphic's area is too large and you reduce the size using the width and height attributes, you are not changing the file size of the image—only the area that the browser reserves for the graphic. The user is still downloading the original graphic file; no time is saved. Also, if you do not maintain the ratio of width to height, you distort the image. Figure 7-11 shows an image in its actual size, the size after changing the width and height values in proportion to one another, and the distorted size caused by incorrect width and height values.

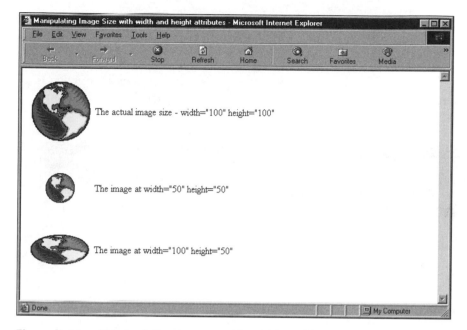

Figure 7-11   Manipulating images with width and height attributes

In the following code for the three images, the width and height attributes are highlighted:

```
<! globe 1 >
<img src="globe1.gif" width="100" height="100"
alt="globe">

<! globe 2 >
<img src="globe1.gif" width="50" height="50" alt="globe">

<! globe 3 >
<img src="globe1.gif" width="100" height="50" alt="globe">
```

However, the ability to manipulate image size using the width and height attributes comes in handy in certain circumstances. When creating a layout mock-up, you can test image sizes by manipulating the code.

Sizing Graphics for the Page

One way to keep file sizes small is to size graphics appropriately. Few things are more annoying than opening a new Web page and waiting to download a large 600 × 400-pixel image. One of the easiest ways to make your graphics download quickly is to keep their dimensions small and appropriate to the size of the page. Figure 7-12 shows a variety of image sizes at an 800 × 600 screen resolution.

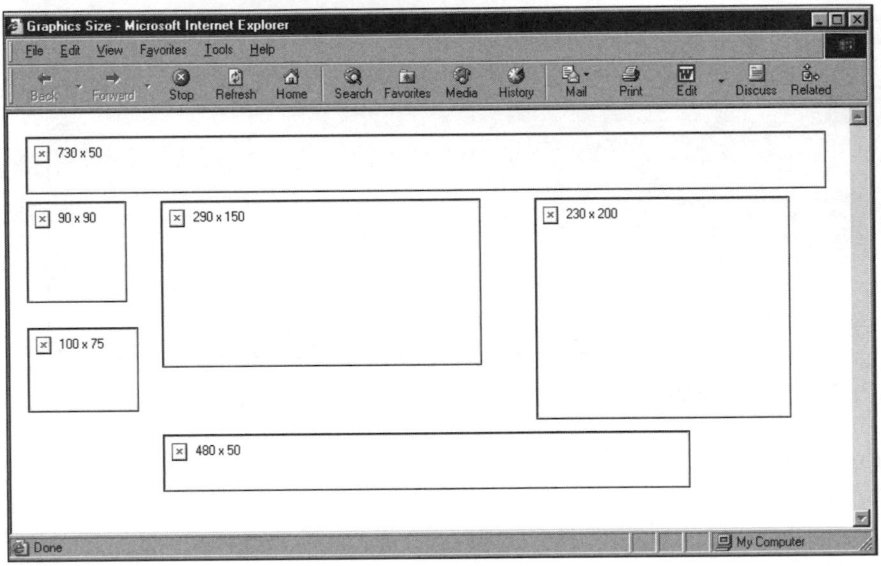

Figure 7-12   Sample graphics sizes at 800 x 600 screen resolution

Use these sample image sizes as guidelines when you size your graphics. It is also useful to think of image size in relation to the number of columns in your layout; size your graphics to occupy one, two, or more columns of the page.

Removing the Hypertext Border from an Image

When you create a hypertext image, the browser's default behavior is to display the hypertext border around the image, as shown in Figure 7-13. This border appears blue before—and purple after—you click the image. In a well-designed site, this border is unnecessary because users often use their mouse to point to each image to see whether the hypertext cursor appears. Another reason to abandon the display of hypertext borders is that their color may not complement your graphic. To remove the hypertext border, add the border="0" attribute to your <img> tag.

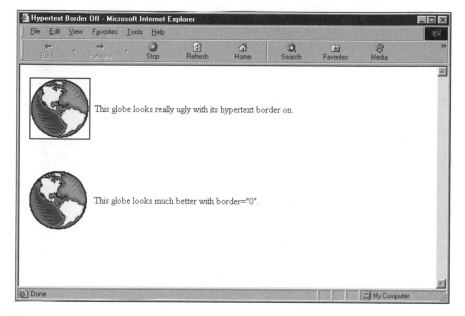

Figure 7-13   Removing the hypertext border from an image

Here is the code for the second globe, which has the hypertext border turned off in both standard HTML and CSS:

```
<! Standard HTML >
<img src="globe1.gif" width="100" height="100" alt="globe"
border="0" align="middle">

<! CSS >
<img src="globe1.gif" width="100" height="100" alt="globe"
style="border: none" align="middle">
```

Aligning Text and Images

You can align text along an image border using the align attribute. The default alignment of the text and image is bottom-aligned, which means the bottom of the text aligns with the bottom edge of the image. You can change the alignment by using either the top or middle values. Figure 7-14 shows all three alignment values.

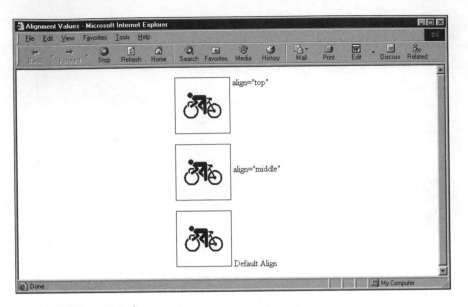

Figure 7-14   Text alignment

The following code shows the three types of alignment and their CSS equivalents:

```
<! Standard HTML >

<img src="cycle.gif" align="top" border="1">
<img src="cycle.gif" align="middle" border="1">
<img src="cycle.gif" border="1">

<! CSS >
<img src="cycle.gif" style="vertical-align: top"
border="1">
<img src="cycle.gif" style="vertical-align: middle"
border="1">
<img src="cycle.gif" border="1">
```

The align attribute can also be used to wrap text around images. Figure 7-15 shows two images (the images are turned off), the first left-aligned and the second right-aligned.

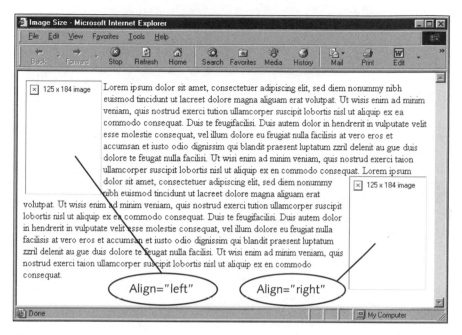

Figure 7-15   Text wrapping

The following code shows both <img> elements and the CSS equivalents:

```
<! Standard HTML >
<img src="planning.jpg" width="125" height="184"
alt="125 x 184 image" align="left">

<img src="planning.jpg" width="125" height="184"
alt="125 x 184 image" align="right">

<! CSS >
<img src="planning.jpg" width="125" height="184"
alt="125 x 184 image" style="float5: left">


<img src="planning.jpg" width="125" height="184"
alt="125 x 184 image" style="float: right">
```

Adding White Space Around Images

Add white space around your images to reduce clutter and improve readability. As shown in Figure 7-16, the default spacing is very close to the image.

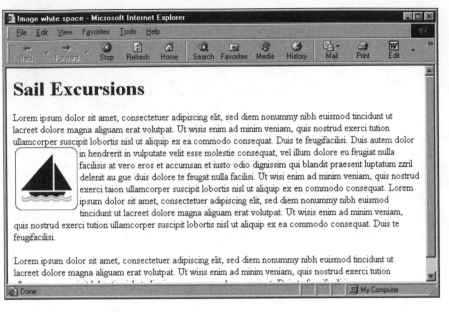

Figure 7-16   Default image spacing

To increase the white space around an image, you can add the vspace and hspace attributes to the <img> element and set the values to a pixel amount. In Figure 7-17, 15 pixels of space are specified for both attributes. Vspace affects both the top and bottom sides, while hspace affects both left and right sides. The code looks like this:

```
<img align="left" alt="sailboat" border="0"
hspace="15" vspace="15" src="sail.gif">
```

You also can add white space into the graphic itself using graphic editing software.

Cascading Style Sheets offers more control over image white space. You can apply the margin properties to individual sides of an image. The following code shows an image with a 12-point margin on the right and bottom sides, floating to the left of text:

```
<img alt="sailboat" border="0" style="margin-right: 12pt;
margin-bottom: 12pt; float: left" src="sail.gif">
```

Using Single-Pixel Rules

Single-pixel lines or rules are single-color GIFs that are very tiny—1px by 1px in size. You can change a single-pixel rule to any size by using the width and height attributes, yielding reusable horizontal or vertical lines of varying thickness that you can use to enhance your Web page's layout. A variety of these single-pixel rules are available for your use on the *Principles of Web Design* Companion Web site. Figure 7-18 shows the same single-pixel black graphic stretched to different shapes and sizes by changes in the width and height attributes in the <img> element.

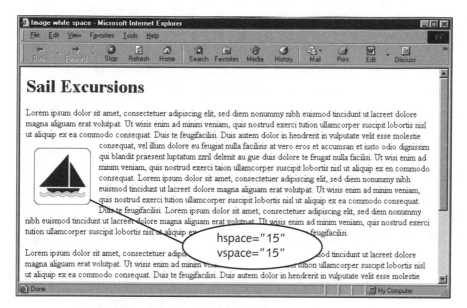

Figure 7-17   Adding white space around an image

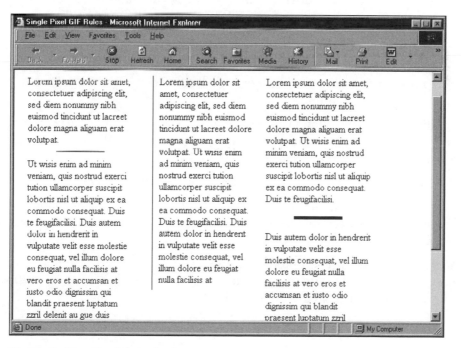

Figure 7-18   Single-pixel rules

7

Here is the code for the three rules. Notice that each src attribute references the same graphic:

Column One:

```
<img src="blackpix.gif" width="80" height="1" vspace="10">
```

Column Two:

```
<img src="blackpix.gif" width="1" height="350" align=
"left" hspace="10">
```

Column Three:

```
<img src="blackpix.gif" width="80" height="5">
```

Using Background Images

You can use the background attribute to the <body> element to tile images across the background of a Web page. Any image can be used as a background graphic, though many are not appropriate for the task. In too many Web sites, complicated background graphics distract the user. If your site includes a lot of text, avoid dark or complex backgrounds. Most text does not read well against a background image unless the image is light enough to provide a good contrast for the text, as illustrated in Figure 7-19. Instead of using a dark, busy image to tile a page background, choose a light, simple image. The Web provides many images that you can use to create seamless backgrounds that do not interfere with your text. Use background images creatively to provide an identifying theme for your site, to frame your content at different screen resolutions, or to provide a light, textured background.

Cascading Style Sheets allows you more control over background image tiling than standard HTML. To apply a background image, use the <body> element as the selector with the background property as follows:

```
body {background: url(images\texture4.jpg);}
```

Note the URL syntax in the rule. The path and filename are contained in parentheses. The default for CSS background graphics is the same as using the background attribute: the image tiles indefinitely across the page.

The CSS background-repeat property allows you to create a single column or row of the image, rather than tiling the image completely across the page. Figure 7-20 shows the background image repeated on the y-axis.

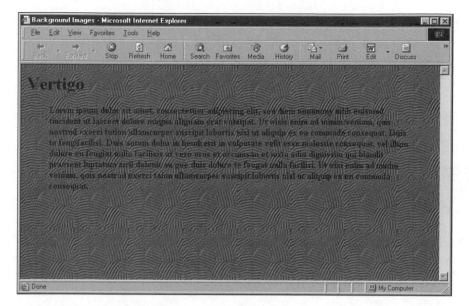

Figure 7-19   Avoid complicated backgrounds for text-oriented pages

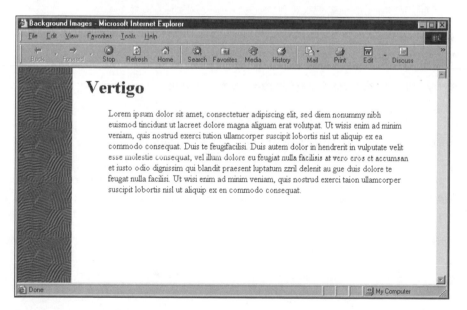

Figure 7-20   Background graphic repeated on y-axis

Here is the rule for repeating the graphic on the y-axis:

```
body {background: url(texture4.jpg);
background-repeat: repeat-y;}
```

You also can tile across the x-axis, as shown in Figure 7-21.

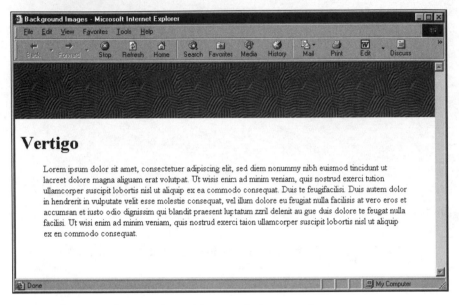

Figure 7-21   Background graphic repeated on x-axis

Here is the rule for repeating the graphic on the x-axis:

```
body {background: url(texture4.jpg);
background-repeat: repeat-x;}
```

You also can use the background-position property to change the position of the background graphic. For example, you can create a right-aligned repeat on the y-axis, as shown in Figure 7-22.

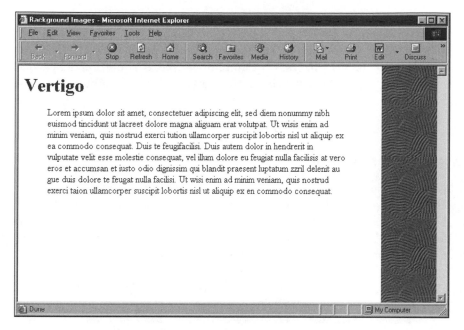

Figure 7-22   Background graphic right-aligned on y-axis

Here is the rule for right-aligning the background:

```
body {background: url(texture4.jpg); background-
repeat: repeat-y; background-position: right;}
```

WORKING WITH HEXADECIMAL COLORS

HTML uses hexadecimal numbers to express RGB color values. Hexadecimal numbers are a base-16 numbering system, so the numbers run from 0 through 9 and then A through F. When compared with a standard base-10 numbering system, hexadecimal looks strange because it includes letters in the numbering scheme. Do not let hexadecimal numbers put you off; all you need is a cross-reference, or better yet, a Web page that lists all the colors. The *Principles of Web Design* Companion Web site has an online color chart. Some HTML reference books have a printed color chart of hexadecimal colors, but in general, you always should use an online color resource for checking color values because you will get a much more realistic view of the actual color.

Browser-safe hexadecimal colors are always made up of the following two-digit color values: 00, 33, 66, 99, CC, and FF. Therefore, 0066FF is a browser-safe color, but 0F66FF is not.

Hexadecimal color values are six-digit numbers; the first two define the red value, the second two define the green, and the third two define the blue. You can use these values in a variety of elements with either the bgcolor attribute or the color attribute to define color in your Web pages. Cascading Style Sheets also accepts hexadecimal color values. Hexadecimal values should always be contained in quotes and preceded by a number sign as shown:

```
<body bgcolor="#ffffff">
```

Universal Color Names

Although you can use color names for many hexadecimal colors, some browsers do not support them; when in doubt, you are better off using hexadecimal values. The 16 basic color names shown in Table 7-5, however, are recognized by most browsers and stated in the W3C HTML 4.01 specification. As you can see from the hexadecimal codes, not all of these colors are browser-safe, so make sure to test your work.

Table 7-5 Color names recognized by most browsers (highlighted colors are browser-safe)

Color Name	Hex	Color Name	Hex
Aqua	00FFFF	Navy	000080
Black	000000	Olive	808000
Blue	0000FF	Purple	800080
Fuchsia	FF00FF	Red	FF0000
Gray	808080	Silver	C0C0C0
Green	008000	Teal	008080
Lime	00FF00	White	FFFFFF
Maroon	800000	Yellow	FFFF00

As described earlier in this chapter, make sure that your hexadecimal colors are browser-safe. There are many shareware tools and Web sites that can help you with hexadecimal colors. For example, Clear Ink's Palette Man Web site at *www.paletteman.com* offers an interactive color chooser.

To use these universal color names, state the color in the attribute value, as in the example below:

```
<body bgcolor="yellow">
```

Setting Background Page Color

One of the simplest ways to work with hexadecimal color is to specify a background color for your pages. Use the bgcolor attribute in the <body> element or, with

Cascading Style Sheets, use the background-color property with body as the selector. The following code examples show the background color set to white.

Standard HTML:

```
<body bgcolor="#ffffff">
```

Cascading Style Sheets:

```
body {background-color: #ffffff}
```

Remember to use a color that will provide a good contrast for reading your text.

Using Background Color in Tables

You can use background color in tables for different purposes, all by using the bgcolor attribute. The table <table>, table row <tr>, table header <th>, and table data <td> elements all accept the bgcolor attribute. Following are a few examples.

Setting Table Background Color

You can easily set a background color for an entire table by adding the bgcolor attribute to the beginning <table> tag. Figure 7-23 shows an example. 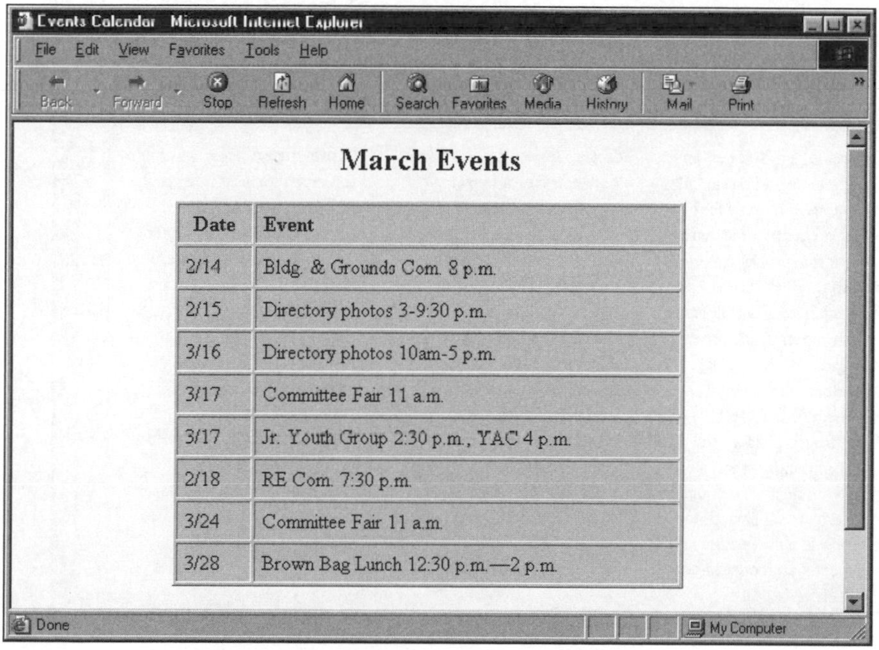

Figure 7-23   Table background color

The <table> element code for the table in Figure 7-23 follows. The bgcolor attribute sets the color.

```
<table cellpadding="5" border bgcolor="#33ffff"
width="400">
```

You can work with the following three layers when designing your pages:
1. The foreground layer contains your content (text and images).
2. The middle layer displays the image specified in the background attribute. The specified image tiles repeatedly. With Cascading Style Sheets you have more control over the tiling of the image.
3. The background layer displays the bgcolor value.

Creating Reverse Text

By using the bgcolor attribute to set the background color, you can create reverse text in table cells. Figure 7-24 shows the first row in the table with the bgcolor attribute set to red, blue, and green, respectively in each cell, and the text color set to white.

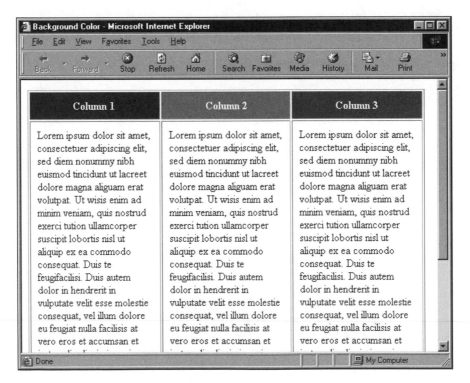

Figure 7-24   Table cell reverse

In this example the <font> element is setting the text color, but a CSS rule would accomplish the same result. The code for the Column 1 cell looks like this:

```
<th bgcolor="#0000ff"><font color="#ffffff">column 1
</font></th>
```

Changing Link Colors

You can change your hypertext link colors using hexadecimal values or standard color names. The following three attributes all reside within the <body> element. These attributes are deprecated in favor of CSS but are still commonly used.

- *link*—The unvisited link color. The default is blue.

- *alink*—The active link color. This is the color that displays when the user points to a link and holds down the mouse button. The default is red.

- *vlink*—The visited link color. The default is purple.

Here is an example of the syntax:

```
<body link="cc3399" vlink="9900ff">
```

Now that you have the capability of changing link colors, do not rush out and change all your links to different colors until you think about the consequences for your users. They probably are expecting the default blue and purple links. However, many sites do change their links to match their design color scheme. Changing link colors is acceptable as long as you maintain color consistency and preserve the contrast between the new and visited link colors to provide a recognizable difference to the user.

7

WORKING WITH IMAGES AND COLOR

In this set of steps you will add an image and hexadecimal color information to a Web page.

To add the image to the Web page:

1. Copy the **sail.htm** file and the **sail.gif** file from the Chapter07 folder on your Data Disk.

2. Save the files to your work folder using the same filenames.

3. Start Notepad or another text editor and open the file **sail.htm**.

4. Add an <img> element to the page immediately after the opening <p> tag, as shown in the following code, where the <img> element is shaded:

```
<html>
<head>
<title>Sailing</title>
</head>
```

```
<body>
<h1>Sail Excursions</h1>
<p><img src="sail.gif">Lorem ipsum dolor sit amet,
consectetuer adipiscing elit, sed diem nonummy nibh
euis mod tincidunt ut lacreet dolore magna aliguam erat
volutpat. Ut wisis enim ad minim veniam, quis nostrud
exerci tution ullamcorper suscipit lobortis nisl ut
aliquip ex eacommodo consequat. Duis te feugifacilisi.
Duis autem dolor inhendrerit in vulputate velit esse
molestie consequat,vel illum dolore eu feugiat nulla
facilisis at vero eros et accumsan et iusto odio
dignissim qui blandit praesent luptatum zzril delenit au
gue duis dolore te feugat nulla facilisi. Ut wisi enim ad
minim veniam, quis nostrud exerci taion ullamcorper
suscipit lobortis nisl ut aliquipex en commodo
consequat. Lorem ipsum dolor sit ame,consectetuer
adipiscing elit, sed diem nonummy nibh euismod tincidunt
ut lacreet dolore magna aliguam erat volutpat. Ut wisis
enim ad minim veniam, quis nostrud exerci tution
ullamcorper suscipit lobortis nisl ut aliquip ex
eacommodo consequat.</p>
</body>
</html>
```

5. Save the file and view it in the browser. It should look like Figure 7-25.

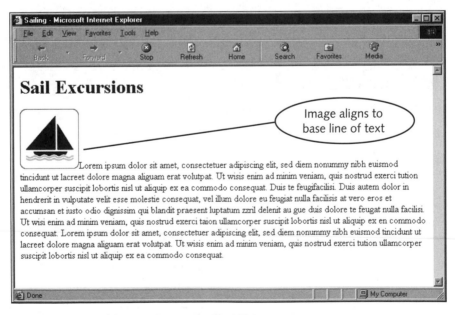

Figure 7-25   Adding an image to the Web page

6. Add attributes to the image to provide size and alternate text information. The image width and height are both 100 pixels. The alt and title attributes can contain any text you choose to describe the image, such as "sailboat image." The following code fragment shows the attribute additions.

```
<img src="sail.gif" width="100" height="100"
alt="sailboat image" title="sailboat image">
```

7. Wrap the text around the image by adding a CSS style rule to the image. Use the style attribute with the float property set to "left" as shown in the following code fragment:

```
<img src="sail.gif" width="100" height="100" alt=
"sailboat image" title="sailboat image" style=
"float: left;">
```

8. Save the file and view it in the browser. When you view the file it looks like Figure 7-26.

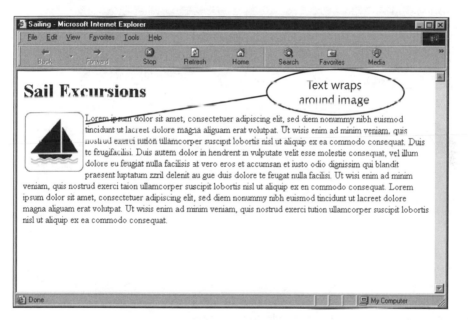

Figure 7-26   Floating the image to the left of text

9. Adjust the right margin of the image by adding a margin-right property to the style attribute. Set the measurement value to 20px as shown in the following code:

```
<img src="sail.gif" width="100" height="100" alt=
"sailboat image" title="sailboat image" style="float:
left; margin-right: 20px;">
```

10. Save the file and view it in the browser. It should look like Figure 7-27.

11. Add a style attribute to the <h1> element to change the color to a deep blue. The hexadecimal code is #0000ff. The following code fragment shows the <h1> element with the style attribute.

```
<h1 style="color: #0000ff">Sail Excursions</h1>
```

12. Finish the page by setting the background color to a light blue. Add a style attribute to the body element and set the background color to light blue, hexadecimal value #ccffff as shown in the following code fragment:

```
<body style="background-color: #ccffff;">
```

13. Save the file and close the editor. Then view the finished page in the browser. It should look like Figure 7-28, with a deep blue heading and light blue page background. The complete code for the page follows.

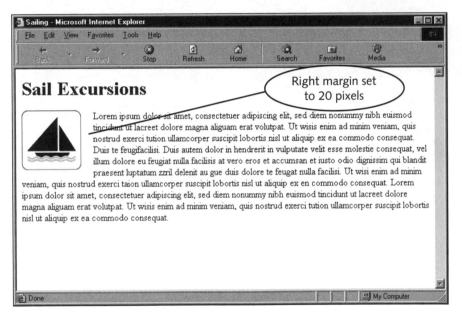

Figure 7-27   Adding a right margin to the image

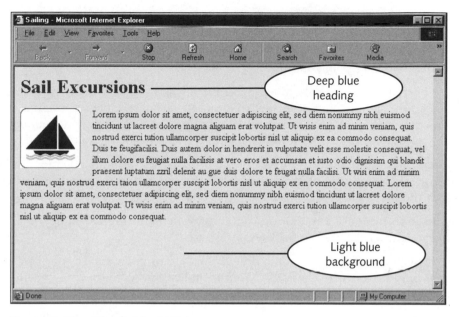

Figure 7-28   The finished Web page

```
<html>
<head>
<title>Sailing</title>
</head>
<body style="background-color: #ccffff;">
<h1 style="color: #0000ff">Sail Excursions</h1>
<p><img src="sail.gif" width="100" height="100" alt="sail
boat image" title="sailboat image" style="float:left;
margin right: 20px">Lorem ipsum dolor sit amet,
consectetuer adipiscing elit, sed diem nonummy nibh
euismod tincidunt ut lacreet dolore magna aliguam erat
volutpat. Ut wisis enim ad minim veniam, quis nostrud
exerci tutionullamcorper suscipit lobortis nisl ut
aliquip ex ea commodo consequat. Duis te feugifacilisi.
Duis autem dolor in hendrerit in vulputate velit esse
molestie consequat, vel illum dolore eu feugiat nulla
facilisis atvero eros et accumsan et iusto odio dignissim
qui blandit praesent luptatum zzril delenit au gue duis
dolore te feugat nulla facilisi. Ut wisi enim ad minim
veniam, quis nostrud exerci taion ullamcorper suscipit
lobortis nisl ut aliquip ex en commodo consequat. Lorem
ipsum dolor sitamet, consectetuer adipiscing elit, sed
diem nonummy nibh euismod tincidunt ut lacreet dolore
magna aliguam erat volutpat. Ut wisis enim ad minim
veniam, quis nostrud exerci tutionullamcorper suscipit
lobortis nisl ut aliquip ex ea commodo consequat.
</p>
</body>
</html>
```

CHAPTER SUMMARY

To create an engaging, accessible, and informative Web site, you must use graphics wisely. Keep the following points in mind:

❑ You currently can use only three image file formats on the Web: GIF, JPG, and PNG. These formats all compress images to create smaller files. Unless you choose the appropriate file format, your image will not compress and appear as you expect. SVG is a new file format from the W3C that offers vector-based graphics for the Web.

❑ Your computer monitor displays color by mixing the three basic colors of light: red, green, and blue. Colors vary widely from one monitor to another, based on both the user's preferences and the exact brand of equipment.

❑ Most monitors have a resolution of 72 dpi. When creating, scanning, or importing images, always change the final resolution to 72 dpi.

❑ Most Web designers use graphic design software to resize images or convert them from one file format to another. More complex tasks could include changing color depth or adding transparency to an image.

❑ Use the <img> element to display images in a browser. It is a replaced element, meaning that the browser replaces the <img> element with the image file referenced in the src attribute. The browser treats the image as a character; normal image alignment is to the baseline of the text. Images that are within a line of text must have spaces on both sides or the text will touch the image.

❑ Reduce image size to the appropriate dimensions for a Web page. If you must use a larger image, let the user view a thumbnail first, and provide the file size information.

❑ Work with a limited Web-safe palette when creating graphics.

❑ HTML uses hexadecimal numbers to express RGB color values. Hexadecimal color values are six-digit numbers; the first two define the red value, the second two define the green value, and the third two define the blue value. You can use these values in a variety of elements with either the bgcolor attribute or the color attribute to define color in your Web pages. Cascading Style Sheets also accepts hexadecimal color values.

❑ Test your work on different browsers and computing platforms, as they render colors differently. Test at different color depths as well.

REVIEW QUESTIONS

1. What are the three image file formats you can use on a Web site?

2. Which file formats support 24-bit color?

3. Explain a file's color depth control.

4. How many colors does GIF support?

5. What is lossless file compression?

6. Which file formats support transparency?

7. What are the drawbacks of using animated GIFs?

8. Explain lossy image compression.

9. What image characteristics can you control using the JPG format?

10. What are the display characteristics of an interlaced image?

11. What are some options for acquiring images for your site?

12. Which image format should you use for a two-color company logo?

13. Which image format should you use for a photograph?

14. Which image format should you use for text with a gradient drop-shadow?

15. What happens when you display a 24-bit image on an 8-bit monitor?

16. What three attributes should you always include in the image tag? Why?

17. What is the attribute and value for removing the hypertext border from an image?

18. How many layers can you work with when designing pages?

19. Which table elements accept the bgcolor attribute?

HANDS-ON PROJECTS

1. Practice using the align image attribute:

   a. Download an image from the *Principles of Web Design* Companion Web site or find an image of your own.

   b. Add text around the image. Experiment with the align attribute and its values to view the way text wraps.

   c. Test the work in multiple browsers to verify that the text wraps consistently.

2. Practice using the spacing image attributes:

   a. Download an image from the *Principles of Web Design* Companion Web site or find an image of your own.

   b. Add text around the image. Experiment with the hspace and vspace attributes to add white space around the image.

   c. Test the work in multiple browsers to verify that the text spacing is consistent.

3. Practice using width and height image attributes:

   a. Download an image from the *Principles of Web Design* Companion Web site or find an image of your own.

   b. Build a simple page that contains text and multiple images. Do not include the width and height attributes in the <img> tag.

   c. With the images turned off in your browser, view the page.

   d. Add the appropriate width and height information to the <img> tag for each image.

e. Again, turn the images off in your browser and view the page. Note the differences between the two results and the way your layout is affected.

4. Download the transparent spacer GIF from the *Principles of Web Design* Companion Web site (transpix.gif).

a. Build a simple layout.

b. Test the capabilities of the transparent spacer GIF. Change the width and height attributes to manipulate the size of the image and its spacing on the page.

5. Download one of the single-color pixel graphics from the *Principles of Web Design* Companion Web site (bluepix.gif, redpix.gif, blackpix.gif, graypix.gif).

a. Build a simple layout.

b. Test the capabilities of the single-pixel GIFs. Change the width and height attributes to manipulate the size of the images and their use on the page.

6. Experiment with background color in tables. Use the bgcolor attribute at different levels of a sample table to add color. Test the result in both Internet Explorer and Netscape Navigator. Note the differences and similarities in the ways that the browsers handle table color.

7. Browse the Web for sites that make effective use of background images. Choose a Web site and write a short design description of how the background images enhance the site.

8. Browse the Web for sites that make effective use of color. Pick a site that has a definite color scheme and write a short design critique that explains how the use of color enhances the site.

CASE PROJECT

Gather or create the boilerplate graphics to use on the different pages of your site. These include any banner, navigation, section, or identifying graphics. Add these graphics to the test pages of your site. Test the images in multiple browsers to make sure they display properly.

Determine the color choices for your Web site. Pick the colors you will use for text, background color in tables, and page backgrounds. If you will be using single-color graphics, such as lines or bullets, create them now.

Establish graphics standards for your Web site, including but not limited to the following:

❑ Decide whether you will use a standard amount of white space around each graphic.

❑ Determine exactly which img attributes should be included in all <img> tags.

❑ Formulate a standard for all alt and title attributes.

❑ Formulate a lowest-common-denominator set of image standards for your site. This will be used as the display standard for testing your graphics.

Write a short standards document that can be provided to anyone contributing to the site.

8

HTML FRAMES

When you complete this chapter, you will be able to:

♦ Understand frames

♦ Understand frame syntax

♦ Use targeting in framesets

♦ Plan frame content

The HTML frame elements let you partition the canvas area of the browser into multiple windows called **frames**. Each frame can display a separate, independent HTML document. The use of frames has become a subject of controversy on the Web because in many cases, framed Web sites are poorly designed. They detract from the user's experience with long download times and confusing navigation. The judicious use of frames, however, can enhance your Web site, allowing consistent simultaneous display of navigation information and content. Frames can be the right solution for specific information problems or for organizing large quantities of content. This chapter explains how to work with frames to display your information effectively.

UNDERSTANDING FRAMES

HTML frames were introduced by Netscape for the 2.0 release of its browser. Frames now are supported in a wide variety of browsers. Controversial since their inception, frames can polarize Web designers, some lauding the benefits, others characterizing frames as unnecessary. As you will see, frames can work well if you use them correctly. Far too many Web sites use frames just because they are available, with no real benefit to the user.

Frames allow you to divide the browser window into independent windows, each displaying a separate HTML document. Figure 8-1 shows an example of a framed set of pages that contains three independent frames.

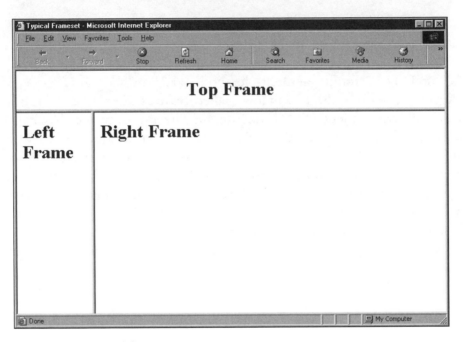

Figure 8-1   Typical frameset

Each of these frames displays a separate HTML file. To create this frameset, you would first create the individual HTML files, and then create the HTML file containing the frame code that holds the three documents together.

Frame Benefits

Frames offer a number of benefits, including allowing users to scroll independently in one frame without affecting the contents of an adjoining frame. This is an ideal way to present large collections of information that are hard to navigate using the traditional single-page browser display. For example, Figure 8-2 shows a frameset that displays a table of contents in one frame, search tools in another, and content in a third.

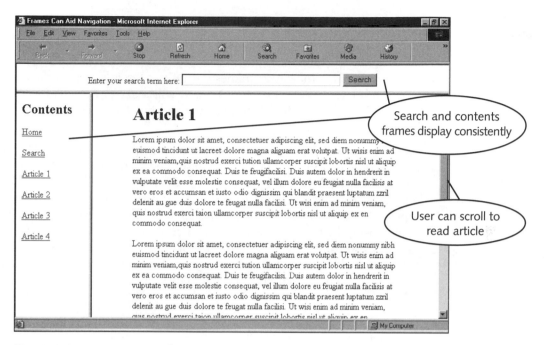

Figure 8-2 Frames can aid navigation

Because the frames can be scrolled independently, the table of contents and search tool are always visible to the user. This may be exactly the type of additional function you need to solve an information design problem.

Frames work best when you keep them simple. Two or three frames per frameset should be enough to accommodate your information needs. More frames will clutter the screen, making it difficult for your reader to find information.

Frame Drawbacks

Frames present a variety of drawbacks that you need to consider before organizing your content with frames.

- *Bookmarks*—Although the newer browsers solve this problem, many browsers do not let the user bookmark individual pages from a Web site. Because the pages are all referenced from a single HTML frames file, the user cannot return to an exact page within a site, only to the main framed page.

- *Download overhead*—Because the browser is loading more than one document, the initial download time can be higher for a framed set of documents than for a single HTML document.

- *Confusing navigation*—Users can become confused if you build complicated framed document sets without enough navigation choices to let users jump to the page of their choice. The Back button in the browser only lets the user load the previous page displayed within the frame, which may not be what the user expects.

- *Visual confusion*—Too many frames within the browser window (each with its own scroll bar) can confuse the user and will make poor use of the available screen. Limit the number of frames to avoid breaking the browser window into too many sections.

- *Frames and search engines*—Frameset code contains no actual content; the content is contained in the HTML files displayed in the frames. Because search engines that read the content of a page for indexing will find no information on a framed page, it is a good idea to avoid using a framed document as the top-level page for your Web site. Instead, provide a standard HTML page as your top-level page and use the framed content at a lower level of the Web site. You also can use the <noframes> element (described later in this chapter) to provide content for search engines. For more tips on working with framed pages and search engines, see "Working with Search Engines" in the "Publishing and Maintaining Your Web Site" chapter.

- *User preferences*—Users can force their browsers to display a page outside of your frameset. Make sure that your pages can stand alone if for some reason a user chooses to display a page on its own. You may want to add a simple text-based navigation bar on each page that is not viewable within the framed document, but can be used to navigate your Web site if a user breaks out of the frameset. You also may want to give the user a choice to navigate your Web site either with or without frames by adding links on the main page to framed and unframed versions of your Web site.

FRAME SYNTAX

HTML frameset documents contain the code that assembles the frames and their contents. Frameset documents themselves have no actual content; therefore they have no <body> element.

The <frameset> Element

The <frameset> element is the container for the frameset code. The cols and rows attributes let you specify the characteristics of the frameset. You can specify a frameset as either cols or rows, but not both. The width (specific to columns) and height (specific to rows) can be expressed as either a percentage value or pixel count in the cols and rows attributes. As with tables, percentage widths build frames relative to the browser window size.

Absolute pixel widths are fixed regardless of the browser size. The following code is an example of a simple frameset document that divides the browser canvas into two rows:

```
<html>
<head>
<title>Frame Rows</title>
</head>
<frameset rows="20%,80%">
<frame src="top.htm">
<frame src="bottom.htm">
</frameset>
</html>
```

Figure 8-3 shows the result of this code.

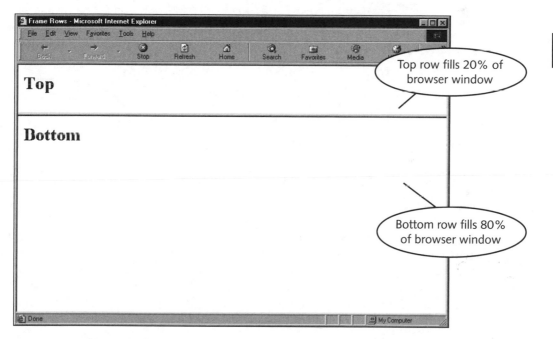

Figure 8-3   Two-row frameset

The <frame> Element

Re-examine the code for Figure 8-3. The <frame> element determines the contents of each frame. Row framesets fill top to bottom. The first <frame> element points to the file to display in the top row, and the second <frame> element points to the file for the bottom row.

The <frame> element is empty. The src attribute provides the location of the file that displays within the frame. Other attributes to the <frame> tag let you name the frame for targeting, decide whether frames have a scroll bar, and specify whether the user can resize the frame. These attributes are described later in this chapter.

In Figure 8-4, the frameset is divided into two column frames.

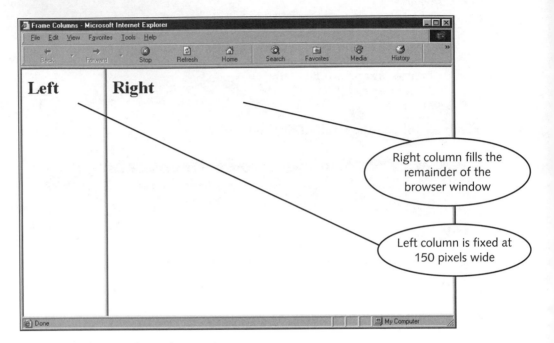

Figure 8-4   Two-column frameset

In this frameset the left column is 150 pixels wide; the right column defaults to the remainder of the browser window size. In the following code, note the syntax in the opening <frameset> tag. The cols attribute determines the width of the columns. The first value sets the left column to 150 pixels. The asterisk (*) character tells the browser to fill the right column to the remainder of the browser window.

```
<html>
<head>
<title>Frame Columns</title>
</head>
<frameset cols="150,*">
<frame src="left.htm">
<frame src="right.htm">
</frameset>
</html>
```

Because the left column is set to a fixed width, it will remain unchanged regardless of the user's browser size or screen resolution. Also note that in column framesets, the frames fill left to right. The first <frame> element fills the left column and the second fills the right column.

 Even though most browsers can display frames, it still is a good idea to add <noframes> content to help search engines index your framed content. When encountering a framed set of pages, some search engines look for the <noframes> element for content information.

The <noframes> Tag

The <noframes> tag lets you provide an alternate page for users who do not have a frames-compliant browser. You can enclose the contents of a standard Web page, contained in a set of <body> tags, within the <noframes> element. This alternate page code follows the frameset code in the HTML file:

```
<html>
<head>
<title>Frames</title>
</head>
<frameset cols="75%, 25%">
    <frame name="index" src="index.htm">
    <frame name="title" src="title.htm">
<noframes>
<body>
(alternate page HTML code)
</body>
</noframes>
</frameset>
</html>
```

8

Nesting Frames

Figure 8-5 shows a rows frameset that contains a nested columns frameset in the second row.

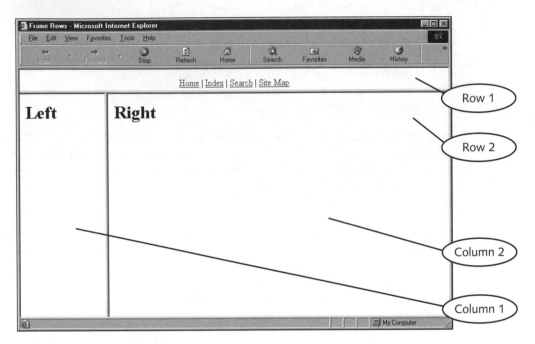

Figure 8-5   Nested frameset

Nesting allows you to break the screen into both row and column frames. The following code shows the nesting of the framesets:

```
<html>
<head>
<title>Frame Rows</title>
</head>
<frameset rows="40,*">
<frame src="topnav.htm"> <! this is row 1 >
<frameset cols="20%,80%"> <! the nested frameset fills the
  2nd row >
<frame src="left.htm"> <! this is column 1 >
<frame src="right.htm"> <! this is column 2 >
</frameset>
</frameset>
</html>
```

Notice in the previous code that two closing </frameset> tags are necessary to close both framesets.

Restricting Resizing

By default, the user has the option of resizing your frames by clicking and dragging the frame border. In most situations you probably want to restrict resizing so the user sees the frameset in the way you intended. Figure 8-6 shows a frameset that the user has resized by clicking and dragging the frame border.

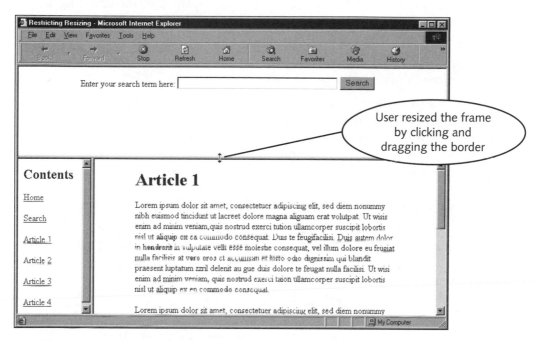

Figure 8-6   Default allows the user to resize the frame

Under most circumstances, you probably want to restrict the user's ability to resize your frames. To restrict resizing, add the noresize attribute to the <src> elements in your frameset, as shown in the following code:

```
<html>
<head>
<title>Restricting Resizing</title>
</head>
<frameset rows="50,*">
<frame src="search.htm" noresize>
    <frameset cols="135,*">
    <frame src="contents.htm" noresize>
    <frame src="article1.htm" noresize>
    </frameset>
</frameset>
</html>
```

Controlling Scroll Bars

By default, scroll bars in frames are set to appear automatically if the content is not accessible within the frame window. In most cases this is the best setting for scroll bars, because you will not need to worry about them. No matter the user's browser size or screen resolution, if scroll bars are necessary they will appear. Sometimes, however, you may want to control whether scroll bars display. Use the scrolling attribute in the <frame> element to control scroll bars. The valid values are "yes," "no," or "auto," which is the default setting.

Figure 8-7 shows a three-frame frameset. Notice that the top frame displays a scroll bar even though no additional content follows the search text box.

The browser displays a scroll bar, because the height of the top frame is slightly smaller than the browser finds necessary to display the contents. One way to solve this problem is to change the height of the frame. Because this frame looks good at this height, however, you can remove the scroll bar by adding the scrolling="no" attribute to the <frame> element. Figure 8-8 shows the result of the attribute addition.

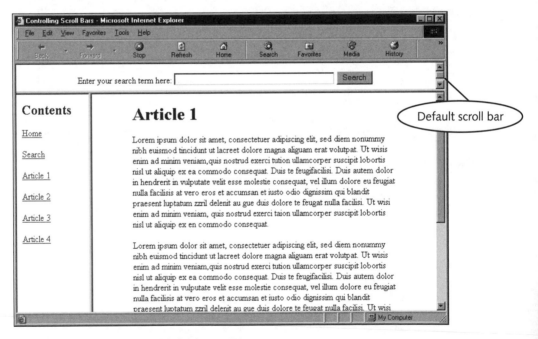

Figure 8-7   Unnecessary default scroll bar

Figure 8-8 Frame with no scroll bar

The scroll bar is no longer displayed, which enhances the look of the frameset. Also, because a scroll bar indicates additional information, omitting the scroll bar reflects the content of this page more accurately. The code for the complete frameset follows:

```
<html>
<head>
<title>Controlling Scroll Bars</title>
</head>
<frameset rows="50,*">
<frame src="search.htm" scrolling="no">
<frameset cols="135,*">
<frame src="contents.htm">
<frame src="article1.htm">
</frameset>
</frameset>
</html>
```

Controlling Frame Borders

As with tables, you can choose not to display frame borders, or to remove the default border spacing between frames entirely. This technique lets you create seamless frames with no visible dividing line, unless a scroll bar pops up. Figure 8-9 shows an example of a two-frame frameset with the frame borders turned off.

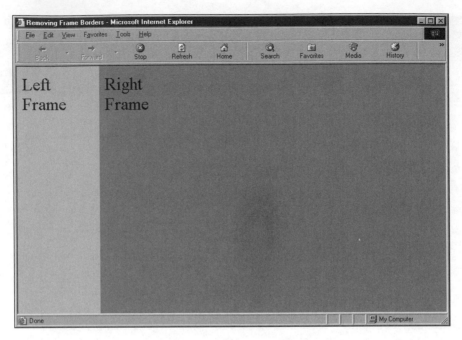

Figure 8-9   Frame borders turned off

To make sure that the frame border and spacing are turned off for both Netscape Navigator and Internet Explorer, set the border attribute to "0", as shown in the code for the previous frameset:

```
<html>
<head>
<title>Removing Frame Borders</title>
</head>
<frameset cols="150,*" border="0">
<frame src="leftgray.htm">
<frame src="rightgray.htm" name="content">
</frameset>
</html>
```

Older browsers are not consistent regarding the attributes to be used to turn off frame borders. Netscape Navigator 4.0 requires frameborder="no" and border="0" attributes. Internet Explorer 5.0 can correctly interpret frameborder="no", but you need to set framespacing="0" to remove the default border spacing between frames. All of these attributes reside in the opening <frameset> tag. If you have trouble with frame borders, test these attributes in your code.

Controlling Frame Margins

Two frame attributes let you control the pixel width of both the vertical and horizontal margins in a frame. The marginwidth attribute lets you control the left and right margins, while marginheight affects the top and bottom margins. Setting these attributes to zero (0) removes the margins entirely, allowing your content to touch the sides of the frame. You most likely would use these attributes in combination with the frame border attributes described in the previous section.

Add the marginheight and marginwidth attributes to the <frame> element for the frame you want to affect. Figure 8-10 shows a frameset with two different margin settings.

The left frame has both margin attributes set to zero (0). Even so, the top margin still includes some space, due to built-in leading in the line of text. The left margin, however, has been completely removed. In the right column both margins have been set to 30 pixels.

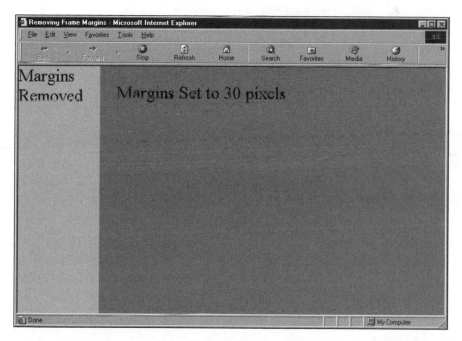

Figure 8-10   Frame borders and margins removed

TARGETING IN FRAMESETS

The power of frames comes from the ability to display information consistently in one frame while the contents of a second frame might change based on the user's choice. By default, a link loads into the same frame in which it was selected. You can change this default behavior and target the destination of a link to another frame in the frameset. In this section you will learn how to target within a simple frameset, as shown in Figure 8-11.

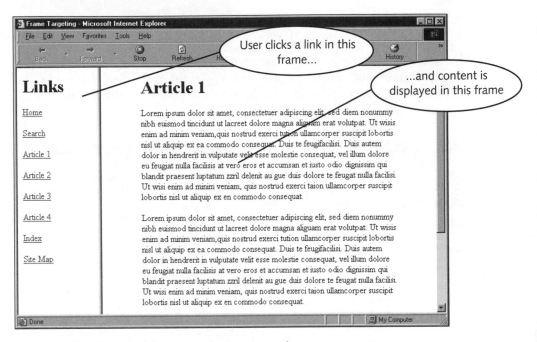

Figure 8-11   Targeting from one frame to another

To target from one frame to another, you must perform two tasks:

1. Name your frames using the name attribute in the <frame> element.

2. Target links to display their content in the named frame.

Naming Frames

To name a frame, add the name attribute to the <frame> element. You do not have to name all of the frames within a frameset, only the frames you want to target. Figure 8-12 shows a frameset with two frames. The right frame is named "main".

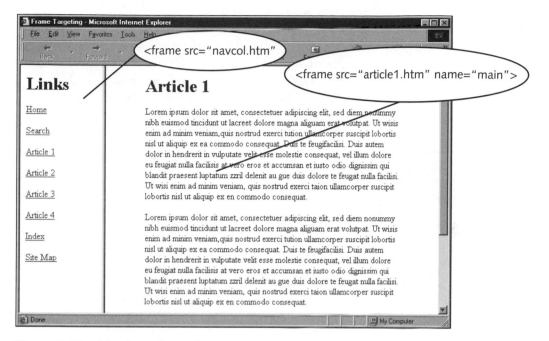

Figure 8-12 Naming a frame for targeting

Here is the HTML code for the frameset illustrated in Figure 8-12:

```
<html>
<head>
<title>Frame Targeting</title>
</head>
<frameset cols="150,*">
<frame src="navcol.htm">
<frame src="article1.htm" name="main">
</frameset>
</html>
```

The name attribute in the second <frame> element names the right frame window "main." You now can target this window to display linked content.

Targeting Named Frames

To target the named frame, you must edit the HTML document that contains the <a> elements and provide target attributes that tell the browser which frame displays the content. You can use the target attribute in either the <base> or <a> elements.

Targeting in the <base> Element

In this example, the HTML document that occupies the left frame window is named "navcol.htm." Adding the <base> element lets you set the default target frame for all of the links in the document. The <base> tag is empty and resides in the <head> section of the document. The code in navcol.htm shows the <base> element.

```
<html>
<head>
<title>Frame Links</title>
<base target="main">
</head>
<body>
<h1>Links</h1>
<p><a href="index.htm">Home</a></p>
<p><a href="search.htm">Search</a></p>
<p><a href="article1.htm">Article 1</a></p>
<p><a href="article2.htm">Article 2</a></p>
<p><a href="article3.htm">Article 3</a></p>
<p><a href="article4.htm">Article 4</a></p>
<p><a href="contindx.htm">Index</a></p>
<p><a href="sitemap.htm">Site Map</a></p>
</body>
</html>
```

Notice that the <base> element contains the target attribute set to "main." This establishes the default window target name for all of the links contained in the file. Any link that the user selects will display in the frame window named "main."

Targeting in the <a> Element

You can override a default base target by using the target attribute in the <a> element. This allows you to target a specific link to a destination different from the base target. You can target a different window within the frameset or use one of the special targeting values in the next section. The following <a> element targets article1.htm to the frame named "frame2."

```
<a href="article1.htm" target="frame2">Article 1</a>
```

Make sure that you match the case of both the target and name attributes, or the browser will not be able to resolve the target name.

Using Special Target Names

There are four special target names that you can use with the target attribute in either the <base> or <a> elements. Table 8-1 lists the special names.

Table 8-1   Special target names

Name	Description
_self	The default behavior for links in a frameset. The linked content is loaded into the same window as the <a> element. You most likely would use this in the <a> element to override a base target.
_blank	Opens a new browser window to display the linked content. However, this can confuse users, who may not realize that they are looking at a new window.
_parent	Lets you break out of a child frameset and display the link in the parent frameset. This name is only useful when you have a link in a frameset that displays an embedded frameset. In most cases using embedded framesets is poor navigation design that can confuse your user.
_top	The most useful of all the special names, _top lets you remove frames and display the linked content in the same, refreshed browser window.

8

Notice that all of these special names begin with an underscore. Any other target name that begins with an underscore will be ignored by the browser.

Special target names can help you in a variety of situations. For example, you can use them when you link to other sites from within a frameset. Figure 8-13 shows the Harvard University Art Museum site shown within a framed site.

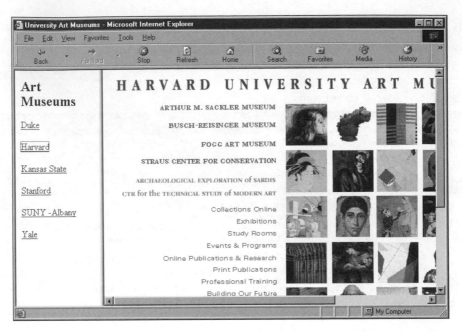

Figure 8-13 Harvard University Art Museum site shown within a framed site

As you can see, loading the Harvard University Art Museum Web site within a frameset does not work well. The size of the frame is too small to display the Web site properly, forcing the user to scroll horizontally to view the entire page. You can solve this problem by using special target names to break out of the frameset. There are two ways to handle this problem:

- Use _blank to load the Web page in a new browser window.
- Use _top to load the Web page to the top of the existing window.

Using _blank

The _blank special target name lets you load the linked content into a new instance of the browser. Figure 8-14 shows the results, with the newly launched browser window overlapping the window that contains the link.

Notice that the Back button is not available in the new browser window, because this is the first page in the new window. Not being able to use Back can be frustrating to users who rely on it for navigation.

Figure 8-14   Using _blank launches a second browser window

Remember that the targeting information is in the file that contains the links, not the frameset file. In this example, the _blank target name resides in the <base> element, setting the default target for all of the links within the file. The following code shows the use of _blank in the left navigation column of Figure 8-14.

```
<html>
<head>
<title>Art Museum Links</title>
<base target="_blank">
</head>
<body>
<h2>Art Museums</h2>
<p><a href="http://www.duke.edu/web/duma/">Duke</a></p>
<p><a href="http://www.artmuseums.harvard.edu/">Harvard</a
></p>
<p><a href="http://www.ksu.edu/bma/">Kansas State</a></p>
<p><a href="http://www.stanford.edu/dept/suma/">Stanford</
a></p>

<p><a href="http://www.albany.edu/museum/">SUNY -
  Albany</a></p>

<p><a href="http://www.yale.edu/yuag/">Yale</a></p>
</body>
</html>
```

This code contains one flaw. Using _blank as the default target name means that every link in this window will launch a new browser window. Before long, the user's computer either will run out of memory or the screen will become cluttered by overlapping windows. For this reason, limit the use of _blank for special purposes, or do not use it at all.

If you decide to use _blank, you can help users by letting them know that clicking the link will open a new browser window.

Using _top

Using _top as a special target name displays the linked content in a non-framed window using the same instance of the browser. Figure 8-15 shows the results.

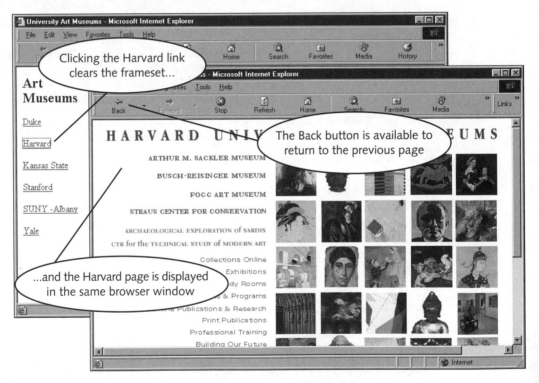

Figure 8-15   Using _top loads content at the top level of the same window

The browser clears the frameset and loads the Harvard page in the same window. The Back button is available if the user wants to return to the previous page. Because the browser maintains only one open window, there is no additional memory overhead or confusion for the user. This effect is hard to reproduce on paper, so use the sample files on the *Principles of Web Design* Companion Web site to see an example.

PLANNING FRAME CONTENT

The variable nature of the World Wide Web affects your framed pages. If you are planning on building a framed site, you must prepare your content for display within a frameset. Frameset display is affected by the base screen resolution you use to code your framed pages. You must decide on the lowest common denominator screen resolution that will display the frameset effectively.

Frames and Screen Resolution

Frame scroll bars and borders add to the screen space requirements of frames. Many Web designers who incorporate frames into sites build them for a base resolution of 800 × 600, forcing users to change their screen resolutions in order to view the content. Even if you decide to code for a higher resolution, you always should test at a 640 × 480 resolution, because some users will view your Web site at this resolution. Also, test your work in different browsers. Small differences between the way browsers display frames can affect their look significantly. Figures 8-16 and 8-17 show the Dan Quayle Vice Presidential Museum Web site (*www.quaylemuseum.org/*) at 800 × 600 and at 640 × 480.

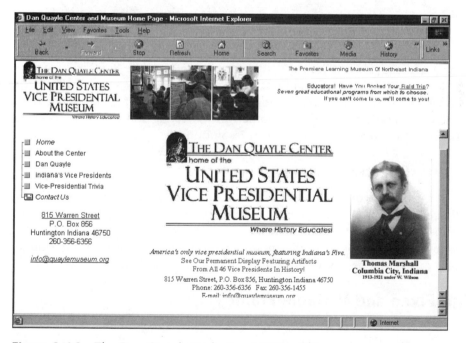

Figure 8-16   The Dan Quayle Web site at 800 × 600

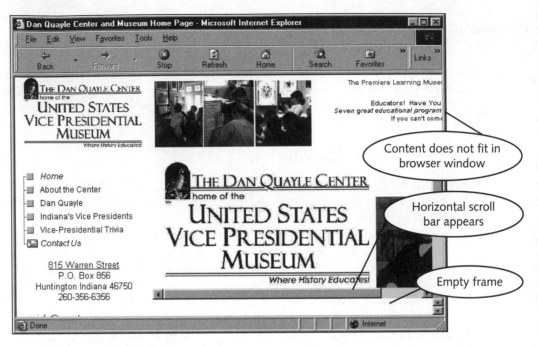

Figure 8-17 The Dan Quayle Web site at 640 × 480

The page design for this Web site is less than perfect at 800 × 600, but if the user views it at 640 × 480 there are additional scroll bars and content that do not fit within the browser window. A blank frame, possibly an error in coding, appears at the bottom of the screen. Clearly this site needs some further testing and tinkering to ensure that the content is viewable at different screen resolutions.

Designing Effective Frames

You must build your pages to fit within the frames in which they will display. You also will need to accommodate different screen resolutions that can affect the size of the frame within the frameset. As with tables, decide whether you will use fixed or relative framesets. You also can choose to mix these two measurement types within a single frameset, which can be the best way to handle multiple screen resolutions.

Mixing Fixed and Variable Frames

Examine the following sample frameset that mixes a fixed frame and a variable frame to accommodate different resolutions.

Here is the code for the sample frameset:

```
<html>
<head>
<title>Designing Frame Content</title>
```

```
</head>
<frameset cols="125,*">
<frame src="leftfxd.htm">
<frame src="article1.htm" name="main">
</frameset>
</html>
```

Notice that the code for the left column is fixed at 125 pixels. The asterisk (*) wildcard character sets the right column to a variable width that changes based on the browser size. Figure 8-18 shows the frameset at 640 × 480 resolution.

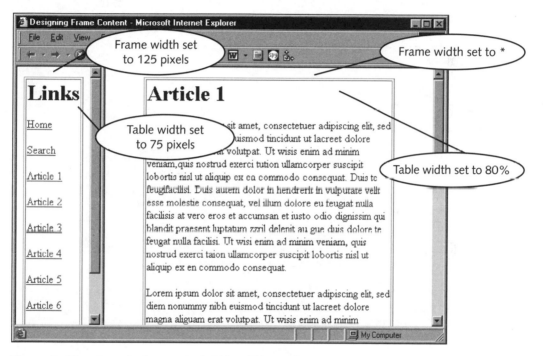

Figure 8-18   Sample frameset at 640 × 480 resolution

Tables in each HTML file keep the content aligned within the frameset. The table borders are turned on so you can see them. The table in the left frame has a fixed width of 75 pixels. The difference between the frame width of 125 and the table width of 75 is taken up by the scroll bar and frame margins. This frame and content will display consistently regardless of the screen resolution. The code for the table in the left frame content, leftfxd.htm, follows:

```
<html>
<head>
<title>Left Fixed Column</title>
<base target="main">
</head>
```

```
<body>
<table width="75" border>
<tr>
<td>
<h1>Links</h1>
<a href="index.htm">Home</a>
<p><a href="search.htm">Search</a></p>
<p><a href="article1.htm">Article 1</a></p>
<p><a href="article2.htm">Article 2</a></p>
<p><a href="article3.htm">Article 3</a></p>
<p><a href="article4.htm">Article 4</a></p>
<p><a href="article5.htm">Article 5</a></p>
<p><a href="article6.htm">Article 6</a></p>
<p><a href="contindx.htm">Index</a></p>
<p><a href="sitemap.htm">Site Map</a></p>
</td>
</tr>
</table>
</body>
</html>
```

The right frame is a variable width; therefore, the content within the right frame is contained in a centered table set to an 80 percent width. The 80 percent width allows for white space on both sides of the text. The code for the right frame content, article1.htm, follows:

```
<html>
<head>
<title>Right Variable Column</title>
</head>
<body>
<div align="center">
<table width="80%" border>
<tr>
<td>
<h1>Article 1</h1>
<p>Lorem ipsum dolor sit amet, consectetuer adipiscing
elit, sed diem nonummy nibh euismod ti . . .(content
abbreviated)</p>
</td>
</tr>
</table>
</div>
</body>
</html>
```

Now look at the same frameset at an 800 × 600 resolution in Figure 8-19.

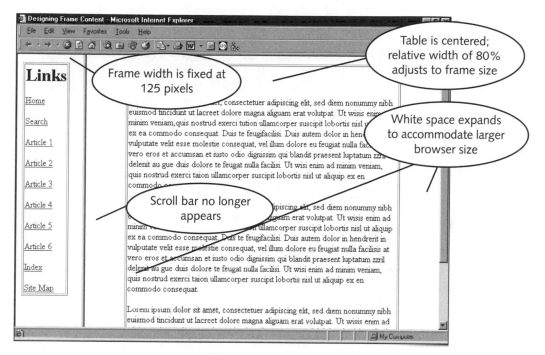

Figure 8-19   Sample frameset at 800 × 600 resolution

The left frame is fixed at 125 pixels. The only difference in the higher resolution is that the scroll bar no longer appears in the left frame. The right column still has centered content with white space on both sides of the text. Because the table in the right frame is variable, it adjusts to the new screen resolution.

If you are building a row frameset, you can use this combined fixed and variable coding method. Set one row to a fixed width and let the second row default to the remainder of the browser canvas, as shown in the following code:

```
<html>
<head>
<title>Fixed/Variable Rows</title>
</head>
<frameset rows="50,*">
<frame src="search.htm" scrolling="no">
<frame src="article1.htm">
</frameset>
</html>
```

This code creates the page shown in Figure 8-20.

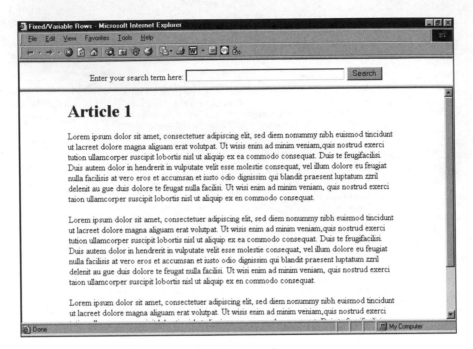

Figure 8-20   Fixed top row, variable second row

The top row is 50 pixels high. The second row fills the browser window regardless of screen resolution.

A final example of the fixed/variable method is a common three-row frameset. In this set the top and bottom rows contain navigation, while the middle row contains content. The top and bottom rows are fixed and the middle row is variable. Here is the code:

```
<html>
<head>
<title>Fixed/Variable Rows</title>
</head>
<frameset rows="50,*,35">
<frame src="search.htm" scrolling="no">
<frame src="article1.htm" name="main">
<frame src="botmnav.htm" scrolling="no">
</frameset>
</html>
```

Figure 8-21 shows this frameset.

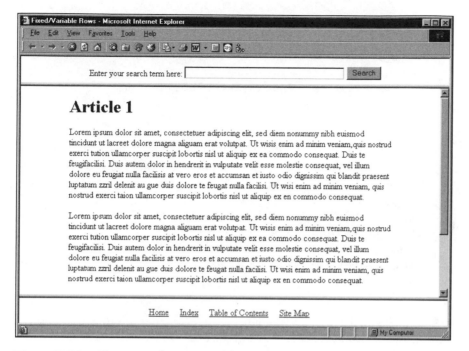

Figure 8-21   Three-row frameset with variable middle row

WORKING WITH FRAMESETS

In this set of steps you will build a frameset that contains links to a small web of pages. The frameset will include a navigation and content frame, with the links targeted from one window to another within the frameset.

To build the frameset:

1. Copy the following files from the Chapter08 folder on your Data Disk:
   - frame.htm
   - hot.htm
   - new.htm
   - navigate.htm
   - info.htm
   - order.htm
   - welcome.htm

2. Save the files to your work folder using the same filenames.

3. Start Notepad or another text editor and open the file **frame.htm**. It contains the following code:

```
<html>
<head>
<title>Frameset Practice</title>
</head>

</html>
```

4. Add the <frameset> element, defining a frameset with two columns. Set the left column to 140 pixels and the right column to 80%, as shown in shaded text in the following code:

```
<html>
<head>
<title>Frameset Practice</title>
</head>
<frameset cols="140, 80%">

</frameset>
</html>
```

5. Add the first <frame> element, with a src attribute that selects the file navigate.htm.

```
<html>
<head>
<title>Frameset Practice</title>
</head>
<frameset cols="140, 80%">
<frame src="navigate.htm">
</frameset>
</html>
```

6. Add the second <frame> element, with a src attribute that selects the file welcome.htm.

```
<html>
<head>
<title>Frameset Practice</title>
</head>
<frameset cols="140, 80%">
<frame src="navigate.htm">
<frame src="welcome.htm">
</frameset>
</html>
```

7. Save the file and view it in the browser. It should look like Figure 8-22.

Figure 8-22 The practice frameset

8. Test the links in the navigation frame. When you click a link, the page loads to the default window rather than the content window, as shown in Figure 8-23.

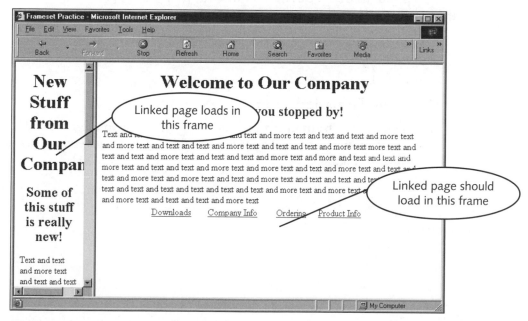

Figure 8-23 Default linking behavior

9. Correct the linking behavior by adding targeting. In the file frame.htm, add names to the frames as shown in the following code, and then save the file.

```
<html>
<head>
<title>Frameset Practice</title>
</head>
<frameset cols="140, 80%">
<frame src="navigate.htm" name="navigate">
<frame src="welcome.htm" name="content">
</frameset>
</html>
```

10. In Notepad or your text editor, open the file **navigate.htm** from your work folder. In the head section of the file add the <base> element with a target attribute that selects the content frame, as shown in the following code:

```
<html>
<head>
<title>Navigator</title>
<base target="content">
</head>

<body>

<h3>Navigate<br>from here</h3>

<p><a href="new.htm">What's New</a></p>

<p><a href="hot.htm">What's Hot</a></p>

<p><a href="info.htm">Company Info</a></p>

<p><a href="order.htm">Ordering</a></p>

</body>
</html>
```

11. Save the file **navigate.htm**.

12. Open the file **frame.htm** in your browser. When you test the links in the navigation frame, the linked pages should display in the content frame, as shown in Figure 8-24.

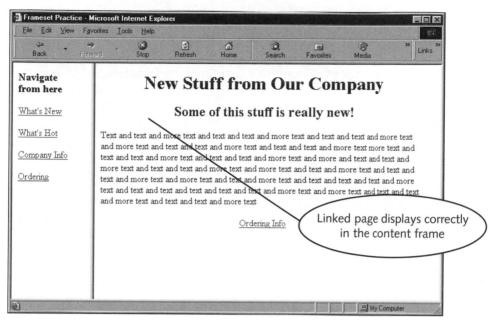

Figure 8-24   The completed frameset

CHAPTER SUMMARY

Using frames judiciously can enhance your Web site, allowing you to consistently display navigation information and content concurrently. Frames can be the right solution for specific information problems or for providing large collections of content. Keep the following in mind as you work with frames:

❏ Frames allow you to divide the browser window into independent windows, each displaying a separate HTML document. Frames allow users to scroll in one frame without affecting the contents of an adjoining frame. This is an ideal way to present large quantities of information that are hard to navigate using the traditional single-page browser display.

❏ Although frames offer a number of benefits, you should use them judiciously. Make sure that your content benefits from the use of frames, and build simple framesets with no more than two or three frames.

❏ Frames present drawbacks that you need to consider before organizing your content with frames. These drawbacks include the inability to bookmark pages, increased download times, potential navigation and visual confusion, and the inability of search engines to find framed documents.

❏ Because frameset documents have no content, they are not the best choice for the top-level page of your Web site. Consider using a standard HTML page for the top level, and then link to your framed content.

❏ HTML frameset documents contain the code that assembles the frames and their contents. The <frameset> element is the container for the frameset code. Because frameset documents themselves have no actual content, they have no <body> element.

❏ <frame> is an empty element that determines the contents of each frame. The src attribute provides the location of the file that displays within the frame. Other attributes to the <frame> tag let you name the frame for targeting, specify whether frames have a scroll bar, and indicate whether the user can resize the frame.

❏ Use the <noframes> element to contain alternate information about your Web site for users with browsers that cannot display frames.

❏ You can designate one frame that displays unchanging information while the contents of a second frame change based on the user's choice. By default, a link loads into the same frame from which it was selected. You can change this default behavior and target the destination of a link to another frame in the frameset. To target from one frame to another, you first must name your frames using the name attribute in the <frame> element, and then target links to display their content in the named frame.

❏ Use special target names to solve unique design problems, favoring _top over _blank whenever possible.

❏ Frameset display is affected by the base screen resolution you use to code your framed pages. Decide on the lowest common denominator screen resolution that will display the frameset effectively. You also can build framesets using a combination of fixed and variable frame widths to accommodate different screen resolutions.

❏ Test your work. Different browsers and screen resolutions may affect the look of your framesets.

REVIEW QUESTIONS

1. What is the main benefit of using frames?
2. Why do framesets add to initial download time?
3. Name two ways in which frames might confuse users.
4. Why do search engines have problems with framesets?
5. What are the two attributes you use to structure the look of a frameset?
6. How does the order of the <frame> element within the <frameset> affect the display of the frameset?
7. What is the purpose of the <noframes> element?
8. What is the benefit of the noresize attribute?
9. What is the default setting for the scrolling attribute?
10. List the correct attributes to the <frameset> element that will remove the frame borders in both Netscape Navigator and Internet Explorer.

11. What are the two tasks you must perform to add targeting to a frameset?

12. Which element lets you set a default target for all links in a document?

13. List the four special target names.

14. Are target names case-sensitive?

15. Which special target name is the default behavior for links in a frameset?

16. What is the major drawback of the _blank special target name?

17. How can you control the display of content within a frameset?

18. What additional browser elements can affect the display of your frameset?

19. How can you accommodate frameset display at varying screen resolutions?

HANDS-ON PROJECTS

1. Browse the Web for a mainstream Web site that you think effectively uses frames.

   a. Test the site at different resolutions.

   b. Test the site in at least two different browsers.

   c. Navigate the site and judge the effectiveness of the navigation and content presentation.

   d. Write a summary of your findings.

2. Browse the World Wide Web for a framed mainstream Web site that you think would benefit from not using frames.

   a. Test the Web site at different resolutions.

   b. Test the Web site in at least two different browsers.

   c. Navigate the Web site and judge the effectiveness of the navigation and content presentation.

   d. Write a design critique and suggest ways in which the Web site could be redesigned without using frames.

3. Visit the *Principles of Web Design* Companion Web site and download some of the sample frame content files.

   a. Build a two-column frameset that contains a fixed left navigation frame and a variable right content frame.

   b. Target all of the links in the left frame to the right content frame.

   c. Restrict the user's ability to resize the frames.

   d. Test your work in different browsers and at different resolutions.

8

4. Visit the *Principles of Web Design* Companion Web site and download some of the sample frame content files.

   a. Build a two-row frameset that contains a fixed top navigation frame and a variable bottom content frame.

   b. Target all of the links in the top frame to the bottom content frame.

   c. Completely remove the frame borders.

   d. Test your work in different browsers and at different resolutions.

5. Visit the *Principles of Web Design* Companion Web site and download some of the sample frame content files.

   a. Build a simple two-row or two-column frameset, or use one of the framesets from Project 3 or 4. Add links to your navigation frame that point to live Web sites.

   b. Add a special target name that will load the linked Web sites into a new browser window.

   c. Test the links and view the browser's behavior.

   d. Test the results in different browsers.

6. Visit the *Principles of Web Design* Companion Web site and download some of the sample frame content files.

   a. Build a simple two-row or two-column frameset, or use one of the framesets from Project 3 or 4. Add links to your navigation frame that point to live Web sites.

   b. Add a special target name that will load the linked Web sites at the top level of the existing browser window.

   c. Test the links and view the browser's behavior.

   d. Test the results in different browsers.

CASE PROJECT

Determine whether frames will enhance the effectiveness of your Web site and presentation of your content. Write a design summary that states how your Web site would benefit from the use of frames, and include a sketch of the structure and navigation of your proposed framed Web site. Discuss targeting behavior and how you would handle links to sites outside of your own. Discuss whether you would have a framed page or standard HTML page for the top-level page of your Web site.

If you determine that your Web site would benefit from frames, build a test frameset. Include some sample content pages. Test your frameset at different resolutions and in different browsers. Code your frameset to work at both 640 × 480 and 800 × 600 resolutions. If the testing shows positive results, adopt the frameset for your completed Web site.

9

WORKING WITH FORMS

When you complete this chapter, you will be able to:

♦ Understand how forms work

♦ Understand form syntax

♦ Build forms within tables

♦ Build and test a sample form

This chapter covers the HTML form elements. Forms let you build interactive Web pages that collect information from a user and process it on the Web server. You can use forms to gather information and create databases, or to send customized responses to your users. Forms collect—but do not process—data. The data processing must be performed on the Web server that hosts the form. Forms are the basis for online commerce; without them users would not be able to enter customer address, credit card, and ordering information on the Web.

UNDERSTANDING HOW FORMS WORK

Figure 9-1 shows a typical form. You can use a variety of different input elements for the form based on the type of information you want to gather from your user. Forms usually contain basic HTML formatting tags such as <p> and <br>. Forms can also be built within tables, which helps control their visual layout.

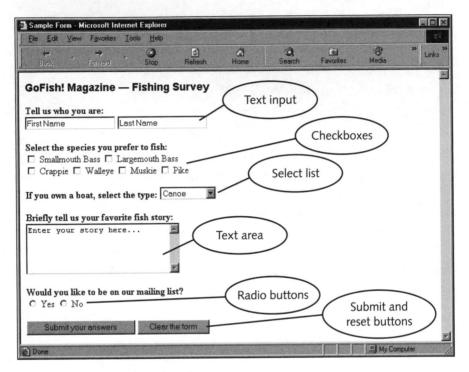

Figure 9-1   A sample HTML form

The HTML form itself is the interface for the user to enter data, but all of the actual data processing is performed on the server using applications that usually reside in the Common Gateway Interface (CGI). The **Common Gateway Interface** is the communications bridge between the Internet and the server. Using programs called scripts, CGI can collect data sent by a user via the Hypertext Transfer Protocol (HTTP) and transfer it to a variety of data processing programs, including spreadsheets, databases, or other software running on the server. The data processing software then can work with the data and send a response back to CGI, and then on to the user, as shown in Figure 9-2.

The programs that transfer the data are called CGI scripts, which can be written in a variety of programming languages. If you are not already familiar with writing CGI scripts, enlist the assistance of a programmer, unless you want to master programming skills in addition to your HTML skills. You can also download public-domain CGI scripts from the Web and use them on your site. These freely available software programs usually come with instructions.

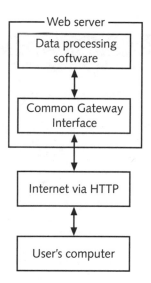

Figure 9-2   Common Gateway Interface architecture

 A good source for CGI scripts is Matt's Script Archive at *www.scriptarchive.com* and the CGI Directory at *www.cgidir.com*.

9

UNDERSTANDING FORM SYNTAX

Five basic form elements are commonly used and supported by the major browsers. These are <form>, <input>, <select>, <option>, and <textarea>. HTML 4.01 introduced five new form elements: <button>, <fieldset>, <label>, <legend>, and <optgroup>. In this section you will learn how to use these elements.

Using the Forms Element

The <form> element is the container for creating a form, as the <table> element is the container for the elements that create a table. Form has a number of attributes that describe how the form data will be handled, as described in Table 9-1.

Table 9-1   Form attributes

Attribute	Description
action	The URL of the application that will process the form data. This URL usually points to a CGI script file.
enctype	The content type used to submit the form to the server (when the value of method is "post"). For most forms you will not need to use this attribute.

Table 9-1   Form attributes (continued)

Attribute	Description
method	Specifies the http method that will be used to submit the form data. The default value is "get." Get—The form data is appended to the URL specified in the action attribute. Post—The form data is sent to the server as a separate message.
accept	A comma-separated list of content types that a server processing this form will handle correctly. For most forms you will not need to use this attribute.
accept-charset	A list of allowed character sets for input data that is accepted by the server processing this form. For most forms you will not need to use this attribute.

The <form> element by itself does not create a form. It must contain **form controls** (such as input elements) and possibly formatting elements as well to control the look of the form. A variety of different form controls are available for collection information, as described in the following sections. The following code shows a typical <form> element with some of the attributes listed in Table 9-1.

```
<form action="http://someserver/cgi_bin/script.cgi"
method="post">
```

Creating Input Objects

The <input> element defines many of the form input object types. Table 9-2 lists the available object types. You specify the object type with the type attribute.

Table 9-2   Input element types

Type Attribute Value	Description
Text	Creates a text entry field that lets the user enter a single word or a line of text. This is the default object type.
Password	Creates the same type of text entry field created by the value "text," but the user entry is masked by asterisks.
Checkbox	Checkboxes are on/off toggles that the user selects. These are best used with multiple-choice questions. Multiple checkboxes can contain the same name, grouping them together so that users can select multiple values for the same property.
Radio	Radio buttons let a user choose one value from a range of values. When radio buttons are grouped together with the same name, only one choice can be selected.
Submit	Sends the form data to the server using the transmission method specified in the <form> element. Every form needs a submit button.

Table 9-2 Input element types (continued)

Type Attribute Value	Description
Reset	Clears the form of any user-entered data and returns it to its original state.
Hidden	This type adds a control that is not displayed in the browser. This is useful for sending additional information with the form data that may be needed for processing.
Image	You can add a graphic button to the form, rather than the default button, with this type.
Button	This type creates a button that has no default behavior. The button's function is usually defined by a script. When the user pushes the button the script function is triggered.
File	This type lets the user select a file that is submitted with the form.

Creating Text Boxes

The text entry box is the most commonly used form element. The default text box is 20 characters long, although this can be changed with the size attribute. The user can enter an unlimited number of characters in the text box even though they exceed the visible length. You can constrain the user's entry of text with the maxlength attribute and supply a default value for the text with the value attribute. The following code shows a simple form with two text boxes.

```
<form action="http://someserver/cgi_bin/script.cgi"
method="post">

<b>Tell us who you are:</b><br>

<input type="text" name="firstname" size="20"
maxlength="35" value="First Name">

<input type="text" name="lastname" size="20"
maxlength="35" value="Last Name">

</form>
```

This code creates the two text box inputs shown in Figure 9-3.

Creating Checkboxes

Checkboxes are on/off toggles that the user can select. Checkboxes can be grouped together with the name attribute, allowing the user to select multiple values for the same property.

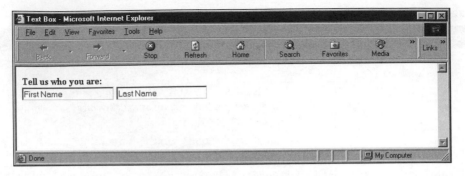

Figure 9-3   Text box inputs

In the following code, the various fish species checkboxes are grouped together with the name attribute set to "species." Notice that the checkboxes are grouped within a <p> element. This code creates the form shown in Figure 9-4.

```
<form action="http://someserver/cgi_bin/script.cgi" method=
"post">
<b>Tell us who you are:</b><br>

<input type="text" name="firstname" size="20" maxlength=
"35" value="First Name" >

<input type="text" name="lastname" size="20" maxlength=
"35" value="Last Name"><br>

<p><b>Select the species you prefer to fish:</b><br>

<input type="checkbox" name="species" value="smbass">
Smallmouth Bass

<input type="checkbox" name="species" value="lgbass">
Largemouth Bass <br>

<input type="checkbox" name="species" value="crappie">
Crappie

<input type="checkbox" name="species" value="walleye">
Walleye

<input type="checkbox" name="species" value="muskie">
Muskie

<input type="checkbox" name="species" value="pike"> Pike
</p>

</form>
```

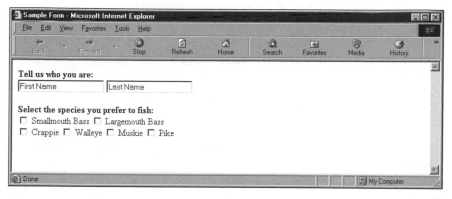

Figure 9-4   Checkbox inputs

You can force a checkbox to be checked by default with the checked attribute. The following code fragment shows the syntax for this attribute.

```
<input type="checkbox" name="species" value="pike" checked
> Pike
```

Creating Radio Buttons

Radio buttons are like checkboxes, but only one selection is allowed. When radio buttons are grouped with the name attribute, only one value can be selected to be "on," while all other values must be "off." You can choose one of the radio buttons to be preselected with the "checked" attribute.

In the following code, the "Yes" and "No" radio buttons are grouped together with the name attribute set to "list." The user can choose only one of the two values. The "Yes" value is preselected with the checked attribute. This code creates the form shown in Figure 9-5.

```
<form action="http://someserver/cgi_bin/script.cgi" method
="post">
<b>Tell us who you are:</b><br>
<input type="text" name="firstname" size="20" maxlength=
"35" value="First Name" >

<input type="text" name="lastname" size="20" maxlength=
"35" value="Last Name"><br>

<p><b>Select the species you prefer to fish:</b><br>

<input type="checkbox" name="species" value="smbass">
Smallmouth Bass

<input type="checkbox" name="species" value="lgbass">
Largemouth Bass <br>
```

```
<input type="checkbox" name="species" value="crappie">
Crappie

<input type="checkbox" name="species" value="walleye">
Walleye

<input type="checkbox" name="species" value="muskie">
Muskie

<input type="checkbox" name="species" value="pike"> Pike
</p>

<p><b>Would you like to be on our mailing list?</b><br>
<input type="radio" name="list" value="yes" checked> Yes
<input type="radio" name="list" value="no"> No
</p>

</form>
```

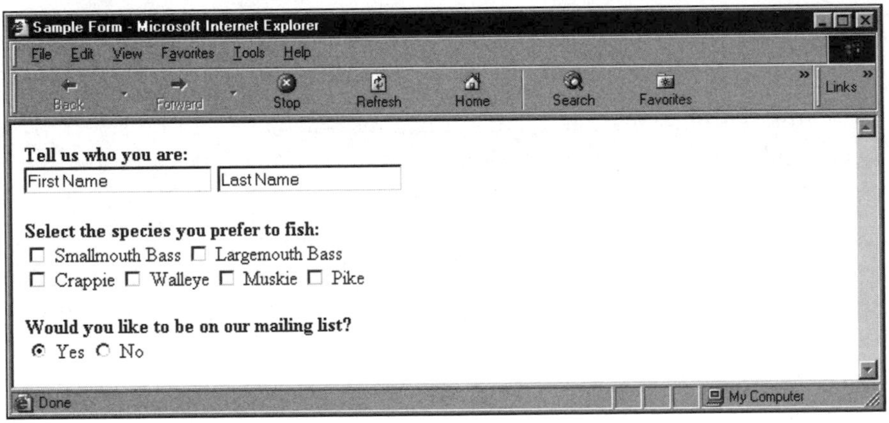

Figure 9-5   Radio button inputs

 Use checkboxes when you want to create a question to which multiple answers are allowed. Use radio buttons when you want users to choose only one answer.

Creating Submit and Reset Buttons

The submit and reset button input types let the user choose whether to send the form data to be processed or clear the form and start over. These are predefined functions that are activated by the button type. Set the input type to either "submit" or "reset." The default button text values are "Submit Query" and "Reset." You can use the value attribute to customize the button text.

The following code shows the addition of submit and reset buttons with customized button text. Figure 9-6 shows the result of the code.

```
<form action="http://someserver/cgi_bin/script.cgi"
method="post">
<b>Tell us who you are:</b><br>
<input type="text" name="firstname" size="20" maxlength=
"35" value="First Name" >

<input type="text" name="lastname" size="20" maxlength=
"35" value="Last Name"><br>

<p><b>Select the species you prefer to fish:</b><br>

<input type="checkbox" name="species" value="smbass">
Smallmouth Bass

<input type="checkbox" name="species" value="lgbass">
Largemouth Bass <br>

<input type="checkbox" name="species" value="crappie">
Crappie

<input type="checkbox" name="species" value="walleye">
Walleye

<input type="checkbox" name="species" value="muskie">
Muskie

<input type="checkbox" name="species" value="pike"> Pike
</p>


<p><b>Would you like to be on our mailing list?</b><br>
<input type="radio" name="list" value="yes" checked> Yes
<input type="radio" name="list" value="no"> No
</p>

<input type="submit" value="Submit your answers"> <input
type="reset" value="Clear the form">

</form>
```

Creating a Custom Event Button

You can create customized buttons that you can use with programming languages such as JavaScript. This type of button differs from the reset and submit buttons because it does not have a predefined function. When a user clicks the button, the event activates a function contained in some associated program. In the following code fragment the button has a customized value of "Calculate." Figure 9-7 shows the button in the browser.

```
Click the calculate button to total your order:
<input type="button" value="Calculate">
```

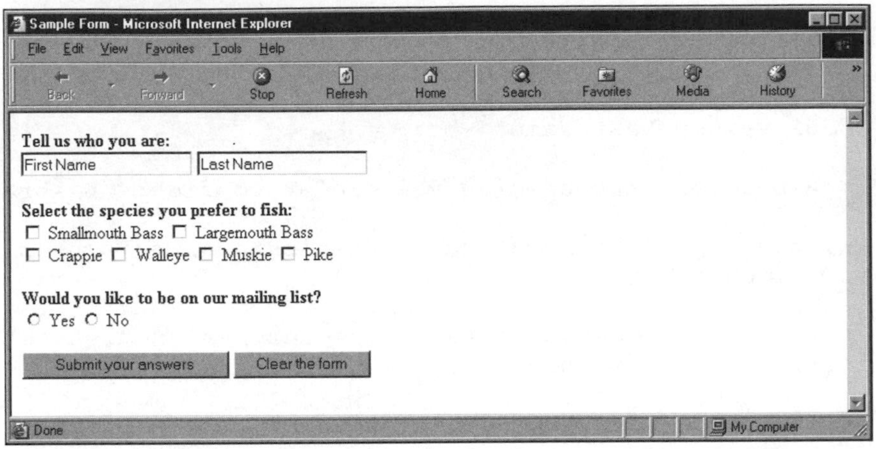

Figure 9-6   Submit and reset input buttons

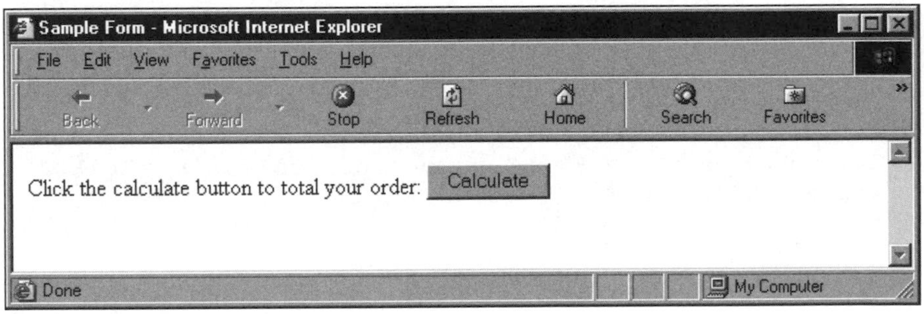

Figure 9-7   A customized button

Creating an Image for the Submit Button

You can choose an image file and use it instead of the default button image for the submit button. The image type works only for the submit function. Make sure that the image you choose is an acceptable Web file format (GIF, PNG, or JPG). The src attribute contains the location of the image file. Remember to include an alt attribute as you would with any other image.

The following code shows the use of an image for the submit button. Figure 9-8 shows the result.

```
<h3>Click the button to find out more:</h3>
<input type="image" src="submit.gif" alt="submit button">
```

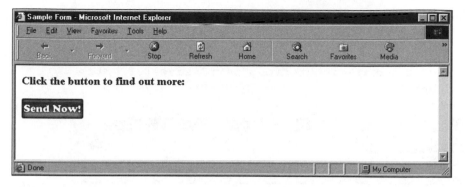

Figure 9-8   Using an image for the submit button

Letting the User Submit a File

The file type input object lets users select a file on their own computer and send it to the server. This type lets you create a text input area for the user to enter a filename. The length of the text input is specified with the size attribute. The file type automatically includes a browse button that lets users browse for a file in their computer's directory system.

The following code shows the file input type. The result is shown in Figure 9-9.

```
Use the browse button to select your file:<br>
<input type="file" size="30">
```

Figure 9-9   File type input

Creating a Password Entry Field

The password type input object works like a text input box, with the additional feature that the entered text is hidden by asterisks rather than shown on the screen. This is a very low level of password protection, as the password is only protected from users looking at the screen. The password itself is sent to the server as plain text, and anyone with network access could read the password information. If you use passwords, check with your system administrator to see whether you can send passwords over a secure Internet connection.

The following code shows the use of the password type input. Figure 9-10 shows the result.

```
Enter your user name and password:<br>
user name: <input type="text" size="30"><br>
password: <input type="password" size="30">
```

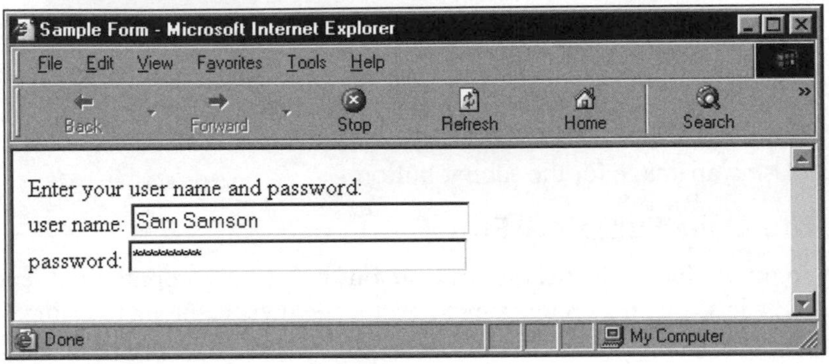

Figure 9-10   Password type input

Using the Select Element

The <select> element lets you create a list box or scrollable list of selectable options. The <select> element is a container element for the <option> element. Each <option> element contains a list value.

The following code shows the standard type of list box list; the user can choose one value. Figure 9-11 shows the result of the code. Notice that the first option in the list is the value that appears in the list box text area.

```
<b>If you own a boat, select the type:</b>
<select name="boats">
<option>Canoe</option>
<option>Jon Boat</option>
<option>Kayak</option>
<option>Bass Boat</option>
<option>Family Boat</option>
</select>
```

You can select the default value in a list by adding the selected attribute to an <option> element. In the following list, "Bass Boat" is the default value.

```
<b>If you own a boat, select the type:</b>
<select name="boats">
<option>Canoe</option>
<option>Jon Boat</option>
<option>Kayak</option>
<option selected>Bass Boat</option>
```

```
<option>Family Boat</option>
</select>
```

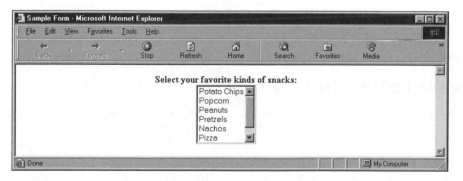

Figure 9-11   The select list box list

You can also choose to let the user pick multiple values from the list by adding the multiple attribute to the <select> element. This results in a scrollable list rather than a list box list. The following code and Figure 9-12 show the use of the multiple attribute. The size attribute specifies how many of the list options are visible at a time.

```
<p align="center"><b>Select your favorite kinds of snacks:
</b><br>
<select name="snacks" multiple size="6">
<option>Potato Chips</option>
<option>Popcorn</option>
<option>Peanuts</option>
<option>Pretzels</option>
<option>Nachos</option>
<option>Pizza</option>
<option>Fries</option>
</select>
</p>
```

Figure 9-12   A scrollable select list

Grouping List Options

You can group and label sets of list options with the <optgroup> element and label attribute. The result is a heading for a series of options within a list. Figure 9-13 shows the result of using the <optgroup> element. The browser determines the format of the labels, but they are usually bold italic. The code for the page follows.

```
<p align="center"><b>Select your favorite kinds of snacks:
</b><br>
<select name="snacks" multiple size="7">
<optgroup label="Salty Snacks">
<option>Potato Chips</option>
<option>Popcorn</option>
<option>Peanuts</option>
<option>Pretzels</option>
</optgroup>
<optgroup label="Hot Snacks">
<option>Nachos</option>
<option>Pizza</option>
<option>Fries</option>
</optgroup>
</select>
</p>
```

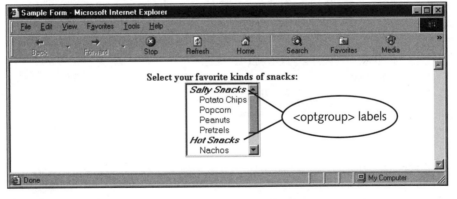

Figure 9-13 Grouping list options

Using the textarea Element

The <textarea> element lets you create a larger text area for user input than the <input> text type object described previously. You can specify the width and height of the text area with the cols and rows attributes. Because of browser differences, text entered in a text area does not wrap automatically; the user must press the Enter key at the end of each line of text. You can set the wrap attribute to "virtual" to force the text to wrap automatically in the user's browser window. Any text you enter in the <textarea> element appears as the default text in the user's browser.

The following code shows a text area set to 30 columns wide by five rows high. Figure 9-14 shows the result of the code.

```
<p><b>Briefly tell us your favorite fish story:</b><br>
<textarea name="fishstory" rows="5" cols="30">
Enter your story here...
</textarea>
</p>
```

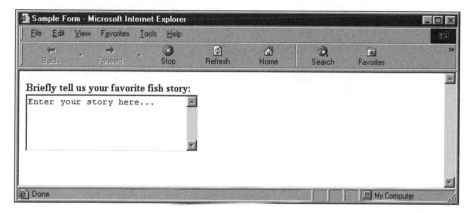

Figure 9-14   Text area element

Creating Input Groupings

You can use the <fieldset> and <legend> elements to create groupings of different types of input elements. The <fieldset> element contains the input elements, while the <legend> element contains a label for the grouping. These two elements help make your forms more readable and increase their accessibility to alternate browsers. Figure 9-15 shows the use of the <fieldset> and <legend> elements. The code for the page follows.

Figure 9-15   Grouping and labeling input elements

```
<form action="http://someserver/cgi_bin/script.cgi" method
="post">
<fieldset>
<legend><b>Select the species you prefer to fish:</b>
</legend>
<input type="checkbox" name="species" value="smbass">
Smallmouth Bass
<input type="checkbox" name="species" value="lgbass">
Largemouth Bass <br>
<input type="checkbox" name="species" value="crappie">
Crappie
<input type="checkbox" name="species" value="walleye">
Walleye
<input type="checkbox" name="species" value="muskie">
Muskie
<input type="checkbox" name="species" value="pike"> Pike
</fieldset>

<br>

<fieldset>
<legend><b>Select the rod type you prefer to use:</b>
</legend>
<input type="checkbox" name="species" value="ltspin">
Light Spinning
<input type="checkbox" name="species" value="mdspin">
Medium Spinning <br>
<input type="checkbox" name="species" value="hvspin">
Heavy Spinning
<input type="checkbox" name="species" value="fly"> Fly
<input type="checkbox" name="species" value="btcas"> Bait
Casting
</fieldset>
</form>
```

BUILDING FORMS WITHIN TABLES

Most forms need some type of formatting to increase their legibility. As you have seen in the form samples in this chapter, forms need at least basic formatting elements, such as <br> and <p>, to place form elements on separate lines and add white space. Even with these basic formatting elements, the look of your form may not be acceptable. Figure 9-16 shows a typical form. Notice how the basic left justification of the form elements gives a ragged look to the form.

In contrast to Figure 9-16, the form in Figure 9-17 has been placed within a table, producing a visually more appealing form that is easier for the user to follow when entering data.

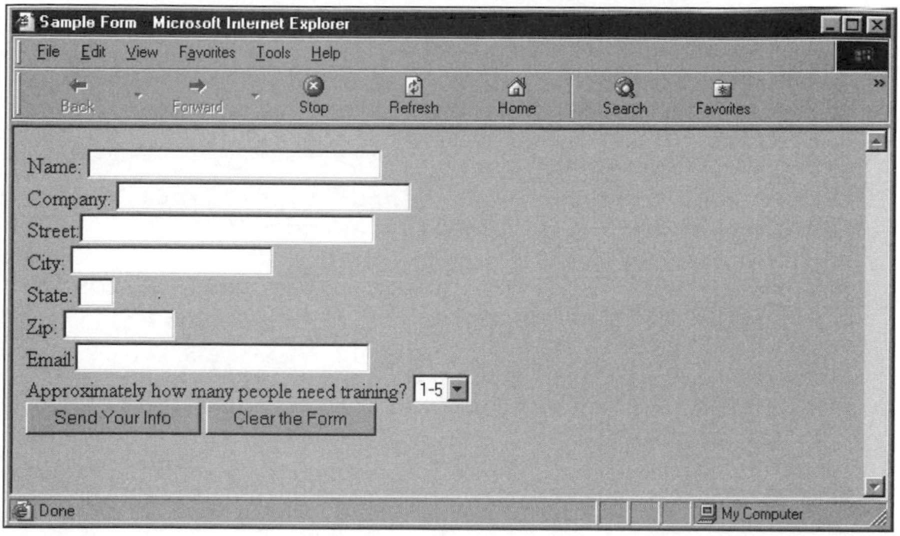

Figure 9-16 Typical form layout

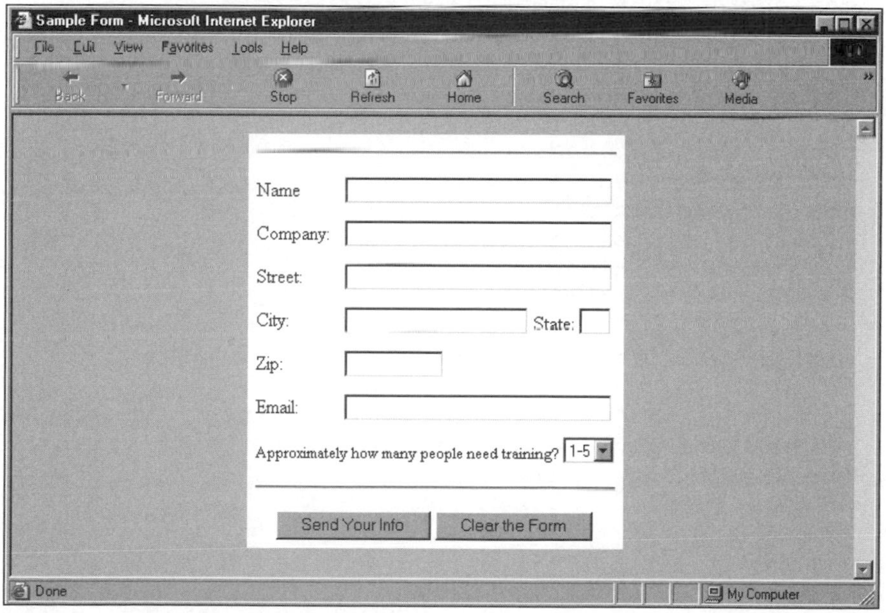

9

Figure 9-17 Form layout enhanced with a table

Placing a form within a table is no different from placing standard HTML content within a table. Usually the <form> element will contain the table, which in turn contains each of the individual form input elements. The following code builds the form in Figure 9-17.

```
<div align="center">
<form method="post" action="http://someserver/cgi_bin/
script.cgi" >
```

```
<table cellpadding="5" border>
<tr><td colspan="2"><hr></td></tr>

<tr><td>Name</td><td><input type="text" size="30"
maxlength="256" name="name"></td></tr>

<tr><td>Company:</td><td> <input type="text" size="30"
maxlength="256" name="company"></td></tr>

<tr><td>Street:</td><td><input type="text" size="30"
maxlength="256" name="street"></td></tr>

<tr><td>City:</td><td><input type="text" size="20"
maxlength="256" name="city">State:<input type="text" size=
"2" maxlength="2" name="state"></td></tr>

<tr><td>Zip:</td><td><input type="text" size="10"
 maxlength="256" name="zip"></td></tr>

<tr><td>Email:</td><td><input type="text" size="30"
maxlength="256" name="email"></td></tr>
<tr><td colspan="2"><font size="2">Approximately how many
people need training?</font><select name="numstudent" size=
"1">
<option selected>1-5
<option>10</option>
<option>20</option>
<option>30</option>
<option>40</option>
<option>50</option>
</select></td></tr>

<tr><td colspan="2"><hr></td></tr>

<tr><td align="center" colspan="2"><input type="submit"
value="Send Your Info"> <input type="reset" value="Clear
the Form"></td> </tr>

</table>
</form>
</div>
```

BUILDING AND TESTING A SAMPLE FORM

In the following set of steps you will build a form for an online job search service. Users of the service will enter address and personal information into the form, and may attach a copy of their resume.

To begin building a sample form:

1. Copy the file **form.htm** from the Chapter09 folder on your Data Disk.

2. Save the file to the Chapter09 folder in your work folder using the same filename.

3. Open the file in your HTML editor and examine the code. The file contains only the default HTML elements and an empty <form> element, as shown in the following code:

```
<html>
<head>
<title>Personal Information Form</title>
</head>
<body>
<form action=... method="post">
</form>
</body>
</html>
```

4. Begin building the form by adding three text input elements, one each for the user's name, e-mail address, and telephone number. Set the size and name attribute values as shown in the following code. Use <br> to format the text input elements and labels.

```
Name:<br><input size="30" name="name"><br>
Email:<br><input size="30" name="email"><br>
Phone:<br><input size="30" name="phone">
```

5. Group this set of fields with a <fieldset> and accompanying <legend> element, as shown in the following code.

```
<fieldset>
<legend>Contact Information</legend>
Name:<br><input size="30" name="name"><br>
Email:<br><input size="30" name="email"><br>
Phone:<br><input size="30" name="phone">
</fieldset>
```

6. Save form.htm and leave it open for the next set of steps. Then view the file in the browser; it should now look like Figure 9-18.

9

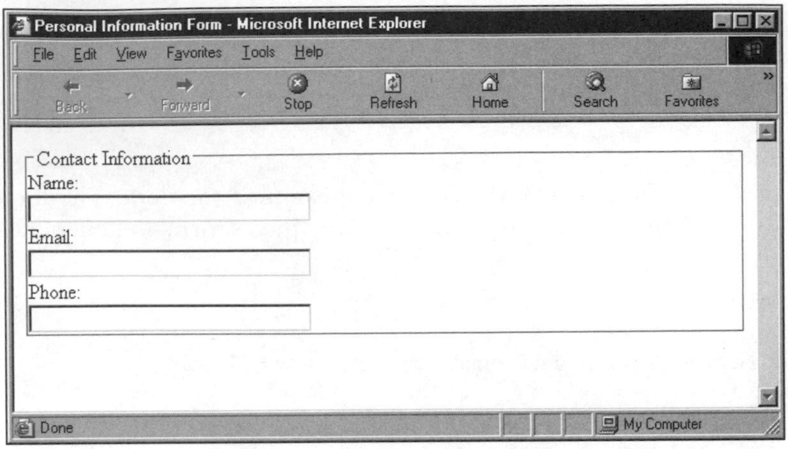

Figure 9-18   Form with three text input elements

Adding a List Box List and Radio Buttons

Continue to build the form by adding two more input elements to collect information from the user. You will add a list box of job position options and a question with a yes or no answer.

To continue building the form:

1. Continue working in the file **form.htm**.

2. Add a select element with four blank option tags as shown in the following code. Place this code after the closing fieldset tag from the previous procedure.

   ```
   <p>
   Select the type of position you desire:
   <select name="position">
   <option>
   <option>
   <option>
   <option>
   </select>
   </p>
   ```

3. Fill in a value for each option as shown in the following code:

   ```
   <p>
   Select the type of position you desire:
   <select name="position">
   <option>Part-time contract</option>
   <option>Full-time contract</option>
   <option>Part-time permanent</option>
   <option>Full-time permanent</option>
   </select>
   </p>
   ```

4. Beneath the select list, add the following question:

```
<p>
Are you willing to relocate?
</p>
```

5. Add two input elements with the type set to "radio" to create radio buttons. Use a <br> element to place the radio buttons under the question text.

```
<p>
Are you willing to relocate? <br>
Yes <input type="radio">
No <input type="radio">
</p>
```

6. Add a value attribute for each element. Set the value for the Yes button to "yes." Set the No button to "no." Also, add a name attribute that groups the radio buttons together with a value of "relocate."

```
<p>
Are you willing to relocate?<br>
Yes <input type="radio" value="yes" name="relocate">
No <input type="radio" value="no" name="relocate">
</p>
```

7. Save form.htm and leave it open for the next set of steps. Then view the file in the browser; it should now look like Figure 9-19.

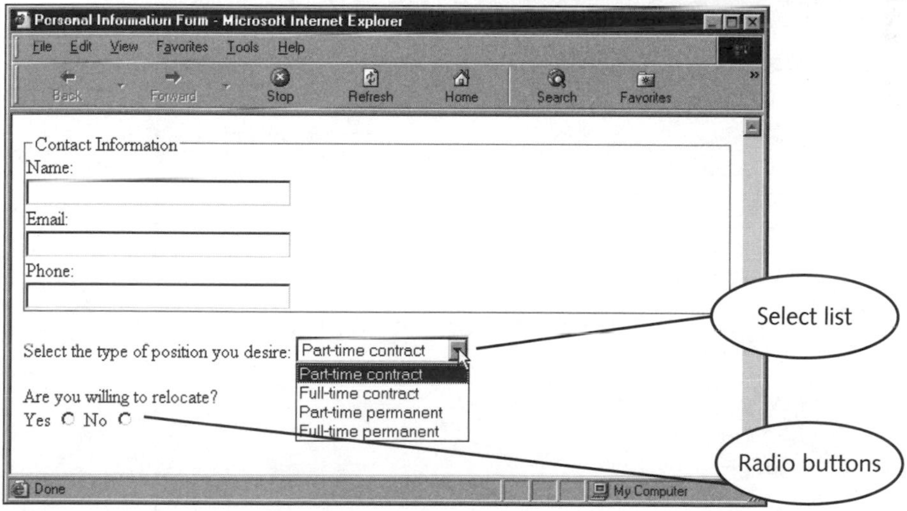

Figure 9-19   Adding a select list and radio buttons

Adding a File Element and Submit Button

You will add a file type input element that lets users attach their resume file to the form data. Then you will finish the form by adding the submit and reset buttons.

To continue building the form:

1. Continue working in the file **form.htm**.

2. Add an input element with the type set to "file." Also, add the explanatory text before the file input element, as shown in the following code.

```
<p>Use the browse button to find and attach your resume
file:</p>
<p><input type="file" name="resume"></p>
```

3. Add a <fieldset> element and accompanying <legend> element, as shown in the following code.

```
<fieldset>
<legend>Submit your resume</legend>
<p>Use the browse button to find and attach your resume
file:</p>
<p><input type="file" name="resume"></p>
</fieldset>
```

4. Save form.htm and leave it open for the next set of steps. Then view the file in the browser; it should now look like Figure 9-20.

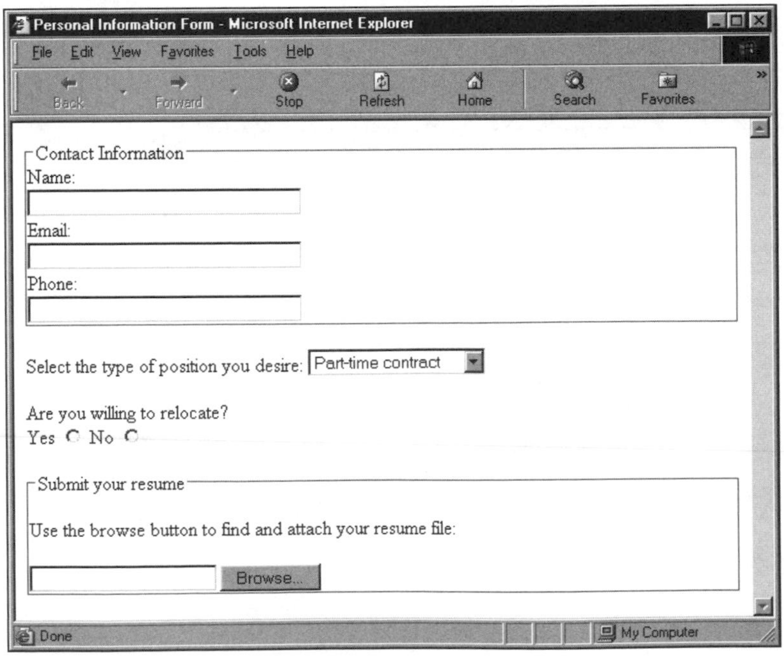

Figure 9-20   Adding a file type input element

5. Finish the form by adding submit and reset button element types and setting values for each button, as shown in the following code.

```
<br>
<input type="submit" value="Send your info">
<input type="reset" value="Clear the form">
```

6. Save form.htm, close it, and then view the file in the browser. The complete form should now look like Figure 9-21.

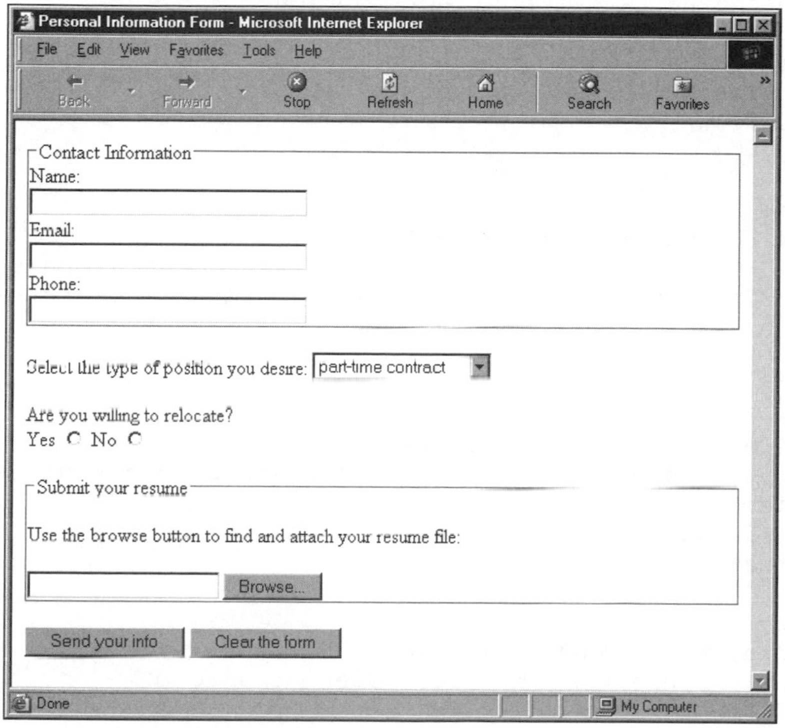

Figure 9-21   The completed form

The complete code for the page follows.

```
<html>
<head>
<title>Personal Information Form</title>
</head>

<body>
<form action=... method="post">
```

```
<fieldset>
<legend>Contact Information</legend>
Name:<br><input size="30" name="name"><br>
Email:<br><input size="30" name="email"><br>
Phone:<br><input size="30" name="phone">
</fieldset>
<p>
Select the type of position you desire:
<select name="position">
<option>Part-time contract</option>
<option>Full-time contract</option>
<option>Part-time permanent</option>
<option>Full-time permanent</option>
</select>
</p>

<p>
Are you willing to relocate? <br>
Yes <input type="radio" value="yes" name="relocate">
No <input type="radio" value="no" name="relocate">
</p>

<fieldset>
<legend>Submit your resume</legend>
<p>Use the browse button to find and attach your resume
file:</p>
<p><input type="file" name="resume"></p>
</fieldset>

<br>
<input type="submit" value="Send your info">
<input type="reset" value="Clear the form">
</form>
</body>
</html>
```

CHAPTER SUMMARY

A usable forms interface is the result of choosing the correct form elements for the type of data you are requesting and designing a clear and readable form. Keep the following points in mind:

❑ You will need to work with some type of server-based software program to process the data from your form.

❑ You have a variety of form elements to choose from when building a form. Use the correct type of form element for the type of data you are gathering. For example, use checkboxes for multiple-choice questions. For a long list of choices, use a select list.

❏ The <fieldset> and <legend> elements let you create more visually appealing forms that have logical groupings of input elements with a title.

❏ You can avoid the ragged look of forms by placing them within tables to control the alignment of input elements.

REVIEW QUESTIONS

1. Where does the forms processing software usually reside?
2. What are the five commonly supported form elements?
3. What does the action attribute in the <form> element contain?
4. What are the two possible values of the <form> method attribute?
5. How can you group multiple checkboxes together?
6. How are radio buttons different from checkboxes?
7. How do you control the length of a user's entry in a text input element?
8. How do you enter default text in a text input element?
9. How do you force a checkbox to be selected by default?
10. What button must be included with every form?
11. How do you change the default button image for the submit button?
12. What input type lets the user attach a file to the form data?
13. What is the security problem with the password input type?
14. What are the two types of select lists?
15. What attributes let you specify the width and height of the <textarea> element?

9

HANDS-ON PROJECTS

1. In this exercise you will build text box form elements.
   a. Open the file **form.htm** from the Chapter09 folder on your Data Disk.
   b. Save the file as **textbox.htm** to the Chapter09 folder in your work folder.
   c. Open the file in your HTML editor and examine the code. The file contains only the default HTML elements and an empty <form> element.
   d. Build the form shown in Figure 9–22. Refer to the following table for each form element's attribute values.

Name	Size	Maxlength
Street	20	35
City	20	35
State	2	35
Zip	10	35

2. In this exercise you will build checkbox form elements.

   a. Open the file **form.htm** from the Chapter09 folder on your Data Disk.

   b. Save the file as **checkbox.htm** to the Chapter09 folder in your work folder.

   c. Open the file in your HTML editor and examine the code. The file contains only the default HTML elements and an empty <form> element.

   d. Build the form shown in Figure 9-23.

   e. Group the checkboxes with a name attribute set to "flavor."

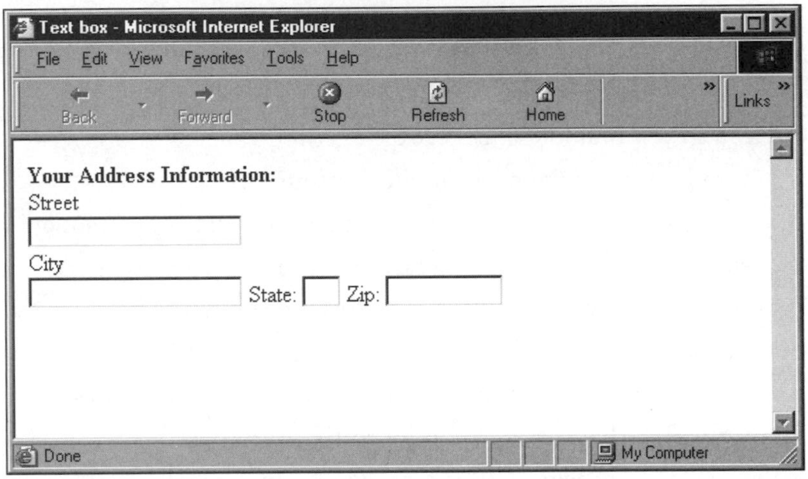

Figure 9-22

Figure 9-23

3. In this exercise you will build radio button form elements.

   a. Open the file **form.htm** from the Chapter09 folder on your Data Disk.

   b. Save the file as **radio.htm** to the Chapter09 folder in your work folder.

   c. Open the file in your HTML editor and examine the code. The file contains only the default HTML elements and an empty <form> element.

   d. Build the form shown in Figure 9-24.

   e. Make sure that "Yes" is the checked choice.

   f. Group the radio buttons with a name attribute set to "offer."

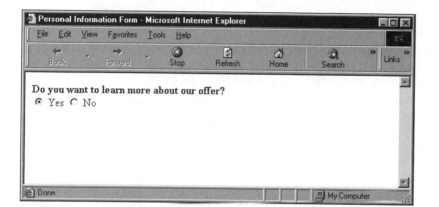

Figure 9-24

4. In this exercise you will build a text area form element.

   a. Open the file **form.htm** from the Chapter09 folder on your Data Disk.

   b. Save the file as **textarea.htm** to the Chapter09 folder in your work folder.

   c. Open the file in your HTML editor and examine the code. The file contains only the default HTML elements and an empty <form> element.

   d. Build the form shown in Figure 9-25. The text area is 6 rows × 35 columns.

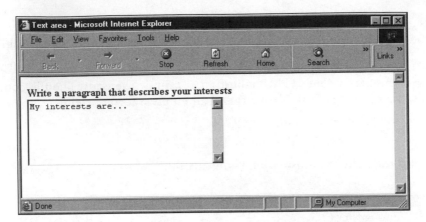

Figure 9-25

5. In this exercise you will build a select form element.

   a. Open the file **form.htm** from the Chapter09 folder on your Data Disk.

   b. Save the file as **select.htm** to the Chapter09 folder in your work folder.

   c. Open the file in your HTML editor and examine the code. The file contains only the default HTML elements and an empty <form> element.

   d. Build the form shown in Figure 9-26.

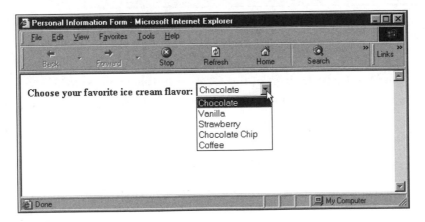

Figure 9-26

CASE PROJECT

Build a user feedback form for your project Web site. You can refer to the sample feedback form in Chapter 3 for ideas. Customize the types of questions you ask to match the content of your site. Create both scaled questions and open-ended questions for your users. For example, ask users to rate the navigation of your site on a scale of 1 to 5, and also include a text area input where they write about their experience of navigating your Web site. Although you will not be able to activate the form (because you don't have an appropriate script to process the data), you can demonstrate the types of questions you would ask users to find out more about their habits when they visit your site.

9

10

PUBLISHING AND MAINTAINING YOUR WEB SITE

When you complete this chapter, you will be able to:

♦ Publish your Web site

♦ Test your Web site

♦ Refine and update your content

♦ Attract notice to your Web site

You have done all the hard work, and now it is time to publish your Web site. Your first important decision is to choose a Web hosting service to host your Web site. You also need to know how to transfer your files from the computer you used to develop your Web page to the Web server. After the Web site is established, you should test it with the help of a variety of users and update or refine it as needed. Finally, you should make sure your Web site gets noticed. This chapter describes the details of publishing and maintaining a Web site.

PUBLISHING YOUR WEB SITE

To make your Web site live, you transfer your Web site files to a **Web server**, a computer connected to the Internet and running server software. The software lets the computer use the Hypertext Transfer Protocol to serve HTML files to Web browser clients. Unless your company or organization has a Web server, you must use the services of a Web hosting provider. After you choose a server to host your files, you will need to select file transfer software and upload the Web site files from your development machine to the Web server.

Choosing a Web Hosting Service Provider

One of the most important choices you will make is your Web hosting service or **Internet Service Provider (ISP)**. This is the company that hosts your Web pages on a Web server, making them available to anyone who knows your URL. ISPs provide dial-up access and most offer Web server space as part of the access package. Small Web sites (around 15-20 pages of content) do not need much more than 1 or 2 MB of server space to hold all of the HTML pages and graphics. Your ISP should provide at least 10 MB of space so your Web page has room to grow. Larger or more complex sites need more server space, especially if you have downloadable files, archives, lots of graphic content, or databases. **Web hosting services** provide Web server space only, and will be more capable of hosting a complex commercial site.

Shopping for an ISP can be a confusing experience, as no two are exactly alike. Do some research and learn about offerings from different vendors. The following sections discuss the features you should seek in an ISP.

Tips for America Online (AOL) users — As a subscriber, you are allowed 10 MB of Web server space, but you cannot have your own domain name. You also may experience slower connections to the Web because so many AOL subscribers are connected during peak times. If you are spending a lot of time on the Web, subscribe to a regular dial-up account from an ISP and then access AOL using your Internet connection. AOL currently charges less for users that "BYOA" (bring your own access), because they are not using AOL's network to access the Internet.

Easy Dial-Up

Choose an ISP that allows you to connect to its network by placing a local phone call. Make sure that your provider has enough Points of Presence to make dialing easy. **Points of Presence (POPs)** are dial-up access points to your service provider's network. Your service provider should have at least one POP available so you can dial a local number to access the network. Major ISPs, such as AT&T, have POPs throughout the United States.

A local ISP will cover only the area that includes its subscriber base. Try to match the size of your ISP to the size of your company—a local company does not need the services of a national ISP.

You should not receive a busy signal when you dial up to get Internet access. Unfortunately, you probably will not find out about access problems until after you have become a customer. Do not hesitate to change ISPs if you are not satisfied with ease of access.

Free Utility Software

Your ISP should provide you with a **File Transfer Protocol (FTP)** application for uploading files. Some ISPs provide HTML editors and other software as well. Some of this software may be shareware, so if you decide to keep it, remember to register with the author.

Accessible Technical Support

Technical support is not a feature, but an absolute necessity. Make sure that your ISP has competent, accessible customer service. When you are checking into ISPs, call and talk with someone in customer service. Tell them how experienced you are with computers, and let them know what you hope to accomplish (such as set up a Web site, transfer files, etc.). Note how long you are on hold when waiting to speak with customer service. Local ISPs may not have a large staff, but they probably have fewer subscribers. National ISPs have so much volume that they may keep you on hold for an unacceptable length of time.

Additional E-mail Addresses

All access accounts come with at least one e-mail address, called a Post Office Protocol 3 (POP3) account. If you are part of a group, you may want an account that has more than one mailbox so that each person can receive his or her own e-mail.

Personal versus Commercial Accounts

Personal ISP accounts generally are less expensive than business accounts. However, you have less disk space, fewer features, and a more complex URL, such as *www.webserver.com/users/yourname/*. Once you buy a domain name, your ISP usually upgrades you to a commercial account. Commercial accounts pay more for services, so make sure you do receive more, such as some of the features listed below.

SQL Database Support

If you are planning on any type of electronic commerce or customized data presentation, you need database support. Databases that understand **Structured Query Language (SQL)** are the most common and powerful type of database.

10

Secure Socket Layer (SSL) Support

The **Secure Socket Layer (SSL)** is an Internet communications protocol that allows encrypted transmission of data between the user and the server. SSL is necessary if you are planning to set up an electronic commerce site or transmitting other sensitive data. Encrypting the data ensures the information cannot be read if the transmission is intercepted.

DSL Support

To take advantage of DSL, you need a network card for your computer and a DSL modem. DSL providers usually offer a "free" modem with the service. Check to make sure that the monthly fee does not include the equipment costs for the modem. Because DSL is an "always-on" connection, there is an increased security risk that your network is vulnerable to hackers. If your DSL provider does not offer network security, you will have to purchase a network security device, known as a DSL gateway router, to protect your computer with a security firewall.

Registering a Domain Name

Domain names are managed by The Internet Corporation for Assigned Names and Numbers (ICANN). ICANN has agreements with a number of vendors to provide domain name registration services. Until recently, Network Solutions was the only vendor of domain names. As more vendors become available, the market for domain names has become more competitive. You can visit Network Solutions to see whether a domain name is available, but you may want to shop around to get the best price. The site (*www.networksolutions.com*) contains a simple form that lets you check to see whether a domain name is already registered. If the domain name is available, you can register online. Domain names currently must be renewed every two years.

For an additional fee, your ISP often can register your Web site and provide Network Solutions with all the details, such as the server's primary and secondary Internet Protocol (IP) addresses. If you prefer, you can save the cost of doing this by filling out the online forms yourself, but you still need to contact your ISP to get the IP addresses.

ISP Comparison Checklist

Use the following checklist when you compare ISPs.

- Is the ISP local or national?
- Does the ISP have enough local POPs in your area code?
- Is space available on the ISP's Web server for your Web site?
- Does the ISP offer technical support? When is support staff available?
- How many e-mail addresses do you get with an account?

- Does the ISP provide software, such as an FTP client?

- Does the ISP support the latest connection technologies? (See the "Bandwidth Concerns" section in Chapter 1.)

- Does the ISP offer enhanced services, such as SQL database support, Secure Socket Layer (SSL), CGI scripting, and DSL support?

 Backing up your files — Always keep a backup of your Web site files in case you have any problems during FTP transmissions, or if you accidentally delete or overwrite existing files. Of course, if you ever accidentally delete or overwrite files on your local computer, you always can use your Web site files as a backup.

Using the File Transfer Protocol to Upload Files

To publish your pages on the Web, you must send your HTML code, image, and other files to the Web server. To do this, you need File Transfer Protocol (FTP) software, often called an FTP client. Some HTML authoring software, such as Microsoft FrontPage 2000 and Macromedia Dreamweaver, include built-in software packages that let you upload files to your Web server if your ISP supports these features. You also can choose from many shareware FTP programs to upload your files. Visit your favorite shareware site, such as Shareware.com, and search for FTP clients. Figure 10-1 is from the WS_FTP Pro application developed by Ipswitch Software (*www.ipswitch.com*), but most FTP clients work on the same principles.

When you have decided which FTP software to use, contact your ISP's customer service department and ask for the correct FTP address for the Web server. You also need your account name and password, which in most cases will automatically point your FTP program to the proper directory on the server.

To upload your files, start your FTP program and connect to your Web server using the FTP information provided by your service provider. Your password allows you write access to your directory on the Web server. Once the FTP client has connected to the Web server, you have the option of choosing the files you want to transfer. The FTP client usually displays directories on both the local and remote computers. Figure 10-1 shows the FTP client with both local and remote system information.

10

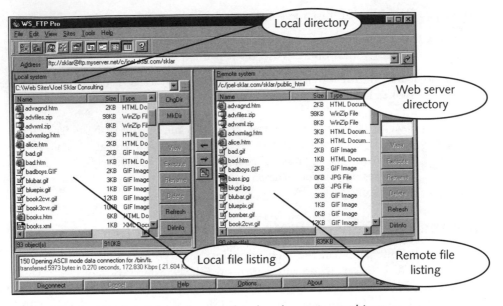

Figure 10-1   FTP dialog box showing local and remote machines

Select the files that you want to upload in your local directory listing and transfer them to the Web server. You also can transfer files from the Web server to your computer. The first time you go live with your Web site, you must transfer all the files. Later you will need to upload only the files that you have updated. Once the files have reached the Web server, they are available for access immediately on the Web.

After you find an ISP and publish your Web site to the World Wide Web, it is time to test your Web site in the real-life Internet environment.

TESTING YOUR WEB SITE

Even though you performed tests throughout the development of your Web site, you need to continue testing after you post your files live on the Web. If possible, load your files to the Web server and test them before making your URL available for users to access the Web site. If you have enough server space, you may want to establish a testing area on the Web site. You can do this by creating a subdirectory in your public HTML directory. Do not publicize the URL so that your testing area can remain private.

Make sure that you maintain the exact directory structure on the Web server that you used on your development computer to ensure that all relative file paths are correct. You can read more about this in Chapter 3.

Testing Considerations

Always test in as many different environments as possible. Remember to test for the following Web design variables:

- Multiple browsers—Test in as many browsers as you can to make sure your work is portable and displays consistently.

- Multiple operating systems—If you can, test on different operating systems. If you have a PC as a development machine, use a Macintosh for testing, and vice versa. You even can run different versions of UNIX on a PC, if necessary. Because computer chip development moves at a lightning pace, machines become outdated quickly. You can find discounted and used machines that often are Internet-capable as long as they have an updated modem. Because these machines will not be used to develop Web sites (only to view them), you do not need the latest or most powerful hardware.

- Connection speeds—Do not rely on the same connection speed when testing your Web site, especially if you work in a corporate environment where the connection to the Internet usually is faster than the average user's. Go to a friend's house, library, or Internet café and access your Web site from there. Test for download times at different connection speeds. According to Wired News (www.wirednews.com), 33% of Web users will leave a Web site if a page takes longer than eight seconds to load. Make sure your pages download quickly.

- Display types—Test at different screen resolutions and color-depth settings to make sure your colors display consistently. Make sure to test different color depths: 8-bit 256 color, 16-bit high color, and 24-bit true color.

In addition, continually test your links. Click through all the links on your Web site, making sure every one takes the user to the intended destination. Any pages that link outside of your Web site need to be tested on a regular basis to make sure that the destination site has not moved, shut down, or posted content different from what you expect.

User Testing

User testing can be as simple as asking a few colleagues to look at your Web site, or as complex as conducting extensive formalized testing. Some companies invest in special user testing labs with videotaping and one-way mirrors to record user behavior, or software that can track users' mouse movements and eye coordination as they look at your Web site. Even if you do not need this level of sophisticated testing, you should perform some type of user assessment of your work. The goal of user testing is to determine whether your Web site is easy to navigate and provides easy access to content. Following are some considerations to take into account when planning for user testing of your site.

10

Vary Your Subjects

Draw your test subjects from a variety of backgrounds, if possible. Gather test subjects that are representative of your target audience. Find users with varying computing skills and familiarity with the information. Avoid using friends as test users, as they may only compliment your work. You might choose to let users look at the Web site on their own time, but you can learn a lot by watching users interact with your Web site. Make sure to let them navigate and use the Web site without any outside help from you. Just stand back and watch.

Formalize Your Testing

Formalize your testing by creating replicable methods of testing your Web site. Prepare a series of questions that users have to answer after viewing the Web site. Give them a specific task to complete or have them find a particular piece of information. Let them rate the ease of completing such tasks. Compare the results from different users to find any problem areas in navigation. Administer the same testing methods to a variety of users, and watch for trends and consistencies. This lets you compare results or focus on a particular feature of the Web site.

Develop a Feedback Form

Develop a feedback form that users can fill out after they have tested the Web site. Include a set of criteria and let them rate the Web site on a progressive scale, or ask them a series of open-ended questions. You also may want to provide the feedback form online, letting users offer feedback directly from the Web site. Here are some sample questions you might ask.

- Did you find the information you needed?
- Was it easy or difficult to access the information you needed?
- Did you find the Web site visually attractive?
- Did you find the content easy to read?
- Did you find the Web site easy to navigate?
- Did you think the information was presented correctly?
- Did the information have enough depth?
- What area of the Web site did you like the best? Why?
- What area of the Web site did you like the least? Why?
- Would you recommend the Web site to others?

REFINING AND UPDATING YOUR CONTENT

Refine your content and presentation based on your user's feedback. When you are evaluating user feedback, look for trends rather than individual aberrations, such as one person's vehement dislike of your color scheme. Pay particular attention to the ease of access to your information. Users should be able to find what they want quickly.

If you have a commercial site, ask your system administrator to set up a program that analyzes your visitors and their preferences when they visit. This type of reporting program, available on most Web servers, reads the communication logs created by the server and extracts information in a report format. These statistical reports vary from program to program, but they can tell you how often users visit, which pages they request the most, and how your Web site traffic varies from month to month.

Plan for ongoing maintenance of your Web site. This is an area often neglected in initial design and budgeting, but it is vital to the success of the Web site. Plan to add new links, information, and featured content continually. The Web is a live, immediate medium, and you want your Web site to stay fresh. Test your links to other Web sites regularly to make sure they are active. You will annoy your users if you send them to linked content that no longer exists. When you update your pages, inform users on your top-level page or on any page that promises up-to-date information.

Plan for major Web site design changes on a regular basis. Some Web sites reorganize their look on a yearly basis. You can perform ongoing testing and improve your test site while maintaining your live Web site. Pay attention to the trends in the industry by visiting lots of other Web sites. Consider new technologies as they become available and when the bandwidth or browser variables allow you to incorporate them.

10

ATTRACTING NOTICE TO YOUR WEB SITE

After you set up your live Web site, it is time to attract visitors. With the millions of pages on the Web, it can be difficult to get your Web site noticed. It is likely that you are trying to attract specific users to your site—people who use your product or who are interested in the same information. Within this narrow audience, publicize your URL as much as possible, in every collateral medium that you can, including business cards, letterhead, catalogs, mailings, and other media. Give users a reason to visit your Web site by offering something they cannot get in any other medium, such as up-to-the-minute pricing or technical information. Give them a reason to come back to your Web site by making your information accessible and useful.

Working with Search Engines

Other than knowing your URL, consider how visitors will find your Web site. Many who are interested in a specific topic or information will use a **search engine** Web site to look for sites on a related topic. Search engines are software programs that search out and index Web sites in a catalog. The way search engines perform searches and arrange their catalogs differs greatly. You can enhance your Web site to take advantage of search engine behavior. Although the following tips can help, there is no guarantee that your Web site will rise to the top of a search engine listing.

For more information on search engine details, visit the Web site *www.searchenginewatch.com.* This site has search engine listings, reviews, ratings, and tests, as well as hints and tips to get your site listed properly with the major search engines.

Use Meaningful Titles

All the pages of your Web site need pertinent information in the <title> element. Some search engines read only the contents of the <title> for Web site information. Also, the contents of the <title> show up in the user's bookmarks or favorites list. Make sure to use meaningful titles that provide information to the user and accurately reflect your site.

Using <meta> Elements

You can use the <meta> elements on your Web site to raise your Web site listing with certain search engines, meaning your site will show up nearer the top of a list of search results. The <meta> tags will affect your listing with AltaVista, Excite, Inktomi, and HotBot, but other search engines ignore them completely.

<meta> Element Syntax

The <meta> element is an empty element that resides in the <head> section of the HTML document. The <meta> element allows you to specify information about a document that is invisible to the user. Certain programs, such as search engines, can use this information for document cataloging. The <meta> element uses both name and content attributes, among others. The name attribute lets you specify a document property, such as "description" or "keywords." The content attribute contains the property's value. Table 10-1 lists the most commonly used name attribute values.

Table 10-1 <meta> name attribute values

name Attribute Values	Description
Author	The author of the page
Description	A short text-based description of the content of the Web site
Keywords	A comma-separated list of keywords that are potential search terms by which a user might find your site
Generator	The name and version of the page-authoring program that generated the site

The following code shows an example of the <meta> elements in use:

```
<html>
<head>
<meta  name="description" content="Joel Sklar Consulting -
Specializing in Course Development and Delivery on Web-
related topics">
<meta  name="keywords" content="Joel, Joel Sklar, Sklar,
HTML, XML, Web, Course Design, Course Development,
Technical Training, CSS, Cascading Style Sheets, HTML
Resources, XML Resources">
</head>
```

Notice that the code uses one <meta> element for each name and content attribute pair. The description property contains a short description of the Web site. The keywords property contains a list of potential search terms that the user might request.

Be Careful with Frames

Avoid using a frameset at the top level of your Web site if at all possible. Because frameset files have no content, they have no information to offer many search engines. If you need to use frames at the top level of your Web site, make sure to use both <meta> tags and information in the <noframes> element, as described in Chapter 8. Many search engines read the contents of <noframes> if they encounter a frameset. Here is an example of a frameset with appropriate <meta> and <noframes> content.

10

```
<html>
<head>
<title>Joel Sklar Consulting - Main Page</title>
<meta  name="description" content="Joel Sklar Consulting -
 Specializing in Course Development and Delivery on Web-
related topics">
<meta  name="keywords" content="Joel, Joel Sklar, Sklar,
HTML, XML, Web, Course Design, Course Development,
Technical Training, CSS, Cascading Style Sheets, HTML
Resources, XML Resources">
</head>
<frameset cols="150,*">
<frame src="navcol.htm">
<frame src="article1.htm" name="content">
<noframes>
<body>
The Joel Sklar Consulting Web site is a resource for HTML
authors and students.
<p>
You can view a <a href="index2.htm">non-framed</a>
version of the site.
</p>
</body>
```

```
</noframes>
</frameset>
</html>
```

Notice that the <noframes> code includes a link to a non-framed version of the Web site.

Use alt Text with Images

Always add alt information to all of the graphics on your page. Some search engines read the contents of the alt attribute, which is especially useful if you start your page with a graphic. Refer to Chapter 7 for more information on the alt attribute.

Submit URLs to Search Engines

One way to have search engines list your URL is to submit it to each of the popular search engine sites. The site's search engine will search your Web site and index the information. Periodically return to the search engine site and search for your Web site name or pertinent search terms. Some search engines are much faster at this process than others, so you may have to resubmit your URL if you do not see your page listed.

CHAPTER SUMMARY

After you plan, design, and build your Web site, you are ready to publish it on a Web server. Keep the following in mind:

- Publishing your Web site involves transferring files to a Web server. Internet Service Providers (ISPs) provide space on their Web server for their subscribers. You can use a File Transfer Protocol (FTP) application to transfer the files.

- Shop carefully and compare features when you are looking for an ISP or Web host. Consider the future disk space and technology needs of your content.

- Download and learn to use an FTP client for use in the often-repeated task of transferring files to your Web site.

- After your Web site is live, test it against the basic Web variables of browser, operating system, display resolution, and connection speed.

- Test your Web site with a variety of users. Listen carefully to their feedback to identify trouble spots in your information design.

- Plan for the maintenance, upkeep, and redesign of your Web site. Keep your content up to date. Let users know when you have made updates to the Web site.

- To take advantage of search engine behavior, enhance your Web site by using meaningful titles, including <meta> elements, avoiding a frameset at the top level of your Web site, using alt attribute text with images, and submitting your URLs to search engines.

REVIEW QUESTIONS

1. How does a Web site become live?

2. What is the difference between an Internet Service Provider (ISP) and a Web hosting service?

3. What is a Point of Presence (POP)?

4. What is the Secure Socket Layer (SSL)?

5. How will you recreate a first-time user's experience when you are testing your Web site?

6. List the four variables to consider when testing your Web site.

7. Why is it helpful to vary your user testing subjects?

8. What are the benefits of formalizing user testing?

9. What aspect of Web site maintenance often is overlooked?

10. What is a search engine?

11. Where does the content of the <title> element appear to the user?

12. What are the two most common attributes of the <meta> element?

13. Why are frames a problem for search engines?

14. List two methods that help search engines with framed Web sites.

10

HANDS-ON PROJECTS

1. Browse the Web for Internet Service Providers and Web hosting services. A good place to start is The List Web site (*thelist.Internet.com*).

   a. Find three different ISPs in your area.

   b. Prepare a comparison chart listing the major features and drawbacks of each ISP. Include information on pricing options.

   c. Choose the ISP you would use and explain why.

2. Download a shareware FTP program from the Web and set it up on your computer.

3. Write a test plan for your Web site.

   a. Create a section for each design variable.

   b. Spell out the exact steps of the test and the different variables that will be tested. State explicitly which browsers and version should be used, and on which operating system. Detail the different screen resolutions and connection speeds. List the exact pages that should be tested.

   c. Walk through the test procedure to test its validity.

4. Write a sample user feedback questionnaire.

5. Write a maintenance plan for your Web site.

   a. Include a schedule of content updates for the different sections of the Web site.

   b. Include a schedule of design reviews.

   c. Plan for link maintenance.

6. Visit some of the more popular Web search engines, such as AltaVista, Lycos, and Excite. Using each Web site's Help features, try to determine the best methods you can use to get each search engine to index your Web site properly.

CASE PROJECT

If you have access, publish your Web site using an FTP client. (If you cannot post your Web site to the Web, make it available on your computer.) Prepare for a round of user testing. Create a user feedback form and perform user testing on your Web site. Enlist six to ten people to review the Web site and fill out the form. Compile the results and write a paper detailing the results of the testing and what they indicate about the effectiveness of your design. Point out areas that you feel could benefit from the user recommendations. Be sure to list any assumptions you made about the Web site and how users either confirmed or denied these assumptions.

HTML REFERENCE

This appendix includes element descriptions sorted both alphabetically and by category. The elements listed in this appendix are the ones you will use most often, including a list of the Core attributes allowed with the majority of HTML elements and a complete list of character entities. For more detailed information, visit the World Wide Web Consortium Web site at *www.w3.org*.

CORE ATTRIBUTES

The Core attributes are allowed within all of the elements listed in the element tables.

Table A-1 HTML core attributes

Attribute	Definition
id	Specifies a document-wide unique identifier for an element
class	Specifies a class name for an element; the class name can be used to specify style sheet rules
style	Specifies a style sheet rule for the element
title	Specifies a title for the element; contents of the title is displayed in the browser as a pop up; Netscape Navigator 4.x does not support this attribute

ALPHABETICAL HTML REFERENCE

Table A-2 Common HTML elements

Element	Description	Attributes
<!--comment text-->	Allows you to insert a comment to your code. Browsers do not display comments in the Web page. Place the comment within the tag, for example: <!-- This is a comment -->	None
<a>	Allows you to create a clickable hypertext anchor in a document; can be text or an image	Core attributes plus: HREF the target destination in a document NAME the name of a fragment of the document TARGET the window or frame in which the linked document displays
<b>	Allows you to boldface text	Core attributes
<base>	Sets the base URL or target for a page; this is an empty element	Core attributes plus: HREF the absolute or relative original URL for the current document TARGET the default window or frame in which links contained in the document display
<basefont> deprecated	Allows you to set a default size for the body text in the document	COLOR the default text color FACE the default text face SIZE the default text size for the document from 1 to 7; normal browser default is size 3

Table A-2   Common HTML elements (continued)

Element	Description	Attributes
<blockquote>	Indents text on both the left and right margins	Core attributes
<body>	Identifies the body section of the Web page	Core attributes plus: ALINK the color for the currently selected link* BACKGROUND points to the image file that is tiled across the background of the page* BGCOLOR the page background color* LINK the color for unvisited links* TEXT the default text color* VLINK the color for visited links* * deprecated in HTML 4.0
 	Inserts a line break, forcing text to the next line; this is an empty element	Core attributes plus: CLEAR when used with a floating image, forces text to appear at the bottom of the image
<caption>	Indicates that the text appears as the caption of a table	Core attributes plus: ALIGN the alignment of the caption, either top or bottom; top is the default
<center> deprecated	Centers text or images horizontally on the page	None
<div>	Indicates a division within the document	Core attributes plus: ALIGN the horizontal alignment of the contents of the division
<em>	Emphasizes text, usually as italic; browser determines the text style	Core attributes
<font> deprecated	Allows you to specify the font size for any string of text; range of sizes is 1 to 7, with 3 being the default	SIZE sets the font size COLOR sets the text color FACE sets the font typeface
<frame>	Defines specific information for each frame in the frameset	Core attributes plus: FRAMEBORDER the width of the frame's border MARGINHEIGHT the margin height in pixels MARGINWIDTH the margin width in pixels NORESIZE prevents the user from resizing the frame by dragging the frame border NAME sets a targeting name for the frame

A

Table A-2   Common HTML elements (continued)

Element	Description	Attributes
		SCROLLING determines whether scroll bars appear SRC specifies the sources HTML file for the frame's content
<frameset>	Defines the column and row characteristics of the frames in the frameset	Core attributes plus: COLS separates the frameset into columns ROWS separates the frameset into rows (Both of these attributes need percentage or pixel values to specify the frame width or height)
<h1> - <h6>	Defines text as a heading level; <H1> is the top-level heading and the largest text	Core attributes plus: ALIGN the alignment of the heading text
<head>	Identifies the Head section of the Web page, which is reserved for information about the document, not document content	Three attributes that are not commonly used: PROFILE specifies the location of one or more meta data profiles about the document LANG specifies the base language for the document DIR specifies the default text direction
<hr>	Inserts a horizontal rule on the page; this is an empty element	Core attributes plus: WIDTH the length of the rule in pixels SIZE the height of the rule in pixels ALIGN horizontal rule alignment; default is center NOSHADE turns off the default 3-D shading of the rule
<html>	Identifies the file as an HTML file	None
<i>	Italicizes text	Core attributes
<img>	Inserts an image into a Web page	Core attributes plus: WIDTH specifies the width of the image in pixels HEIGHT specifies the height of the image in pixels SRC the URL that points to the image file; this attribute is required ALIGN allows you to wrap text around the image; valid values are left, middle, and right

Table A-2   Common HTML elements (continued)

Element	Description	Attributes
		ALT allows you to specify an alternate string of text if the image cannot be displayed by the browser BORDER the border for the image; set this attribute to zero (0) to remove a hypertext border on an anchor image HSPACE the horizontal white space in pixels on the left and right sides of an image VSPACE the vertical white space in pixels on the top and bottom of an image
`<li>`	Marks an individual list item; this is an empty tag	Core attributes
`<link>`	Defines a relationship between the document and external resources, such as a style sheet	Core attributes plus: TYPE the type of external resource HREF the URL of the external resource REL describes the relationship from the current document to the anchor specified by the href attribute
`<meta>`	Used within the document HEAD to provide information	NAME the meta information name, such as keyword or description CONTENT the content of the named information type
`<noframe>`	Contains content that is viewable by browsers that do not support frames	Core attributes
`<ol>`	Creates a numbered indented list	Core attributes
`<p>`	Marks the beginning of a new block of text	Core attributes plus: ALIGN the horizontal alignment of the paragraph content
`<pre>`	Preserves the formatting and spacing of text as typed in the source code; displays the text in a monospace font, different from the standard browser text	Core attributes
`<span>`	Serves as an inline division, used to apply a style class or rule to text	Core attributes
`<strong>`	Emphasizes text, usually as bold; browser determines the text style	Core attributes

Table A-2   Common HTML elements (continued)

Element	Description	Attributes
<style>	Used within the HEAD section to contain CSS style rules	TYPE specify the type of style language; for CSS, use text/CSS as the value
<sub>	Subscripts text	Core attributes
<sup>	Superscripts text	Core attributes
<table>	Marks the beginning and end of a table	Core attributes plus: ALIGN floats the table to the left or right of text* BORDER specifies whether a border is displayed for a table BGCOLOR the background color of the table* CELLPADDING the amount of space in pixels between the border of the cell and the cell content on all four sides CELLSPACING the amount of space in pixels between the table cells on all four sides HEIGHT the height of the table* WIDTH the width of the table, either to a fixed pixel width, or percentage relative width* *deprecated in HTML 4.0
<td>	Marks an individual table cell	Core attributes plus: ALIGN the horizontal alignment for table cells within the table row VALIGN the horizontal alignment for table cells within the row BGCOLOR the background color of the table row* ROWSPAN the number of rows spanned by a cell COLSPAN the number of columns spanned by a cell *deprecated in HTML 4.0
<th>	Forces the contents of a cell to display as bold and centered	Core attributes plus: ALIGN the horizontal alignment for table cells within the table row VALIGN the vertical alignment for table cells within the row BGCOLOR the background color of the table row* *deprecated in HTML 4.0

Table A-2   Common HTML elements (continued)

A

Element	Description	Attributes
		ROWSPAN the number of rows spanned by a cell COLSPAN the number of columns spanned by a cell
<title>	Specifies the title of the Web page; title text appears in the browser title bar and as the bookmark or favorites text	Two attributes that are not commonly used: LANG specifies the base language for the document DIR specifies the default text direction
<tr>	Marks a row of cells in a table	Core attributes plus: ALIGN the horizontal alignment for table cells within the table row VALIGN the vertical alignment for table cells within the row BGCOLOR the background color of the table row* *deprecated in HTML 4.0
<tt>	Specifies monospace text, usually Courier	Core attributes
<u> deprecated	Underlines text	Core attributes
<ul>	Creates a bulleted indented list	Core attributes

CATEGORICAL HTML REFERENCE

The following is a quick reference for the HTML elements and attributes used in this book, listed by category.

Global Structure Elements

Table A-3   HTML structure elements

Element	Description	Attributes
<body>	Identifies the Body section of the Web page	Core attributes plus: ALINK the color for the currently selected link* BACKGROUND points to the image file that is tiled across the background of the page* BGCOLOR the page background color* LINK the color for unvisited links* TEXT the default text color* VLINK the color for visited links * deprecated in HTML 4.0

Table A-3   HTML structure elements (continued)

Element	Description	Attributes
<div>	Indicates a division within the document	Core attributes plus: ALIGN the horizontal alignment of the contents of the division
<h1> - <h6>	Defines text as a heading level; <H1> is the top level heading and the largest text	Core attributes plus: ALIGN the alignment of the heading text
<head>	Identifies the Head section of the Web page, which is reserved for information about the document, not document content	Three attributes that are not commonly used: PROFILE specifies the location of one or more meta data profiles about the document LANG specifies the base language for the document DIR specifies the default text direction
<html>	Identifies the file as an HTML file	None
<meta>	Used within the document Head to provide information	NAME the meta information name, such as keywords or description CONTENT the content of the named information type
<span>	Serves as an inline division, used to apply a style class or rule to text	Core attributes
<title>	Specifies the title of the Web page; title text appears in the browser title bar and as the bookmark or favorites text	Two attributes that are not commonly used: LANG specifies the base language for the document DIR specifies the default text direction

Text Elements

Table A-4   HTML text elements

Element	Description	Attributes
<blockquote>	Indents text on both the left and right margins	Core attributes
 	Inserts a line break, forcing text to the next line; this is an empty element	Core attributes plus: CLEAR when used with a floating image, forces text to appear at the bottom of the image
<em>	Emphasizes text, usually as italic; browser determines the text style	Core attributes
<p>	Marks the beginning of a new block of text	Core attributes plus: ALIGN the horizontal alignment of the paragraph content

Table A-4   HTML text elements (continued)

Element	Description	Attributes
<pre>	Preserves the formatting and spacing of text as typed in the source code; displays the text in a monospace font, different from the standard browser text	Core attributes
<strong>	Emphasizes text, usually as bold; browser determines the text style	Core attributes
<sub>	Subscripts text	Core attributes
<sup>	Superscripts text	Core attributes

List Elements

Table A-5   HTML list elements

Element	Description	Attributes
<li>	Marks an individual list item; this is an empty tag	Core attributes
<ol>	Creates a numbered indented list	Core attributes
<ul>	Creates a bulleted indented list	Core attributes

Table Elements

Table A-6   HTML table elements

Element	Description	Attributes
<caption>	Indicates that the text appears as the caption of a table	Core attributes plus: ALIGN the alignment of the caption, either top or bottom; top is the default
<table>	Marks the beginning and end of a table	Core attributes plus: ALIGN floats the table to the left or right of text* BORDER specifies whether a border is displayed for a table BGCOLOR the background color of the table* CELLPADDING the amount of space in pixels between the border of the cell and the cell content on all four sides CELLSPACING the amount of space in pixels between the table cells on all four sides HEIGHT the height of the table* WIDTH the width of the table, either to a fixed pixel width or percentage relative width *deprecated in HTML 4.0

Table A-6   HTML table elements (continued)

Element	Description	Attributes
<td>	Marks an individual table cell	Core attributes plus: ALIGN the horizontal alignment for table cells within the table row VALIGN the vertical alignment for table cells within the row BGCOLOR the background color of the table row* ROWSPAN the number of rows spanned by a cell COLSPAN the number of columns spanned by a cell *deprecated in HTML 4.0
<th>	Forces the contents of a cell to display as bold and centered	Core attributes plus: ALIGN the horizontal alignment for table cells within the table row VALIGN the vertical alignment for table cells within the row BGCOLOR the background color of the table row* ROWSPAN the number of rows spanned by a cell COLSPAN the number of columns spanned by a cell *deprecated in HTML 4.0
<tr>	Marks a row of cells in a table	Core attributes plus: ALIGN the horizontal alignment for table cells within the table row VALIGN the vertical alignment for table cells within the row BGCOLOR the background color of the table row* *deprecated in HTML 4.0

Link Elements

Table A-7   HTML link elements

Element	Description	Attributes
<a>	Allows you to create a clickable hypertext anchor in a document; can be text or an image	Core attributes plus: HREF the target destination of the hypertext link NAME names a fragment of the document TARGET the window or frame in which the linked document displays
<base>	Sets the base URL or target for a page; this is an empty element	Core attributes plus: HREF the absolute or relative original URL for the current document TARGET the default window or frame in which links contained in the document display

Table A-7 HTML link elements (continued)

Element	Description	Attributes
<link>	Defines a relationship between the document and external resources, such as a style sheet	Core attributes plus: TYPE the type of external resource HREF the URL of the external resource

Inclusion Element

Table A-8 HTML inclusion element

Element	Description	Attributes
<img>	Inserts an image into a Web page	Core attributes plus: WIDTH specifies the width of the image in pixels HEIGHT specifies the height of the image in pixels SRC the URL that points to the image file; attribute is required ALIGN allows you to wrap text around the image; valid values are left, middle, and right ALT allows you to specify an alternate string of text if the image cannot be displayed by the browser BORDER the border for the image; set this attribute to zero (0) to remove a hypertext border on an anchor image HSPACE the horizontal white space in pixels on the left and right sides of an image VSPACE the vertical white space in pixels on the top and bottom of an image

Style Sheet Element

Table A-9 Style sheet element

Element	Description	Attributes
<style>	Used within the Head section to contain CSS style rules	TYPE specifies the type of style language; for CSS, use text/CSS as the value

Formatting Elements

Table A-10 HTML formatting elements

Element	Description	Attributes
<b>	Boldfaces text	Core attributes
<basefont> deprecated	Allows you to set a default size for the body text in the document	COLOR the default text color FACE the default text face SIZE the default text size for the document from 1 – 7; the normal browser default is size 3

Table A-10   HTML formatting elements (continued)

Element	Description	Attributes
`<center>` deprecated	Centers text or images horizontally on the page	None
`<font>` deprecated	Allows you to specify the font size for any string of text; range of sizes is 1 to 7, with 3 being the default	SIZE sets the font size COLOR sets the text color FACE sets the font typeface
`<hr>`	Inserts a horizontal rule on the page; this is an empty element	Core attributes plus: WIDTH the length of the rule in pixels SIZE the height of the rule in pixels ALIGN horizontal rule alignment; default is center NOSHADE turns off the default 3-D shading of the rule
`<i>`	Italicizes text	Core attributes
`<tt>`	Specifies monospace text, usually in Courier	Core attributes
`<u>` deprecated	Underlines text	Core attributes

Frame Elements

Table A-11   HTML frame elements

Element	Description	Attributes
`<frameset>`	Defines the column and row characteristics of the frames in the frameset	COLS separates the frame set into columns ROWS separates the frameset into rows (Both of these attributes need percentage or pixel values to specify the frame width or height)
`<noframe>`	Contains content that is viewable by browsers that do not support frames	Core attributes

NUMERIC AND CHARACTER ENTITIES

Table A-12   Numeric and character entities

Character	Character Entity	Numeric Entity	Description
"	"	"	Quotation mark
#	#		Number sign
$	$		Dollar sign
%	%		Percent sign

Table A-12   Numeric and character entities (continued)

Character	Character Entity	Numeric Entity	Description
&	&#38;	&amp;	Ampersand
'	&#39;		Apostrophe
(	&#40;		Left parenthesis
)	&#41;		Right parenthesis
*	&#42;		Asterisk
+	&#43;		Plus sign
,	&#44;		Comma
-	&#45;		Hyphen
.	&#46;		Period (fullstop)
/	&#47;		Solidus (slash)
0	&#48;		Digit 0
1	&#49;		Digit 1
2	&#50;		Digit 2
3	&#51;		Digit 3
4	&#52;		Digit 4
5	&#53;		Digit 5
6	&#54;		Digit 6
7	&#55;		Digit 7
8	&#56;		Digit 8
9	&#57;		Digit 9
:	&#58;		Colon
;	&#59;		Semicolon
<	&#60;	&lt;	Less than
=	&#61;		Equals sign
>	&#62;	&gt;	Greater than
?	&#63;		Question mark
@	&#64;		Commercial at
A - Z	A - Z		Uppercase letters A-Z
[	&#91;		Left square bracket
\	&#92;		Reverse solidus (backslash)
]	&#93;		Right square bracket
^	&#94;		Caret
_	&#95;		Horizontal bar (underscore)
`	&#96;		Acute accent
a-z	a - &#122		Lowercase letters A-Z
{	&#123;		Left curly brace

Table A-12   Numeric and character entities (continued)

Character	Character Entity	Numeric Entity	Description
|	|		Vertical bar
}	&#125;		Right curly brace
~	&#126;		Tilde
			Non-breaking space
¡	&#161;	&iexcl;	Inverted exclamation mark
¢	&#162;	&cent;	Cent sign
£	&#163;	&pound;	British Pound sign
$	&#164;	&curren;	Currency sign
¥	&#165;	&yen;	Yen sign
¦	&#166;	&brvbar;	Broken vertical bar
§	&#167;	&sect;	Section sign
¨	&#168;	&uml;	Spacing diaeresis
©	&#169;	&copy;	Copyright sign
ª	&#170;	&ordf;	Feminine ordinal indicator
«	&#171;	&laquo;	Left-pointing double angle quotation mark
¬	&#172;	&not;	Not sign
	&#173;	&shy;	Soft hyphen
®	&#174;	&reg;	Registered trademark sign
¯	&#175;	&macr;	Macron overline
°	&#176;	&deg;	Degree sign
±	&#177;	&plusmn;	Plus-or-minus sign
²	&#178;	&sup2;	Superscript digit 2
³	&#179;	&sup3;	Superscript digit 3
´	&#180;	&acute;	Acute accent
µ	&#181;	&micro;	Micro sign
¶	&#182;	&para;	Paragraph sign
·	&#183;	&middot;	Middle dot
¸	&#184;	&cedil;	Cedilla
¹	&#185;	&sup1;	Superscript digit 1
º	&#186;	&ordm;	Masculine ordinal indicator
»	&#187;	&raquo;	Right-pointing double angle quotation mark
¼	&#188;	&frac14;	Fraction one-quarter
½	&#189;	&frac12;	Fraction one-half
¾	&#190;	&frac34;	Fraction three-quarters
¿	&#191;	&iquest;	Inverted question mark

Table A-12   Numeric and character entities (continued)

Character	Character Entity	Numeric Entity	Description
À	&#192;	&Agrave;	Capital letter A with grave
Á	&#193;	&Aacute;	Capital letter A with acute
Â	&#194;	&Acirc;	Capital letter A with circumflex
Ã	&#195;	&Atilde;	Capital letter A with tilde
Ä	&#196;	&Auml;	Capital letter A with diaeresis
Å	&#197;	&Aring;	Capital letter A with ring above
Æ	&#198;	&Aelig;	Capital letter AE
Ç	&#199;	&Ccedil;	Capital letter C with cedilla
È	&#200;	&Egrave;	Capital letter E with grave
É	&#201;	&Eacute;	Capital letter E with acute
Ê	&#202;	&Ecirc;	Capital letter E with circumflex
Ë	&#203;	&Euml;	Capital letter E with diaeresis
Ì	&#204;	&Igrave;	Capital letter I with grave
Í	&#205;	&Iacute;	Capital letter I with acute
Î	&#206;	&Icirc;	Capital letter I with circumflex
Ï	&#207;	&Iuml;	Capital letter I with diaeresis
Ð	&#208;	&ETH;	Capital letter ETH
Ñ	&#209;	&Ntilde;	Capital letter N with tilde
Ò	&#210;	&Ograve;	Capital letter O with grave
Ó	&#211;	&Oacute;	Capital letter O with acute
Ô	&#212;	&Ocirc;	Capital letter O with circumflex
Õ	&#213;	&Otilde;	Capital letter O with tilde
Ö	&#214;	&Ouml;	Capital letter O with diaeresis
×	&#215;	&times;	Multiplication sign
Ø	&#216;	&Oslash;	Capital letter O with stroke
Ù	&#217;	&Ugrave;	Capital letter U with grave
Ú	&#218;	&Uacute;	Capital letter U with acute
Û	&#219;	&Ucirc;	Capital letter U with circumflex
Ü	&#220;	&Uuml;	Capital letter U with diaeresis
Ý	&#221;	&Yacute;	Capital letter Y with acute
Þ	&#222;	&THORN;	Capital letter THORN
ß	&#223;	&szlig;	Sz ligature
à	&#224;	&agrave;	Small letter a with grave
á	&#225;	&aacute;	Small letter a with acute
â	&#226;	&acirc;	Small letter a with circumflex
ã	&#227;	&atilde;	Small letter a with tilde

Table A-12   Numeric and character entities (continued)

Character	Character Entity	Numeric Entity	Description
ä	&#228;	&auml;	Small letter a with diaeresis
å	&#229;	&aring;	Small letter a with ring above
æ	&#230;	&aelig;	Small letter ae
ç	&#231;	&ccedil;	Small letter c with cedilla
è	&#232;	&egrave;	Small letter e with grave
é	&#233;	&eacute;	Small letter e with acute
ê	&#234;	&ecirc;	Small letter e with circumflex
ë	&#235;	&euml;	Small letter e with diaeresis
ì	&#236;	&igrave;	Small letter i with grave
í	&#237;	&iacute;	Small letter i with acute
î	&#238;	&icirc;	Small letter i with circumflex
ï	&#239;	&iuml;	Small letter i with diaeresis
d–	&#240;	&eth;	Small letter eth
ñ	&#241;	&ntilde;	Small letter n with tilde
ò	&#242;	&ograve;	Small letter o with grave
ó	&#243;	&oacute;	Small letter o with acute
ô	&#244;	&ocirc;	Small letter o with circumflex
õ	&#245;	&otilde;	Small letter o with tilde
ö	&#246;	&ouml;	Small letter o with diaeresis
÷	&#247;	&divide;	Division sign
o/	&#248;	&oslash;	Small letter o with stroke
ù	&#249;	&ugrave;	Small letter u with grave
ú	&#250;	&uacute;	Small letter u with acute
û	&#251;	&ucirc;	Small letter u with circumflex
ü	&#252;	&uuml;	Small letter u with diaeresis
´y	&#253;	&yacute;	Small letter y with acute
þ	&#254;	&thorn;	Small letter thorn
ÿ	&#255;	&yuml;	Small letter y with diaeresis

B

CSS REFERENCE

This appendix includes the most commonly used CSS property descriptions, sorted both alphabetically and by category. For more detailed information, visit the World Wide Web Consortium Web site at *www.w3.org*.

CSS Notation Reference

Notation	Definition
<>	Words between angle brackets specify a type of value. For example, **<color>** means to enter a color value such as red.
I	A single vertical bar between values means one or the other must occur. For example, **scroll I fixed** means choose scroll or fixed.
II	Two vertical bars separating values means one or the other or both values can occur. For example, **<border-width> II <border-style> II <color>** means any or all of the three values can occur.
[ ]	Square brackets group parts of the property value together. For example, **none I [underline II overline II line-through II blink]** means the value is either none or one of the values within the square brackets.

Alphabetical CSS Property Reference

Property	Values	Default	Applies to
Background (Shorthand property)	<background-color> II <background-image> II <background-repeat> II <background-attachment> II <background-position>	No default for shorthand properties	All elements
Background-attachment	scroll I fixed	Scroll	All elements
Background-color	color name or hexadecimal value I transparent	Transparent	All elements
Background-image	<url> I none	None	All elements
Background-position	[<percentage> I <length>] {1,2} I [top I center I bottom] II [left I center I right]	0% 0%	Block-level and replaced elements
Background-repeat	repeat I repeat-x I repeat-y I no-repeat	Repeat	All elements
Border (Shorthand property)	<border-width> II <border-style> II <color>	No default for shorthand properties	All elements
Border-bottom	<border-bottom-width> II <border-style> II <color>	No default for shorthand properties	All elements

Property	Values	Default	Applies to
Border-bottom-color	<color>	The value of the 'color' property	All elements
Border-bottom-style	none | dotted | dashed | solid | double | groove | ridge | inset | outset	None	All elements
Border-bottom-width	thin | medium | thick | <length>	'Medium'	All elements
Border-color	<color>	The value of the 'color' property	All elements
Border-left (Shorthand property)	<border-left-width> || <border-style> || <color>	No default for shorthand properties	All elements
Border-left-color	<color>	The value of the 'color' property	All elements
Border-left-style	none | dotted | dashed | solid | double | groove | ridge | inset | outset	None	All elements
Border-left-width	thin | medium | thick | <length>	'Medium'	All elements
Border right (Shorthand property)	<border-right-width> || <border-style> || <color>	No default for shorthand properties	All elements
Border-right-color	<color>	The value of the 'color' property	All elements
Border-right-style	none | dotted | dashed | solid | double | groove | ridge | inset | outset	None	All elements
Border-right-width	thin | medium | thick | <length>	'Medium'	All elements
Border-style	none | dotted | dashed | solid | double | groove | ridge | inset | outset	None	All elements
Border-top (Shorthand property)	<border-top-width> || <border-style> || <color>	No default for shorthand properties	All elements
Border-top-color	<color>	The value of the 'color' property	All elements
Border-top-style	none | dotted | dashed | solid | double | groove | ridge | inset | outset	None	All elements

B

Property	Values	Default	Applies to
Border-top-width	thin I medium I thick I \<length\>	'Medium'	All elements
Border-width (Shorthand property)	[thin I medium I thick I \<length\>]	No default for shorthand properties	All elements
Bottom	\<length\> I \<percentage\> I auto	Auto	Positioned elements
Clear	none I left I right I both	None	All elements
Color	\<color\>	Browser-specific	All elements
Display	inline I block I list-item I run-in I compact I marker I table I inline-table I table-row-group I table-header-group I table-footer-group I table-row I table-column-group I table-column I table-cell I table-caption I none	Inline	All elements
Float	left I right I none	None	All elements
Font (Shorthand property)	[\<font-style\> II \<font-variant\> II \<font-weight\>] \<font-size\> [/ \<line-height\>] \<font-family\>	No default for shorthand properties	All elements
Font-family	Font family name (such as Times) or generic family name (such as sans-serif)	Browser specific	All elements
Font-size	\<absolute-size\> I \<relative-size\> I \<length\> I \<percentage\>	Medium	All elements
Font-stretch	normal I wider I narrower I ultra-condensed I extra-condensed I condensed I semi-condensed I semi-expanded I expanded I extra-expanded I ultra-expanded	Normal	All elements
Font-style	normal I italic I oblique	Normal	All elements
Font-variant	normal I small caps	Normal	All elements
Font-weight	normal I bold I bolder I lighter I 100 I 200 I 300 I 400 I 500 I 600 I 700 I 800 I 900	Normal	All elements
Height	\<length\> I \<percentage\> I auto	Auto	Block-level and replaced elements; also all elements except inline images

B

Property	Values	Default	Applies to
Left	<length> | <percentage> | auto	Auto	Positioned elements
Letter-spacing	normal | <length>	Normal	All elements
Line-height	normal | <number> | <length> | <percentage>	Normal	All elements
List-style (Shorthand property)	<keyword> || <position> || <url>	No default for shorthand properties	Elements with 'display' value 'list-item'
List-style-image	<url> | none	None	Elements with 'display' value 'list-item'
List-style-position	inside | outside	Outside	Elements with 'display' value 'list-item'
List-style-type	disc | circle | square | decimal | lower-roman | upper-roman | lower-alpha | upper-alpha | none	Disc	Elements with 'display' value 'list-item'
Margin (Shorthand property)	[<length> | <percentage> | auto]	No default for shorthand properties	All elements
Margin-bottom	<length> | <percentage> | auto	0	All elements
Margin-left	<length> | <percentage> | auto	0	All elements
Margin-right	<length> | <percentage> | auto	0	All elements
Margin-top	<length> | <percentage> | auto	0	All elements
Padding	<length> | <percentage>	0	All elements
Padding-bottom	<length> | <percentage>	0	All elements
Padding-left	<length> | <percentage>	0	All elements
Padding-right	<length> | <percentage>	0	All elements
Padding-top	<length> | <percentage>	0	All elements
Position	static | relative | absolute | fixed	Static	All elements except generated content

Property	Values	Default	Applies to
Right	<length> I <percentage> I auto	Auto	Positioned elements
Text-align	left I right I center I justify	Depends on browser and language direction	Block-level elements
Text-decoration	none I [underline II overline II line-through II blink]	None	All elements
Text-indent	<length> I <percentage>	0	Block-level elements
Text-shadow	none I [<color> II <length> <length> <length>? ,]* [<color> II<length> <length> <length>?]	None	All elements
Text-transform	capitalize I uppercase I lowercase I none	None	All elements
Top	<length> I <percentage> I auto	Auto	Positioned elements
Vertical-align	baseline I sub I super I top I text-top I middle I bottom I text-bottom I <percentage>	Baseline	Inline elements
White-space	normal I pre I nowrap	Normal	Block-level elements
Width	<length> I <percentage> I auto	Auto	Block-level and replaced elements; also all elements except inline elements
Word-spacing	normal I <length>	Normal	All elements
Z-index	auto I integer	Auto	Positioned elements

CSS PROPERTIES BY CATEGORY

Font and Text Properties

Property	Values	Default	Applies to
Color	<color>	Browser-specific	All elements
Font (Shorthand property)	[<font-style> II <font-variant> II <font-weight>] <font-size> [/ <line-height>] <font-family>	No default for shorthand properties	All elements
Font-family	Font family name (such as Times) or generic family name (such as sans-serif)	Browser-specific	All elements
Font-size	<absolute-size> I <relative-size> I <length> I <percentage>	Medium	All elements
Font-style	normal I italic I oblique	Normal	All elements
Font-stretch	normal I wider I narrower I ultra-condensed I extra-condensed I condensed I semi-condensed I semi-expanded I expanded I extra-expanded I ultra-expanded	Normal	All elements
Font-variant	normal I small-caps	Normal	All elements
Font-weight	normal I bold I bolder I lighter I 100 I 200 I 300 I 400 I 500 I 600 I 700 I 800 I 900	Normal	All elements
Letter-spacing	normal I <length>	Normal	All elements
Line-height	normal I <number> I <length> I <percentage>	Normal	All elements
Text-align	left I right I center I justify	Depends on browser and language direction	Block-level elements
Text-decoration	none I [underline II overline II line-through II blink]	None	All elements
Text-indent	<length> I <percentage>	0	Block-level elements
Text-shadow	none I [<color> II <length> <length> <length>? ,]* [<color> II<length> <length> <length>?]	None	All elements

Property	Values	Default	Applies to
Text-transform	capitalize I uppercase I lowercase I none	None	All elements
Vertical-align	baseline I sub I super I top I text-top I middle I bottom I text-bottom I <percentage>	Baseline	Inline elements
Word-spacing	normal I <length>	Normal	All elements

Box Properties

Property	Values	Default	Applies to
Margin (Shorthand property)	[<length> I <percentage> I auto]	No default for shorthand properties	All elements
Margin-bottom	<length> I <percentage> I auto	0	All elements
Margin-left	<length> I <percentage> I auto	0	All elements
Margin-right	<length> I <percentage> I auto	0	All elements
Margin-top	<length> I <percentage> I auto	0	All elements
Padding	<length> I <percentage>	0	All elements
Padding-bottom	<length> I <percentage>	0	All elements
Padding-left	<length> I <percentage>	0	All elements
Padding-right	<length> I <percentage>	0	All elements
Padding-top	<length> I <percentage>	0	All elements
Border (Shorthand property)	<border-width> II <border-style> II <color>	No default for shorthand properties	All elements
Border-bottom	<border-bottom-width> II <border-style> II <color>	No default for shorthand properties	All elements
Border-bottom-color	<color>	The value of the 'color' property	All elements
Border-bottom-style	none I dotted I dashed I solid I double I groove I ridge I inset I outset	None	All elements
Border-bottom-width	thin I medium I thick I <length>	'Medium'	All elements
Border-color	<color>	The value of the 'color' property	All elements

B

Property	Values	Default	Applies to
Border-left (Shorthand property)	\<border-left-width\> || \<border-style\> || \<color\>	No default for shorthand properties	All elements
Border-left-color	\<color\>	The value of the 'color' property	All elements
Border-left-style	none | dotted | dashed | solid | double | groove | ridge | inset | outset	None	All elements
Border-left-width	thin | medium | thick | \<length\>	'Medium'	All elements
Border-right (Shorthand property)	\<border-right-width\> || \<border-style\> || \<color\>	No default for shorthand properties	All elements
Border-right-color	\<color\>	The value of the 'color' property	All elements
Border-right-style	none | dotted | dashed | solid | double | groove | ridge | inset | outset	None	All elements
Border-right-width	thin | medium | thick | \<length\>	'Medium'	All elements
Border-style	none | dotted | dashed | solid | double | groove | ridge | inset | outset	None	All elements
Border-top (Shorthand property)	\<border-top-width\> || \<border-style\> || \<color\>	No default for shorthand properties	All elements
Border-top-color	\<color\>	The value of the 'color' property	All elements
Border-top-style	none | dotted | dashed | solid | double | groove | ridge | inset | outset	None	All elements
Border-top-width	thin | medium | thick | \<length\>	'Medium'	All elements
Border-width (Shorthand property)	[thin | medium | thick | \<length\>]	No default for shorthand properties	All elements
Clear	none | left | right | both	None	All elements
Float	left | right | none	None	All elements
Height	\<length\> | \<percentage\> | auto	Auto	Block-level and replaced elements
Width	\<length\> | \<percentage\> | auto	Auto	Block-level and replaced elements

Background Properties

Property	Values	Default	Applies to
Background (Shorthand property)	\<background-color\> || \<background-image\> || \<background-repeat\> || \<background-attachment\> || \<background-position\>	No default for shorthand properties	All elements
Background-attachment	scroll | fixed	Scroll	All elements
Background-color	color name or hexadecimal value | transparent	Transparent	All elements
Background-image	\<url\> | none	None	All elements
Background-position	[\<percentage\> | \<length\>] {1,2} | [top | center | bottom] | [left | center | right]	0% 0%	Block-level and replaced elements
Background-repeat	repeat | repeat-x | repeat-y | no-repeat	Repeat	All elements

Visual Properties

Property	Values	Default	Applies to
Bottom	\<length\> | \<percentage\> | auto	Auto	Positioned elements
Height	\<length\> | \<percentage\> | auto	Auto	All elements except inline elements
Left	\<length\> | \<percentage\> | auto	Auto	Positioned elements
Position	static | relative | absolute | fixed	Static	All elements except generated content
Right	\<length\> | \<percentage\> | auto	Auto	Positioned elements
Top	\<length\> | \<percentage\> | auto	Auto	Positioned elements
Width	\<length\> | \<percentage\> | auto	Auto	All elements except inline elements
Z-index	auto | integer	Auto	Positioned elements

Classification Properties

Property	Values	Default	Applies to
Display	inline I block I list-item I run-in I compact I marker I table I inline-table I table-row-group I table-header-group I table-footer-group I table-row I table-column-group I table-column I table-cell I table-caption I none	Inline	All elements
List-style-image	<url> I none	None	Elements with 'display' value 'list-item'
List-style-position	inside I outside	Outside	Elements with 'display' value 'list-item'
List-style (Shorthand property)	<keyword> II <position> II <url>	No default for shorthand properties	Elements with 'display' value 'list-item'
List-style-type	disc I circle I square I decimal I lower-roman I upper-roman I lower-alpha I upper-alpha I none	Disc	Elements with 'display' value 'list-item'
White-space	normal I pre I nowrap	Normal	Block-level elements

CSS Measurement Units

Unit	Code Abbreviation	Description
Centimeter	cm	Standard metric centimeter
Em	em	The width of the capital M in the current font, usually the same as the font size
Ex	ex	The height of the letter x in the current font
Inch	in	Standard U.S. inch
Millimeter	mm	Standard metric millimeter
Pica	pc	Standard publishing unit equal to 12 points
Pixel	px	The size of a pixel on the current display
Point	pt	Standard publishing unit; there are 72 points in an inch
Relative	For example: 150%	Sets a font size relative to the base font size. 150% equals one-and-one-half the base font size.

ISO 369 2-Letter Language Codes

Code	Language
AA	Afar
AB	Abkhazian
AF	Afrikaans
AM	Amharic
AR	Arabic
AS	Assamese
AY	Aymara
AZ	Azerbaijani
BA	Bashkir
BE	Byelorussian
BG	Bulgarian
BH	Bihari
BI	Bislama
BN	Bengali Bangla
BO	Tibetan
BR	Breton
CA	Catalan
CO	Corsican

Code	Language
CS	Czech
CY	Welsh
DA	Danish
DE	German
DZ	Bhutani
EL	Greek
EN	English American
EO	Esperanto
ES	Spanish
ET	Estonian
EU	Basque
FA	Persian
FI	Finnish
FJ	Fiji
FO	Faeroese
FR	French
FY	Frisian
GA	Irish
GD	Gaelic Scots Gaelic
GL	Galician
GN	Guarani
GU	Gujarati
HA	Hausa
HI	Hindi
HR	Croatian
HU	Hungarian
HY	Armenian
IA	Interlingua
IE	Interlingue
IK	Inupiak
IN	Indonesian
IS	Icelandic
IT	Italian
IW	Hebrew
JA	Japanese
JI	Yiddish
JW	Javanese

Code	Language
KA	Georgian
KK	Kazakh
KL	Greenlandic
KM	Cambodian
KN	Kannada
KO	Korean
KS	Kashmiri
KU	Kurdish
KY	Kirghiz
LA	Latin
LN	Lingala
LO	Laothian
LT	Lithuanian
LV	Latvian Lettish
MG	Malagasy
MI	Maori
MK	Macedonian
ML	Malayalam
MN	Mongolian
MO	Moldavian
MR	Marathi
MS	Malay
MT	Maltese
MY	Burmese
NA	Nauru
NE	Nepali
NL	Dutch
NO	Norwegian
OC	Occitan
OM	Oromo Afan
OR	Oriya
PA	Punjabi
PL	Polish
PS	Pashto Pushto
PT	Portuguese
QU	Quechua
RM	Rhaeto-Romance

B

Code	Language
RN	Kirundi
RO	Romanian
RU	Russian
RW	Kinyarwanda
SA	Sanskrit
SD	Sindhi
SG	Sangro
SH	Serbo-Croatian
SI	Singhalese
SK	Slovak
SL	Slovenian
SM	Samoan
SN	Shona
SO	Somali
SQ	Albanian
SR	Serbian
SS	Siswati
ST	Sesotho
SU	Sudanese
SV	Swedish
SW	Swahili
TA	Tamil
TE	Tegulu
TG	Tajik
TH	Thai
TI	Tigrinya
TK	Turkmen
TL	Tagalog
TN	Setswana
TO	Tonga
TR	Turkish
TS	Tsonga
TT	Tatar
TW	Twi
UK	Ukrainian
UR	Urdu

Code	Language
UZ	Uzbek
VI	Vietnamese
VO	Volapuk
WO	Wolof
XH	Xhosa
YO	Yoruba
ZH	Chinese
ZU	Zulu

Glossary

Active white space — White space used deliberately as an integral part of your design that provides structure and separates content.

Animated GIF — A Graphics Interchange Format (GIF) file that is capable of storing multiple images along with timing information about the images. This means that you can build animations consisting of multiple static images that play continuously, creating the illusion of motion.

ASCII — The American Standard Code for Information Interchange (ASCII) is the most common format for text files. HTML files are ASCII text files.

Browser-safe colors — The 216 colors shared by PCs and Macintoshes. These colors display properly across both platforms without dithering.

Cache — The browser's temporary storage area for Web pages and images. There are two types of cache: memory cache and hard drive cache.

Canvas area — The part of the browser window that displays the content of the Web page.

Cascading Style Sheets — A style language, created by the W3C, that allows complete specifications of style for HTML documents. CSS allows HTML authors to use over 50 properties that affect the display of Web pages. CSS style information is contained either within an HTML document, or in external documents called style sheets.

CGI — See *Common Gateway Interface*.

CGI script — An application program that runs in the Common Gateway Interface (CGI). CGI scripts often are used to collect data that a user has entered in an HTML form, and then pass it to an application for processing.

Color channel — One of the three basic colors in the RGB color space: red, green, or blue.

Client — Software that communicates with a server. In the Web environment, the Web browser is client software.

Color depth — The amount of data used to create color on a display. The three common color depths are 8-bit, 16-bit, and 24-bit. Not all displays support all color depths.

Common Gateway Interface (CGI) — The communications bridge between the Internet and the server. Using programs called scripts, CGI can collect data sent by a user via the Hypertext Transfer Protocol (HTTP) and transfer it to a variety of data processing programs including spreadsheets, databases, or other software running on the server.

Complete URL — A complete Uniform Resource Locator (URL) is an address of documents and other resources on the Web that includes the protocol the browser uses to access the file, server or domain name, the relative path, and the filename.

CSS — See *Cascading Style Sheets*.

Deprecated elements — Elements that the W3C has identified as obsolete in future releases of HTML.

Dithering — This color mixing process occurs when a browser encounters a color on a Web page that it does not support. The browser is forced to mix the color. The resulting color may be grainy or unacceptable. To avoid dithering, work with browser-safe colors.

Domain name — An identifying name for an organization on the Internet. The domain name is an alias for the actual numeric IP address of the server that hosts the Web site. The domain name also is part of the Uniform Resource Locator (URL) address.

Dots per inch (DPI) — A measure of resolution, the sharpness of a computer display. Also used to refer to the resolution capability of a computer printer.

DPI — See *Dots per inch*.

Extensible Hypertext Markup Language (XHTML) — XHTML is HTML 4.01 reformulated as an application of XML.

Extensible Markup Language (XML) — A meta-language that allows you to create elements that meet your information needs, which significantly distinguishes it from the pre-defined elements of HTML. XML provides a format for describing structured data that can be shared by multiple applications across multiple platforms.

Extensible Style Language (XSL) — A style language created by the W3C for use with the Extensible Markup Language (XML).

External style sheets — ASCII text files that contain style rules written in CSS. External style sheets can be used to set styles for a large number of HTML documents.

Extranet — A private part of a company's intranet that uses the Internet to share securely part of an organization's information.

File Transfer Protocol (FTP) — A standard communications protocol for transferring files over the Internet.

Font — A typeface in a particular size, such as Times Roman 24-point.

Form controls — These are the input elements that make up an HTML form, such as radio buttons, text boxes, and check boxes.

Fragment — A logical segment of an HTML document. You can name the segment using a fragment identifier.

Fragment identifier — The use of the <a> element and NAME attribute to name a segment of an HTML file. You then can reference the fragment name in a hypertext link.

FTP — See *File Transfer Protocol*.

FTP client — A graphical software program that simplifies the task of transferring files using FTP.

GIF — See *Graphics Interchange Format*.

Graphics Interchange Format (GIF) — The Graphic Interchange Format (GIF) is designed for online delivery of graphics. The color depth of GIF is 8-bit, allowing a palette of no more than 256colors. The GIF file format excels at compressing and displaying flat color areas, making it the logical choice for line art and graphics with simple colors.

Grid — A layout device that organizes the Web page, providing visual consistency.

Hexadecimal number — A base-16 numbering system that uses the numbers 0-9 and then the letters A-F. Hexadecimal numbers are used to express RGB color values in HTML.

Hypertext — A nonlinear way of organizing information. When you are using a hypertext system, you can skip from one related topic to another, find the information that interests you, and then return to your starting point or move on to another related topic of interest.

Interlacing — The gradual display of a graphic in a series of passes as the data arrives in the browser. Each additional pass of data creates a clearer view of the image until the complete image is displayed. You can choose an interlacing process when you are creating GIFs.

Internet Service Provider (ISP) — A company that provides Internet access and Web site hosting services to individuals and organizations.

Intranet — A private collection of networks contained within an organization. Intranet users gain access to the Internet through a firewall that prevents unauthorized users from getting in to the intranet.

ISP — See *Internet Service Provider*.

Joint Photographic Experts Group (JPEG or JPG) — A file format, commonly shortened to JPG, designed for the transfer of photographic images over the Internet. JPGs are best for photos and images that contain feathering, complex shadows, or gradations.

JPEG — See *Joint Photographic Experts Group*.

JPG — See *Joint Photographic Experts Group.*

Leading — The vertical white space between lines of type. You can adjust leading with the CSS Line-Height property.

Lossless compression — A file compression method that reduces file size without the loss of any data. GIF and PNG are lossless file formats.

Lossy compression — A file compression method that discards some data in order to gain a smaller file size. The difference in quality of the resulting file is not that noticeable on a computer display. JPG is a lossy file format.

Markup language — A structured language that lets you identify common elements of a document such as headings, paragraphs, and lists.

Meta-language — A language that lets you describe the characteristics of a markup language. The Extensible Markup Language (XML) is a meta-language.

Non-dithering Web palette — The basic Web palette that contains 216 non-dithering colors. The 216 colors are shared by PCs and Macintoshes and often are called browser-safe colors.

Parser — A program built into a browser that interprets the markup tags in an HTML file and displays the results in the canvas area of the browser interface.

Partial URL — A Uniform Resource Locator (URL) that omits the protocol and server name, and only specifies the path to the file relative to one another on the same server.

Pica — A printing measurement unit, equal to 12 points. Picas are a valid measurement unit in Cascading Style Sheets; abbreviated as "pc."

Pixel — The unit of measurement on a computer display. The number of pixels on the display is based on the screen resolution chosen by the user. Pixels are a valid measurement unit in Cascading Style Sheets; abbreviated as "px."

Plug-ins — Helper applications that assist a browser in rendering a special effect.

PNG — See *Portable Network Graphics.*

Point — A printing measurement unit, equal to 1/72nd of an inch. Points are a valid measurement unit in Cascading Style Sheets; abbreviated as "pt."

Points of Presence (POP) — Dial-up access points to your service provider's network. Your service provider should have at least one POP available so you can dial a local number to get access. Major ISPs such as AT&T have POPs throughout the United States, where a local ISP only will cover the area that includes their subscriber base.

POP — See *Points of Presence.*

POP3 — See *Post Office Protocol 3.*

Portable Network Graphic (PNG) — A graphics file format for the Web that supports many of the same features as GIF.

Post Office Protocol 3 (POP3) — A client/server protocol that allows an Internet server to receive and hold e-mail.

Progressive display — The gradual display of a graphic in a series of passes as the data arrives in the browser. Each additional pass of data creates a clearer view of the image until the complete image is displayed.

Progressive JPG — A form of the JPG file format that progressively displays the image in a series of passes as the data arrives in the browser.

RGB color space — The three basic colors of red, green, and blue that computers use to display color.

Scalable Vector Graphics (SVG) — A language for describing two-dimensional graphics using XML. SVG files can contain shapes such as lines and curves, images, text, animation and interactive events.

Screen resolution — The horizontal and vertical height and width of the computer screen in pixels. The three most common screen resolutions (traditionally expressed as width × height) are 640 × 480, 800 × 600, and 1024 × 768.

Secure Sockets Layer (SSL) — Communications software that allows transmission of encrypted secure messages over the Internet.

Server — The name for a computer that runs server software. Server software allows other computers, called clients, to interact with the server to access data. In the Web environment, servers answer requests from client Web browsers for HTML pages and other data.

SGML — See *Standard Generalized Markup Language*.

Shareware — Software that is distributed free so users can try before they buy. Users then can register the software for a relatively small fee compared to software produced commercially. Shareware usually is developed by individuals or very small software companies, so registering the software is important.

Standard Generalized Markup Language (SGML) — A standard system for specifying document structure using markup tags.

Style sheet — An ASCII text file that contains style information for HTML documents, written in either Cascading Style Sheets (CSS) or Extensible Style Language (XSL).

Structured Query Language (SQL) — A programming language that lets you select information from a database.

Typeface — The name of type family, such as Times Roman or Futura Condensed.

Uniform Resource Locator (URL) — The global address of documents and other resources on the Web.

Vector graphics — Images represented as geometrical formulas, as compared with a raster graphics format, which represents images pixel by pixel for the entire image. GIFs and JPGs are raster formats. SVG is a vector graphic format. Vector graphics are scalable and cross-platform compatible.

W3C — See *World Wide Web Consortium*.

Web hosting service — Commercial service that provides Web server space only and may be more capable of hosting a more complex commercial site. This service does not include Internet access.

Web server — A computer connected to the Internet that runs server software. The software lets the computer use the Hypertext Transfer Protocol to serve HTML files to Web browser clients.

Well-formed — A syntactically correct XML or XHTML file.

World Wide Web Consortium (W3C) — Founded in 1994 at the Massachusetts Institute of Technology to standardize HTML. The W3C, led by Tim Berners-Lee, sets standards for HTML and provides an open, non-proprietary forum for industry and academic representatives to add to the evolution of HTML.

XHTML — See *Extensible Hypertext Markup Language*.

XML — See *Extensible Markup Language*.

XSL — See *Extensible Style Language*.

Index

Special Characters

<> (angle brackets), 334
| (vertical bar), 334
|| double vertical bar, 334
[] square brackets, 334

A

absolute paths, 75
accept attribute, <form> element, 276
accept-charset attribute, <form> element, 276
accessibility, 55–56
action attribute, <form> element, 275
active white space, 35–40
<a> element, 318, 326
   targeting in, 254
align attribute, <img> element, 211
   replacing with CSS property, 212
aligning text and images, 219–221
alt attribute
   <img> element, 211, 213–214
   navigation, 111–114
alt text with images, 314
America Online (AOL)
   browser compatibility, 14
   Web hosting services, 304
angle brackets (<>), CSS, 334
animation, GIF, 202–204
AOL. See America Online (AOL)
attribute values, XML, 8
audience definition, 66–69
author attribute, <meta> element, 312

B

background color
   pages, 228–229
   tables, 229–231
background images, 224–227
background properties, CSS, 334, 342
backing up files, 307
banding, 209
bandwidth, 19–21
   cache, 20
   connection technologies, 19–21
   HTML editors, 21
   low, designing for, 30
<base> element, 318, 326
   targeting in, 254

<basefont> element, 318, 327
<b> element, 318, 327
Berners-Lee, Tim, 2
billboard sites, 64
_blank target name, 255, 256–258
block-level attributes, specifying values for space around, 185–187
<blockquote> element, 319, 324
<body> element, 319, 323
   background page color, 228–229
   link colors, 231
bookmarks, frame drawbacks, 241
book titles, CSS, 195–198
border(s)
   frames, 249–250
   hypertext, removing from images, 218–219
border attribute, <img> element, 211
   replacing with CSS property, 212
border properties, CSS, 334–336, 340–341
bottom property, CSS, 336, 342
box properties, CSS, 340–341

 element, 319, 324
button attribute, <input> element, 277

C

cable modems, 20
cache, 20
cameras, digital, 207
canvas area, 11
<caption> element, 319, 325
   HTML tables, 121, 122
Cascading Style Sheets (CSS), 4–5, 120, 172–198
   block-level space values, 185–187
   book title, 195–198
   chapter numbers, 191–193
   chapter titles, 193–194
   credits, 195–198
   document divisions, 189–190
   ISO 369 2-letter language codes, 344–348
   linking to external style sheets, 174
   measurement units, 344
   notation reference, 334
   properties. See CSS properties; font properties

selection techniques, 175–177
solving problems with style sheets, 175
standard paragraphs, 190–191
style rules, 173–174
XHTML, 9
case-sensitivity
   filenames, 71
   XML, 7
catalog sites, 65
catalog structure, 82–83
cell-level table attributes, 123–124
<center> element, 319, 328
centering tables, 134
CGI (Common Gateway Interface), 274–275
CGI scripts, 274, 275
chapter numbers, CSS, 191–193
chapter titles, CSS, 193–194
character entities, 328–332
character exceptions, filenames, 71
checkbox attribute, <input> element, 276
checkboxes, creating, 277–279
clarity, designing for, 30–31
class attribute, 318
class attributes, CSS, 176
classification properties, CSS, 343
clear property, CSS, 336, 341
clip art, 208
cluster structure, 81–82
coding
   browser-specific, 13
   cutting-edge, 13
   lowest common denominator, 13
color, 56, 208–210
   depth, 209
   dithering, 209, 210
   fonts, 171
   hexadecimal. See hexadecimal colors
   non-dithering, 209
   text, specifying, 184
color depth, 209
color property, CSS, 336
columns, spanning in tables, 124–125
column width, page templates, 145–146
<!--comment text--> element, 318

commercial ISP accounts, 305
Common Gateway Interface (CGI), 274–275
compatibility with browsers, 11–14
complete URLs, 73
computer medium, designing for, 28–31
  clarity and easy access to information, 30–31
  look and feel, 28
  low bandwidth, 30
  portability, 28–29
connection speed, 20
content
  amount, 53–55
  frames. *See* frame content
  goals for, 64–66
  refining and updating, 311
  reformatting for online presentation, 57–58
context-based selectors, CSS, 176
contextual links, 105–106
contrast, 56
core attributes, 318
credits, CSS, 195–198
CSS(s). *See* Cascading Style Sheets (CSS)
CSS properties
  background, 342
  border, 334–336, 340–341
  box, 340–341
  classification, 343
  font. *See* font properties
  list, 343
  margin, 337, 340
  padding, 337, 340
  replacing <img> attributes, 212–213
  text, 338, 339–340
  visual, 342
custom event buttons, creating, 281–282

D

database administrators on Web site development teams, 70
default spacing, removing in tables, 131–132
deprecated elements, 11–12
description attribute, <meta> element, 312
designers on Web site development teams, 70
diagraming sites, 77–83
  catalog structure, 82–83
  cluster structure, 81–82
  hierarchical structure, 80–81

linear structure, 78
tutorial structure, 78–79
Web structure, 79–80
dial-up, ease of, 304–305
digital cameras, 207
Digital Subscriber Line (DSL), 19, 20
  ISP support, 306
directory structure, 73–77
display property, CSS, 336, 343
dithering, 209, 210
<div> element, 319, 324
  CSS, 176–177
document(s), well-formed, 7
document divisions, CSS, 189–190
document fragments, external, linking to, 100–103
domain name registration, 306
DOS, filenaming convention, 71
double vertical bar (||), CSS, 334
downloading, frame drawbacks, 241
DSL. *See* Digital Subscriber Line (DSL)

E

ease of access, designing for, 30–31
e-commerce sites, 65
e-mail addresses, provided by ISPs, 305
<em> element, 319, 324
empty elements, XML, 8
enctype attribute, <form> element, 275
end tags, XML, 8
Extensible Hypertext Markup Language (XHTML), 8–10
  benefits, 8–9
  style sheets, 9
  syntax, 10
Extensible Markup Language (XML), 5–8
  data description, 6–7
  syntax, 7–8
Extensible Style Language (XSL), 9
external style sheets, linking to, 174
extranets, 66

F

feature article cell, page templates, 142–143
feedback forms for testing Web sites, 310
<fieldset> element, 287–288
file(s)
  backing up, 307
  individual, linking to, 94–95
file attribute, <input> element, 277
file elements, forms, 294–296

file extensions, 71–72
file formats, graphics. *See* graphics file formats
filenaming conventions, 70–72
file structure, relative, 75–77
File Transfer Protocol (FTP), 305, 307–308
fixed frames, mixing with variable frames, 260–265
fixed resolution design, 15–17
fixed table width
  correct, determining, 129
  page templates, 139–140
  relative table width versus, 126–128
  setting, 139–140
flexible resolution design, 17–18
float property, CSS, 336, 341
font(s)
  available to users, 167–168
  number to use, 166–167
  properties. *See* font properties
  setting color, 171
  specifying alternates, 170
<font> element, 170–172, 319, 328
font families, specifying, 178
font properties, 177–185
  CSS, 336, 339–340
  color, 184
  CSS measurement values, 178–179
  letter spacing, 182–183
  line height, 181–182
  selecting specific fonts and alternates, 178
  size, 179–180
  text background color, 184–185
  text indents, 183–184
  weight, 180–181
font sizes
  number to use, 166–167
  setting with <font> element, 170
  specifying, 179–180
font weight, specifying, 180–181
form(s), 273–297
  building within tables, 288–290
  file elements, 294–296
  <form> element, 275–276
  <input> element, 276–284
  input groupings, 287–288
  list boxes, 292–293
  radio buttons. *See* radio buttons
  sample, building and testing, 290–296
  <select> element, 284–286
  submit buttons. *See* submit buttons
  <textarea> element, 286–287
formatting elements, 327–328

formatting tables, 126–132
  determining correct fixed width, 129
  relative versus fixed table widths,
    126–128
  removing default table spacing,
    131–132
  white space, 130–131
form controls, 276
<form> element, 275–276
fragment identifiers, 96
frame(s), 239–270
  attracting visitors to Web site,
    313–314
  benefits, 240–241
  borders, 249–250
  content. See frame content
  drawbacks, 241–242
  fixed and variable, mixing, 260–265
  <frame> element, 243–245
  <frameset> element, 242–243
  framesets, 265–269. See also
    targeting in framesets
  margins, 251
  nesting, 246
  <noframes> tag, 245
  restricting resizing, 247
  scroll bars, 248–249
  targeting in framesets. See targeting
    in framesets
frame content, 259–265
  effective frame design, 260
  mixing fixed and variable frames,
    260–265
  screen resolution, 259–260
<frame> element, 243–245, 319–320
frame elements, 242–245, 328
frameset(s), targeting in. See targeting
  in framesets
<frameset> element, 242–243,
  320, 328
FTP (File Transfer Protocol), 305,
  307–308

G
generator attribute, <meta>
  element, 312
GIF. See Graphics Interchange
  Format (GIF)
global structure elements, 323–324
global table attributes, 123
graphics. See image(s)
graphics file formats, 202–208
  choosing, 208
  GIF, 202–204, 208

image sources, 207–208
interlacing and progressive display,
  206–207
JPG, 204–205, 208
PNG, 205, 208
SVG, 205–206
graphics for navigation and linking,
  107–114
  alt attribute, 111–114
  icons, 108–111
  text images, 107–108
Graphics Interchange Format (GIF),
  202–204, 208
  animation, 202–204
  transparency, 202
grids to provide visual structure, 34
grouping list options, 286

H
<head> element, 320, 324
height attribute, <img> element, 211
  specifying, 214–217
height property, CSS, 336, 341, 342
hexadecimal colors, 227–231
  changing link colors, 231
  page background color, 228–229
  reverse text, 230–231
  table background color, 229–231
  universal color names, 228
  working with, 231–235
<h1> - <h6> elements, 320, 324
hidden attribute, <input>
  element, 277
hierarchical structure, 80–81
hierarchy, flat, 48–50
<hr> element, 320, 328
hspace attribute, <img> element, 212
  replacing with CSS property, 212
HTML. See Hypertext Markup
  Language (HTML)
HTML coders on Web site development teams, 70
HTML editors, 21
<html> element, 320, 324
HTML frames. See frame(s); targeting
  in framesets
HTML table(s). See table(s)
HTML table code, easy-to-read,
  132–133
hypertext, 5
  to connect facts, relationships, and
    concepts, 90
hypertext borders, removing from
  images, 218–219

Hypertext Markup Language
  (HTML), 1–5
  creation, 2
  frames. See frame(s); targeting in
    framesets
  HTML editors, 21
  limitations, 3
  organizing information, 5
  style sheets, 3–5
  table(s). See table(s) table code, easy-
    to-read, 132–133
  W3C, 2–3

I
ICANN (Internet Corporation for
  Assigned Names and Numbers), 306
icons, navigation, 108–111
id attribute, 318
<i> element, 320, 328
image(s)
  aligning with text, 219–221
  alt text, 314
  avoiding use of text as graphics,
    169–170
  creating for submit buttons, 282–283
  <img> element. See <img> element
  software tools, 210–211
  working with, 231–235
image attribute, <input> element, 277
<img> element, 211–227,
  320–321, 327
  adding white space around images,
    221–222
  aligning text and images, 219–221
  background images, 224–227
  removing hypertext borders,
    218–219
  replacing attributes with style sheet
    properties, 212–213
  single-pixel rules, 222–224
  sizing graphics, 218
  specifying alt and title attribute
    text, 213–214
  specifying image width and height,
    214–217
inclusion element, 327
indents, text, specifying, 183–184
information, manageable segments, 90
information designers on Web site
  development teams, 70
information overload, limiting, 90
<input> element, 276–284
  checkboxes, creating, 277–279
  custom event buttons, 281–282

password entry fields, 283–284
radio buttons, 279–280
reset buttons, 280–281
submit buttons, 280–281
text boxes, 277
user file submission, 283
input groupings, 287–288
Integrated Services Digital Network
(ISDN), 19, 20
interaction, designing for, 42–43
interlaced formats, 206–207
internal linking, 96–97
internal navigation bars, 97–99
Internet Corporation for Assigned
Names and Numbers (ICANN), 306
Internet Service Providers (ISPs),
304–307
comparison, 306–307
services, 304–306
intranets, 13, 66
ISDN (Integrated Services Digital
Network), 19, 20
ISO 369 2-letter language codes,
344–348
ISO 9660 standard, filenaming
convention, 71
ISPs. *See* Internet Service Providers
(ISPs)

J

Joint Photographic Experts Group
(JPG), 204–205, 208

K

keywords attribute, <meta>
element, 312

L

language codes, ISO 369, 344–348
left property, CSS, 337, 342
<legend> element, 287–288
legibility, 168–169
letter spacing, specifying, 182–183
letter-spacing property, CSS, 337, 339
<li> element, 321, 325
linear structure, 78
line height, specifying, 181–182
line-height property, CSS, 339
link(s), 50–53
changing link colors, 231
contextual, 105–106
external document fragments,
100–103
to external style sheets, 174

graphics. *See* graphics for
navigation and linking
to individual files, 94–95
internal, 96–97
link column cells, page templates,
143–145
<link> element, 321, 327
link elements, 321, 326–327
list boxes, forms, 292–293
list elements, 325
list options, grouping, 286
list properties, CSS, 343
list-style properties, CSS, 337
location of information, 44–45
look and feel, 28

M

margin(s), frames, 251
margin properties, CSS, 337, 340
marketing staff on Web site
development teams, 70
markup languages, 3
measurement units, CSS, 344
measurement values, CSS, 178–179
<meta> elements, 321, 324
attracting visitors to Web site,
312–313
meta-languages, 5–6
method attribute, <form>
element, 276
multiple selectors, CSS, 175–176

N

names, hexadecimal colors, 228
naming
frames, 252–253
special target names, 255–258
navigation, 87–115
contextual linking, 105–106
frame drawbacks, 241–242
graphics. *See* graphics for
navigation and linking
limiting information overload, 90
text-based. *See* text-based
navigation
user orientation, 89–90
navigation bars, internal, 97–99
nesting frames, 246
nesting tables, 135–137
nesting XML tags, 7
<noframe> element, 321, 328
<noframes> tag, 245
non-dithering colors, 209
nonprofit organization sites, 65
numeric entities, 328–332

O

<ol> element, 321, 325
online shopping sites, 65
<optgroup> element, 286

P

padding properties, CSS, 337, 340
page banner cell, page templates,
140–141
page length, 90
page templates, 119–161
column width, 145–145
feature article cell, 142–143
fixed width, 139–140
HTML tables. *See* table(s)
link column cells, 143–145
page banner cell, 140–141
tables. *See* formatting tables
three-column, 156–157
three-column main sectioned,
159–160
three-column sectioned, 158–159
three-column with banner,
157–158
two-column, 154–155
two-column with banner, 155–156
page turners, 103–105
paragraphs, standard, CSS, 190–191
_parent target name, 255
parsers, 11
partial URLs, 73
password attribute, <input>
element, 276
password entry fields, 283–284
paths, relative and absolute, 75
<p> element, 321, 324
personal ISP accounts, 305
planning sites, 63–84
audience definition, 66–69
content goal identification, 64–66
development teams, 69–70
diagraming, 77–83
directory structure, 73–77
filename conventions, 70–72
site specification, 64
URLs, 70, 72–73
plug-ins, 13
PNG (Portable Network Graphic),
205, 208
Points of Presence (POPs), 304–305
portability, Web site design, 28–29
Portable Network Graphic (PNG),
205, 208
portal sites, 65
position property, CSS, 337, 342

<pre> element, 321, 325
product support sites, 65
programmers on Web site
  development teams, 70
progressive display of graphics, 206–207
public domain Web sites, images
  available, 207
public interest sites, 65
publishing sites, 64–65
publishing Web sites, 304–308
  domain name registration, 306
  ISPs, 304–307
  uploading files using FTP, 307–308

Q

quotes, XML, 8

R

radio attribute, <input> element, 276
radio buttons
  creating, 279–280
  forms, 292–293
raster graphics, 206
reading patterns, 44–45
refining content, 311
regular telephone line, 20
relative file structure, 75–77
relative paths, 75
relative table width, fixed table width
  versus, 126–128
removing spaces in table content, 133
reset attribute, <input> element, 277
reset buttons, creating, 280–281
resizing frames, restricting, 247
resolution, 57
reverse text, 230–231
right property, CSS, 338, 342
row-level table attributes, 123
rows, spanning in tables, 125–126

S

Scalable Vector Graphics (SVG),
  205–206
scanners, 207
screen, designing for, 56–58
  reformatting content for online
    presentation, 57–58
screen resolution, 14–19
  fixed resolution design, 15–17
  flexible resolution design, 17–18
  frames, 259–260
scroll bars, frames, 248–249
search engines
  attracting visitors to Web site,
    311–312

frames, 242
  submitting URLs, 314
Secure Socket Layer (SSL), ISP
  support, 306
<select> element, 284–286
selecting elements in CSS, 175–177
  with class attribute, 176
  by context, 176
  <div> element, 176–177
  multiple elements, 175–176
  <span> element, 177
_self target name, 255
server administrators on Web site
  development teams, 69
shareware, 69
single-pixel rules, 222–224
site specifications, 64
sizing
  frames, restricting, 247
  graphics, 218
slashes, XML, 8
software
  graphics tools, 210–211
  matching to audience, 69
  provided by ISPs, 305
software programmers on Web site
  development teams, 70
spaces, removing in table content, 133
spacing, default, in tables, removing,
  131 132
<span> element, 321, 324
  CSS, 177
spanning columns in tables, 124–125
spanning rows in tables, 125–126
special interest sites, 65
specifying
  color, 184
  font families, 178
  font size, 179–180
  font weight, 180–181
  letter spacing, 182–183
  line height, 181–182
  text background color, 184–185
  text borders, 187
  text indents, 183–184
  text margins, 186–187
  text padding, 186
  values for space around block-level
    attributes, 185–187
speed, connection, 20
SQL (Structured Query Language),
  ISP Support, 305
square brackets ([]), CSS, 334
src attribute, <img> element, 212
SSL (Secure Socket Layer), ISP
  Support, 306

stacking tables, 134–135
Standard Generalized Markup
  Language (SGML), 2
standard paragraph, CSS, 190–191
stock photo collections, 207
<strong> element, 321, 325
Structured Query Language (SQL),
  ISP support, 305
style attribute, 318
<style> element, 322, 327
style rules, coding for readability, 187
style sheet(s)
  CSS. See Cascading Style Sheets
    (CSS)
  HTML, 3–4
  XHTML, 9
<sub> element, 322, 325
submit attribute, <input> element, 276
submit buttons
  creating, 280–281
  creating images for, 282–283
  forms, 294–296
<sup> element, 322, 325
SVG (Scalable Vector Graphics),
  205–206
syntax, XHTML, 10

T

table(s), 119–137
  background color, 229–231
  building basic structure, 138–139
  building forms within, 288–290
  centering, 134
  defining attributes, 122–124
  easy-to-read table code, 132–133
  elements, 120–122
  formatting. See formatting tables
  nesting, 135–137
  removing extra spaces, 133
  spanning columns, 124–125
  spanning rows, 125–126
  stacking, 134–135
table attributes, 122–124
  cell-level, 123–124
  global, 123
  row-level, 123
<table> element, 322, 325
  HTML tables, 121, 122
  table background color, 229–230
table elements, 325–326
targeting in framesets, 252–258
  naming frames, 252–253
  special target names, 255–258
  targeting named frames, 253–254
task elements, 324–325

<td> element, 322, 326
technical support provided by ISPs, 305
technology, matching to audience, 68
templates. *See* page templates
testing Web sites, 308–310
text
  aligning with images, 219–221
  avoiding use as graphics, 169–170
  reverse, 230–231
  specifying background color,
    184–185
  specifying color, 184
<textarea> element, 286–287
text attribute, <input> element, 276
text-based navigation, 91–105
  internal linking, 96–97
  internal navigation bars, 97–99
  linking to external document frag-
    ments, 100–103
  linking to individual files, 94–95
  page turners, 103–105
  text navigation bars, 92–94
text borders, specifying, 187
text boxes, creating, 277
text images, navigation, 107–108
text indents, specifying, 183–184
text margins, specifying, 186–187
text navigation bars, 92–94
text padding, specifying, 186
text properties, CSS, 338, 339–340
<th> element, 322–323, 326
  HTML tables, 121, 122
three-column main sectioned page
  templates, 159–160
three-column page templates,
  156–157
three-column sectioned page
  templates, 158–159
three-column with banner page
  templates, 157–158
title(s)
  attracting visitors to Web site, 312
  books, CSS, 195–198
  chapters, CSS, 193–194
title attribute, 318
  <img> element, 212, 213–214
<title> element, 323, 324
top property, CSS, 338, 342
_top target name, 255, 258
transitions, smooth, 33–34
transparency, GIF, 202
<tr> element, 326
  HTML tables, 121, 122

<tt> element, 323, 328
tutorial structure, 78–79
two-column page templates, 154–155
two-column with banner page
  templates, 155–156
typography, 165–198
  controlling with CSS. *See* CSS
    (CSS)
  controlling with <font> element,
    170–172
  design principles, 166–170

U

<u> element, 323, 328
<ul> element, 323, 325
unified look, designing for, 31–40
  active white space, 35–40
  grids for visual structure, 34
  smooth transitions, 33–34
Universal Resource Locators
  (URLs), 70, 72–73
  complete, 73
  partial, 73
  submitting to search engines, 314
updating content, 311
uploading files, FTP, 307–308
URLs. *See* Universal Resource
  Locators (URLs)
users
  attracting to Web site, 311–314
  designing for. *See* users, designing for
  fonts available to, 167–168
  frames, 242
  location cues, 89–90
  selecting files to submit, 283
  viewing patterns, 44–45
users, designing for, 40–56
  accessibility, 55–56
  amount of content, 53–55
  guiding user's eye, 45–48
  hierarchy, 48–50
  hypertext linking, 50–53
  interaction between user and Web
    site, 42–43
  location of information, 44–45
user testing, 309–310

V

variable frames, mixing with fixed
  frames, 260–265
vector graphics, 206
vertical-align property, CSS, 338, 340
vertical bar (|), CSS, 334

viewing patterns, 44–45
virtual gallery sites, 65
visual confusion, frames, 242
visual properties, CSS, 342
visual structure, grids to provide, 34
vspace attribute, <img> element, 212
  replacing with CSS property, 212

W

W3C (World Wide Web
  Consortium), 2–3
Web browsers, 11–14
  compatibility issues, 11–14
  cross-browser compatible pages,
    12–13
Web hosting services, 304–306
Web pages, cross-browser compatible,
  12–13
Web servers, 304
Web site, default main page name, 72
Web site development teams, 69–70
Web structure, 79–80
well-formed documents, 7
white space
  active, 35–40
  adding around images, 221–222
  adding in tables, 130–131
white-space property, CSS, 338, 343
width attribute, <img> element, 212,
  214–217
width property, CSS, 338, 341, 342
Windows operating systems,
  filenaming conventions, 71
word-spacing property, CSS, 338, 340
World Wide Web Consortium
  (W3C), 2–3
writers on Web site development
  teams, 70

X

XHTML. *See* Extensible Hypertext
  Markup Language (XHTML)
XML. *See* Extensible Markup
  Language (XML)
XSL (Extensible Style Language), 9

Z

Z-index property, CSS, 338, 342